# A Sourcebook for Classical Logic

# A Sourcebook for Classical Logic

John Tomarchio

The Catholic Education Press
Washington, DC

Copyright © 2022

The Catholic University of America Press

All rights reserved

Library of Congress Cataloging-in-Publication Data

ISBN 978-1-949822-28-1 (paperback)   978-1-949822-29-8 (ebook)

*Now reason is not only able to direct the acts of lower powers, but is also director of its own act.*

*For what is peculiar to the intellective part of the human being is its ability to reflect upon itself.*

*Accordingly, reason is able to reason about its own act.*

Thomas Aquinas,
*In Posteriorem analyticam Aristotelis*

# SOURCEBOOKS
## For Liberal Arts and Sciences

THE AUTHORS

**Aristotle**
*Philosopher and Polymath, Ancient Greece*
384-322 BC

**Augustine**
*Theologian and Bishop of Hippo, Roman North Africa*
354-430

**Maimonides**
**(Moses ben Maim on)**
*Theologian and Torah Scholar, Spain & Egypt*
1138-1204

**Thomas Aquinas**
*Theologian and Polymath, Italy, France, & Germany*
1225-1274

# TABLE OF CONTENTS

*Introduction, xi-xvi*
*Sources, xviii-xix*

## Philosophy of Language
### GRAMMATICA SPECULATIVA

| | | | |
|---|---|---|---|
| AUGUSTINE | I | *De Magistro* I-VII | 1 |
| | II | *De Magistro* VIII-XIV | 27 |
| ARISTOTLE | III | *De interpretatione* I | |
| | | & Aquinas *In De Interpretatione* I.2 | 51 |
| MAIMONIDES | IV | *Guide for the Perplexed* I.50-54 | 57 |
| | V | *Guide for the Perplexed* I.55-60 | 73 |
| AQUINAS | | On Disputed Question Format | 90 |
| | VI | *Summa theologica* Ia 13.1-4 & 4.3 | 93 |
| | VII | *In Metaphysicam Aristotelis* IV.2 | |
| | | & *Summa theologica* Ia 13.5-6 | 107 |
| | VIII | *Summa theologica* Ia 13.12 | |
| | | & *Quaestiones de veritate* 1.1-3 | 119 |
| | IX | *Quaestiones de veritate* 14.1-2 | |
| | | & *Summa theologica* IaIIae 9.1 | 129 |

*The Trivium* from *The Seven Liberal Arts* by Hans Sebald Beham

*Aristotle At His Writing Desk*, by Anonymous Miniaturist

## ORGANON
### ARISTOTLE'S TREATISES ON LOGIC
### OR THE ART OF DIALECTIC

| | | | |
|---|---|---|---|
| An Overview of the *Organon* by Thomas Aquinas, Preface to his *Commentary on Posterior Analytics* | | | 138 |
| I | On Definitions | *Topics* I.1-9 | 141 |
| II | On Reasons | *Posterior analytics* II | 153 |
| III | On Predicates | *Categories* 1-4 | 163 |
| IV | On Propositions | *De interpretatione* 1-6, 11 | 175 |
| V | Opposition & Conversion of Propositions | *De interpretatione* 7-8 & *Prior Analytics* I.1-3 | 183 |
| VI | On Syllogism | *Prior analytics* I.23-25 | 191 |
| A Symbology of the Four Figures of Syllogism | | | 199 |
| VII | 1st Figure | *Prior analytics* I.4 | 201 |
| VIII | 2nd Figure | *Prior analytics* I.5 | 207 |
| IX | 3rd & 4th Figures | *Prior analytics* I.6-7 | 213 |
| X | On Demonstration | *Posterior analytics* I.1-4 | 219 |
| XI | On Premises of Demonstration | *Posterior analytics* I.6-10 & II.19 | 229 |
| XII | On The First Principle | *Metaphysics* IV.3-4 | 241 |
| On Logical Fallacies: Aristotle, *Sophistical Refutations* 1 & 7 | | | 253 |
| & Recollections of Plato's *Meno*. | | | 258 |

*An art seems to be nothing more
than a definite and fixed procedure established by reason
by which human acts reach their due end through fitting means.*

*Now reason is not only able to direct the acts of lower powers,
but is also director of its own act.
For what is peculiar to the intellective part of man
is its ability to reflect upon itself.
For the intellect knows itself.
Accordingly, reason is able to reason about its own act.*

*Thus, just as the art of building or carpentering by which man is enabled
to perform manual acts in an easy and orderly manner
arose from the fact that reason reasoned about manual acts,
so in like manner an art is needed to direct the act of reasoning,
that by it a man when performing the act of reasoning
may proceed in an orderly and easy manner, and without error.*

*This art is Logic, the science of reason.
And it concerns reason not only because it is according to reason,
for that is common to all arts,
but because it is concerned with the very act of reasoning
as with its proper matter.
Therefore it seems to be the art of the arts,
because it directs us in the act of reasoning,
from which all arts proceed.*

Thomas Aquinas
Preface to *In Posteriorem analyticam Aristotelis*

*Dialectica*, from the *Mantegna Tarocchi*

# INTRODUCTION

In this Sourcebook I offer a brief sequence in classical Logic befitting an unspecialized study for students of liberal arts and sciences. The sequence is made up of select texts of the Aristotelian *Organon*, mostly the opening chapters of each treatise, in the traditional order, where Aristotle lays out the primary elements of his overall account of reasoning. Accompanying his more technical and logistical texts are study aids that provide mnemonics and diagrams developed in my classroom in the Great Books Program at St. John's College, Annapolis. The culmination of this Aristotelian sequence is the selections from the *Posterior Analytics* where Aristotle offers an account of how sound reasoning yields true reasoning in the demonstrative reasoning of the theoretical sciences. The aim of this Sourcebook, as of Aristotelian Logic, is search for such knowledge.

I preface this Aristotelian Logic sequence with a propaedeutic sequence in *grammatica speculativa,* borrowing that name from the high Middle Ages. Medieval logicians did not hesitate to call Logic a *grammar*, nor to call it *theoretical*, nor to synthesize those appellations. In terms of our own day, I have renamed it philosophy of language. My sequence in philosophy of language begins with an ancient source to which that metaphysically minded medieval *grammatica speculativa* recurred, namely Augustine's *De magistro* (*On the Teacher*). It is a dialogue between him and his son about the relation of the work spoken to the word thought, and of these to the thing spoken and thought about. I have found that this aporetic dialectic between Augustine and his son is effective in awakening students to the theoretical interest of grammatical and logical questions.

Similarly, theological concerns shared by the Jewish theologian Maimonides and the Catholic Thomas Aquinas motivated their interestingly divergent accounts of human talk about God. Medieval theology's own needs and aims spurred philosophical inquiries into language for purposes of scriptural interpretation, especially figurative interpretation, and more general theories of language were soon elaborated for the purpose. The theological use to which these two medieval theologians put Aristotle's Logic offers, in my judgement, a theoretical orientation to whet student appetite for the technical matter of my Logic sequence proper. I may perhaps be subject to the reproach of reversing the traditional order of arts and sciences by beginning with logical theory and descending to the logical art that is its handmaid, but I fear that the pedagogical prejudices of our day requires such honeying of Logic.

In the traditional division of liberal arts and sciences into seven arts and three sciences, Logic formed with Grammar and Rhetoric a *trivium* to complement the *quadrivium* of Geometry and Astronomy, Arithmetic and Music—the mathematical arts. In this Sourcebook series, I rename the three "trivial" arts Language Arts. That designation might seem to suit Grammar and Rhetoric better then Logic. Is not Logic the study of the forms of thought rather than forms of language? Does it not transcend differences of grammar and idiom between languages toward what they have in common from their common source, namely human reasoning? Is it not precisely this study of the universal figures of reasoning itself that won it the medieval title of handmaiden to the theoretical sciences of Mathematics, Physics, and Metaphysics?

However, it is precisely this ordering to human reason's searches for knowledge of things themselves that makes the classical art of Logic not abstract altogether from natural language. After all, human reason does not in fact reason in the abstract, but in words. In Grammar and Rhetoric, elements and principles of verbal expression are studied first in themselves and then in relation to ends of persuasion. In Logic, such expressive reason turns toward itself in search of the primary elements and operative principles of its own acts of addressing and expressing itself.

Like Physics, and unlike Mathematics, classical Logic wants to abstract from the matter and motions of this or that particular expression, but not from the matter and motion of human expression generally, namely speaking and reasoning. Whereas mathematical sciences want to study the quantitative forms of number and extension in abstraction from matter and motion altogether, physical sciences want to understand the forms of matter *as* they are in motion and affect things in matter and in motion. Therefore, its abstractions, like Logic's, ascend from particulars to universals, however only in order to again descend to them in the end. The physicist is not content to understand his globule as a sphere merely; he is interested in the effects of that shape on matter in motion.

A similar contrast may be drawn between classical Aristotelian Logic and modern formal Logic. For classical Logic, natural human language is its matter, and its motion is human reason's search for knowledge of natural things. That is what Logic wants to explain, not abstract from. Modern Formal Logic, in contrast, so completely abstracts logical soundness or validity from any meaning or truth that it may use mathematical algebraic symbols and equations as its apt mode of discourse. Aristotle's ultimate end of accounting for the necessity and truth of demonstrative reasoning in the sciences is abstracted from in modern formal Logic for study of logical self-consistency merely.

Classical Logic took a canonical form in the *Organon* of Aristotelian treatises on reasoning collated and arranged by editors. This Aristotelian *Organon* constitutes the heart of this Language Arts volume on Logic. The first three treatises of the *Organon* concern such material elements of reasoning as words, sentences, and argument; Aristotle abstracts from these their forms of definition, proposition, and syllogism for analysis in their own right. However, in the last three treatises of the *Organon* he returns to study such logical elements and principles *in use*: in the demonstrations of science, in the persuasions of politics, and in the deceptions of sophistry.

The traditional *Organon* includes treatises on Sophistry and on Rhetoric as well as Logic. As for the former, a mere listing of sophistical fallacies in this volume for completeness' sake proved too dry to be illuminating, so I went in search for examples of interest in Plato's *Meno*, that being a seminal text for my college's Great Books program. I was delighted with what I found. I include my reflections here as my own idiosyncratic contribution, noting that they presuppose acquaintance with Plato's' *Meno*. As for Rhetoric, I found that Aristotle's few opening chapters did not work well in the classroom by themselves, so I have detached them from the traditional Logic sequence and in a separate volume to come filled them out with other texts from other classical authors, to give students a separate and more varied introduction to that dubious art.

The systematic and comprehensive form that ancient Greek Logic took in this Aristotelian *Organon* shaped programs of study in the Western Academy for most of its history. This classical Logic has not been displaced by the rise in the twentieth century of a mathematically formal Logic that so abstracts from the matter of human thought as to substitute algebraic equations for natural language. This latter Logic has proven of use only to particular specialists. Aristotle's Logic remains of use to reasoning humans and human reasoning generally.

What use, exactly? Is it to teach students correct reasoning? I do not think so. The attempt to reduce Logic to canons of correctness systematically presented in logic manuals designed to train students in syllogizing has done for Logic what grammar manuals have done for Grammar, namely rendered it odious. On one hand, I have colleagues with doctorates who have never worked through Aristotle's figures of syllogism in the classroom (if at all) but are quite sure it would be quite boring to do so—sure enough to advocate against study of Logic at all and in favor of the study of Rhetoric in its stead. (*O tempora, o mores!*) On the other hand, I myself earned a doctorate in Philosophy without any study of classical Logic. True, as a graduate student I was required to take a course in formal Logic, but I found it useless for anything but a handful of (uninteresting) articles in Anglo-American Analytic Philosophy, and of no use for decades since.

In sum, as a student I did not find study of Logic, either classical or formal, necessary to reason well. Likewise, as a teacher, I find that most of my students come to the study of Logic already reasoning quite well. Intelligent people can recognize inferences as fallacious or unnecessary without the art of Logic. Logic may well hone logical skills, but it takes them for granted to do so. So, why study Logic?

Is self-understanding enough of a reason? Self-possession? Recognizing sound reasoning is less than understanding what reasoning is, how it works, why it works. To a thinking person, an understanding of the sources of their own reasoning is desirable for its own sake, even apart from all practical intents and purposes. Upon examination, human reason turns out to be a wonder to behold. Tracing its array of works back to its principles is likewise wonderful. In the *Posterior Analytics*, Aristotle likens Logic to a search for "the unit" of reasoning, the unit-measure by which all reasoning may be measured. He discovers that unit in the "middle term," and he discovers that the simplest step common to all and any reasoning relates two other terms to a common middle term.

He goes on to systematically analyze all possible inflections of such a triadic relation, to show which known relations of each extreme term to this middle term allows reason to learn a new relation between the extremes. To advance from relations known to new relations is to advance in knowledge. The very fact that Aristotle's systematic and comprehensive account of reasoning is even possible is itself a wonder. Such understanding of reasoning would be worthy of the reasoner's study in its own right, even if it did not also serve to render individual reasonings even more perspicacious and self-assured than without it.

I came to study classical Logic by a circuitous route and quite belatedly. A Logic sequence is required in a program of liberal arts and sciences where I teach, and I thought a high school manual approach unworthy of college students. A reduction of Logic to rules and exercises for syllogizing did not seem to me worthy of serious students of liberal education. As this was a Great Books program, I turned to the seminal texts of Aristotle's *Organon* for an alternative, and I learned Logic from Aristotle together with my students. We found it wonderful.

Now, Aristotle is a great thinker, but not a great teacher, and though his theoretical claims about human speaking and thinking gave me and my students great matter for discussion, his more logistical texts often proved intractable, until I discovered the mnemonics of those great teachers, the medieval Masters of Arts. Their clever and cleverly succinct code-names for the valid figures of syllogism Aristotle identifies were just the pedagogical fix Aristotle's texts needed. The medieval code-names explicate Aristotle's logical triads of terms into triads of propositions, of two premises and a conclusion. The syllogisms or "connections" become of two premises in a conclusion rather than of two extreme terms through a middle term. It was our use of medieval mnemonics for all the valid forms of propositional syllogism that gave my students a handle on Aristotle's logistical texts. When his triads became more manageable, they even became fun to demonstrate.

These logistical demonstrations proved necessary for a responsible and substantive discussion of Aristotle's more theoretical claims about human reasoning and science. It is my conviction that an approach to Logic as a theoretical art, as a reflective inquiry into the forms and principles of one's own reasoning and all human reasoning, is the approach that befits liberal education in arts and sciences.

Moreover, I am also indebted to medieval masters for a metaphysical turn they gave to Logic in the High Middle Ages. In the Arts faculty of thirteenth century universities there emerged a metaphysical interest in tracing the forms and principles of human reasoning to the forms and principles of being in the things which reason reasons about. Relating language's logical categories to epistemological and metaphysical ones became an innovative project for medieval logicians. They considered how definitions of words are related to concepts of reason, and these to essences of things; how logical propositions relate to judgements of reason, and these in turn to causal dependencies within things; and how syllogism reflects causal relations between things. Such speculative interests made the art of Logic all the more reflective in its own right and all the more consequential for science. It took on the name of *Grammatica Speculativa*, a sort of grammar of thought and the sort of language theory that prefaces Aristotle's *Organon* in this volume.

What little Logic I knew before studying the *Organon* I learned indirectly in just such metaphysical discussions. The interest of such epistemological and metaphysical concerns gave me theoretical motivation for acquiring knowledge of the logical elements presupposed by them—in a word, it whetted my appetite for the art of Logic. It also motivated the development of this Sourcebook.

I am indebted to the open-source Internet for many of the Aristotle translations, and in particular to Perseus Hopper and the Internet Archives. However, this variety of translators posed pedagogical difficulties in class, so I have freely emended the texts for pedagogical purposes, e.g., homogenizing divergent translations of key terms across texts, or adding paragraph divisions to make parts of an argument more salient to the eye. In the case of the *Posterior Analytics*, I found it worthwhile to translate some of the Greek myself. I translated all Aquinas' Latin myself. In digitalizing a translation of Augustine's *De magistro,* I so revised the text in light both of Augustine's Latin and American English that one must regard it as a retranslation of the original translation.

I am indebted to several colleagues and friends at St. John's College, Annapolis, who generously studied this Sourcebook together with me while at the same time trying it with their students in their classrooms. Their experiences, feedback, reflections, and encouragement were invaluable. From Chester Burke, Jason Tipton, Andrew Romiti, Brendon Lasell, I received pedagogical thoughtfulness, theoretical keenness, and most careful proofing, all given freely, collegially, liberally. More, we are all indebted to our student collaborators in these classroom trials, knowing all too well that in leading learning we were not always the learner in the lead.

More practically, I owe a debt of thanks to the erstwhile manager of the College bookstore, Robin Dunn, for having encouraged my publication of this Sourcebook both within and beyond the College. Beyond the College, my lifelong mentor and friend, Dr. Kevin White, showed wonted generosity in introducing my work to the Catholic University Press of America. What began as pedagogical materials for my own classes would not have burgeoned into this sourcebook without the rallying of my spirits by such friends. As Aristotle says, we both act and think better together with friends.

# SOURCES

## TEXTS

ARISTOTLE, *The Categories*, Tr. E.M. Edgehill, Project Gutenberg EBook of The Categories by Aristotle (2008): *gutenberg.org/files/2412/2412-h/2412-h.htm*
— *De interpretatione*, Part 1 and 7-8, Tr. J. Tomarchio, from Greek text of *The Categories of Interpretation*, Ed. Harold P. Cooke, in *Aristotle*, Vol. I ( 325), The Loeb Classical Library, Ed./Tr. G.P. Goold (Harvard University Press, 1938).
— *De interpretatione*, Section I, Parts 1-6 & 11, from The Internet Classics Archive, Works by Aristotle, *On Interpretation*, Tr. E.M. Edgehill: *classics.mit.edu//Aristotle/interpretation.html*
— *Metaphysics*, Bk. IV, Ch. 2, Tr. J. Tomarchio from Greek text of *The Metaphysics*, in The Loeb Classical Library, Ed. G.P. Gould, Aristotle Vol. XVII (Harvard University Press, 1933).
— *Metaphysics*, Bk. IV, Ch. 3-4, Tr. W.D. Ross, from The Internet Classics Archive, Works by Aristotle: *classics.mit.edu//Aristotle/metaphysics.html*
— *On Sophistical Refutations*, Parts I & VII, Tr. W.A. Pickard, from The Internet Classics Archive, Works by Aristotle: *classics.mit.edu/Aristotle/sophist_refut.mb.txt*
— *Posterior Analytics*, Bk. I, Parts 1-4, Tr. J. Tomarchio from Greek text of *Posterior Analytics*, Ed. Hugh Tredennick, *in* The Loeb Classical Library (Harvard University Press, 1960).
— *Posterior Analytics*, Book I, Parts 6-10 & Book II, Part 19, Tr. G.R.G. More, from The Internet Classics Archive, Works by Aristotle: *classics.mit.edu//Aristotle/posterior.html*
— *Posterior Analytics*, Book II, Parts 1-10, retranslated by J. Tomarchio from translation of G.R.G. More, Internet Classics Archive, in light of Loeb texts by. H. Tredennick, in Aristotle Vol. II, The Loeb Classical Library (Harvard University Press, 1960).
— *Prior Analytics*, Bk. I, Parts 1-6 & 23-25, Tr. A.J. Jenkinson (1906), from The Internet Classics Archive, Works by Aristotle: *classics.mit.edu//Aristotle/prior.html*.
— *Prior Analytics*, Book I, Parts 7-9, Tr. J. Tomarchio from Greek text of *Prior Analytics*, Ed. Hugh Tredennick, in Aristotle Vol. I, in The Loeb Classical Library (Harvard University Press, 1960).
— *Topics*, Tr. W.A. Pickard-Cambridge, from the Internet Classics Archive, Works by Aristotle: *classics.mit.edu/Aristotle/topics.1.i.html*

THOMAS AQUINAS, *Commentary on the Posterior Analytics*, Preface, Tr. Fabian Larcher, The Thomistic Institute: *aquinas101.thomisticinstitute.org/aquinas-commentary-on-the-posterior-analytics*
— *In libros Peri hermeneias expositio*, Liber I, Lectio 2, Tr. J. Tomarchio, Leonine text (Marietti, 1955), Ed. Raymundi Spiazzi.
— *In Metaphysicam Aristotelis Commentaria*, Bk. IV, Ch. 2, Tr. J, Tomarchio. Leonine text (Marietti,1935), Ed. M.-R. Cathala.
— *Quaestiones disputatae de veritate*, Qu. I, Art. 1-3; Qu. 14, Art. 1, Tr. J. Tomarchio, Leonine text (Marietti, 1953), Vol. I, Ed. Raymundi Spiazzi.
— *Summa theologiae*, Prima pars, Qu. 13, Art. 1-6, Tr. J. Tomarchio, Leonine text (Marietti, 1948), Vol. 1, Ed De Rubeis, Billuart, P. Faucher.

AUGUSTINE OF HIPPO, *De magistro*, retranslated by J. Tomarchio from *Concerning the Teacher (De magistro)*, Tr. George G. Leckie (D. Appleton—Century Co., c. 1938).

MOSES MAIMONIDES, *The Guide for the Perplexed*, Tr. M. Friedlander, 2nd ed. (George Routledge & Sons—E.P. Dutton & Co., 1904), courtesy of Wikisource.org: */en.wikisource.org/wiki/The_Guide_for_the_Perplexed_(1904)*

## IMAGES

**Title Pages,** Detail figures of *Dialectica, Grammatic,* and *Rhetorica,* from *The Seven Liberal Arts,* by German engraver Hans Sebald Beham, c. 1520, Commons.Wikimedia.org: *commons.wikimedia.org/w/index.php?search=Beham+liberal+arts&title=Special:MediaSearch&go=Go&type=image*
ORGANON TABLE OF CONTENTS: Aristotle at his writing-desk, 1457 Miniature, Manuscript Vienna, Österreichische Nationalbibliothek, Commons.Wikimedia.org: *Aristotle,_Vienna,_Cod._Phil._gr._64.jpg*
SOURCEBOOK INTRODUCTION: *Dialectica* from the *Mantegna Tarocchi*, 15th century, Italy, Nazareth College: *naz.edu/dept/philosophy/liberal-arts-resources/classical-images-gallery/*

# SOURCES

**LANGUAGE I & II** *De Magistro*: *Saint Augustine in his Study*, painting by Sandro Botticelli (1480), Church of Ognissanti, Florence, Italy, Commons.Wikimendia.org: *Sandro botticelli, sant'agostino nello studio, 1480 circa, dall'ex-coro dei frati umiliati, 01.jpg*
—*Saint Augustine at his desk*, engraver and date unknown, Bibliothèque publique et universitaire, Neuchâtel, Switzerland, Commons.Wikimedia.org: *Augustinus 2.jpg*
—French engraving of Augustine in his study, unkown, Bibliothèque publique et universitaire, Neuchâtel, Suisse, Quotescosmos.com: *quotescosmos.com/quotes/Augustine-of-Hippo-quote-12.html*
—Detail of *Vision of St. Augustine* (1502), by Vittore Carpaaccio, Scuola di San Giorgio degli Schiavoni, Venice, Italy, Commons.Wikimedia.org: *Vittore carpaccio, visione di sant'agostino 01.jpg*

**LANGUAGE III** *De interpretione*: Adam telling Eve his names for the animals, *Adduxit ea ad Adam ut videret quid vocaret ea* (1791, Lyon), by Jacques Christophe, in the *Dictionnaire raisonné universel d'histoire naturelle*, Vol. 1 frontis, the National Library of Medicine Digital Collections, Bethesda MD: *resource.nlm.nih.gov/101435550*

**LANGUAGE IV & V** *Guide For The Perplexed:* Illuminated Hebrew manuscript by Samuel Ibn Tibbon, Spain c. 1350, the British Library: *bl.uk/collection-items/maimonides-guide-to-the-perplexed*
—Detail of illuminated manuscipt of the *Guide*, Hebrew translation (1347), in the Royal Library in Copenhagen (Cod. Heb.37), *Maimonides teaching the "measure of men"*, Commons.Wikimedia.org: *Maimonides teaching.jpeg*
—Title Page, source unknown, Commons.Wikimedia.org: *Guide for the Perplexed by Maimonides.jpg*

**LANGUAGE VI-IX** *Summa theologica* **et al.**: *St. Thomas Aquinas Reading* (1510-11), by Fra Bartolmeo, in the Museum di San Marco dell'Angelico, Florence, Italy, Commons.Wikimedia.org: *Saint Thomas Aquinas Reading.png*
—*Allegory of Theology and Metaphysics*, by Giovanni Antonio da Brescia (1500–19), Raimondi school, Rijksmuseum, Belgium: *commons.wikimedia.org/Darafsh*
— *Veritas*, by Cesare Ripa (1560-1622), possibly from his *Nova Iconologia* (1602 illustrated edition), PorcelainsAndPeakcocks.com: *porcelainsandpeacocks.com%2011%06%truth-is-fire-verita-in-art.html*

**LOGIC I, end**: Engraved card of *Logica* from the *Tarocchi* Series C Liberal Arts, #22, by the Master of the E-Series Tarocchi, 15th c. Ferrara, Italy, The Cleveland Museum of Art (not on view), ClevelandArt.org: *clevelandart.org/art/1924.432.22*

**LOGIC II, end**: Engraving of Albert the Great by Jean-Jacques Boissard, in *Icones* (1597-99; first image), Linda Hall Library: *lindahall.org/albertus-magnus/*

**LOGIC VI, end**: *Dialectica*, from *Seven Liberal Arts*, by Johann Sadeler I, 16th c., Elisha Whittelsey Collection, Metropolitan Museum of Art, New York NY, Commons.Wikimedia.org: *Dialectica from Seven Liberal Arts MET DP252336.jpg*

Logic V: Allegory of the Seven Liberal Arts (1635-55), by Cornelis Schut, British Museum, Commons.Wikimedia.org: *Cornelis Schut - Allegorical scene on the seven Liberal Arts.jpg*

**LOGIC VII:** *Dialectica*, from *The Liberal Arts*, by German Georg Pencz (1500-50), Metropolitcan Museum of Art, Commons.Wikimedia.org: *Dialectica,_from_The_Liberal_Arts_MET_DP860349*

**LOGIC VIII, end:** Detail of *Seven Liberal Arts*, Engraving by German Virgilius Solis (1514-62), in the Cleveland Museum of Art, Commons.Wikimedia.org: *Virgilius Solis - Seven Liberal Arts - 1924.680 - Cleveland Museum of Art.jpg*

**LOGIC XII:** *Dialectica*, Engraving by German Virgilius Solis (1514-62), from *Seven Liberal Arts*, National Gallery of Art (not on view), Washington, D.C., Commons.Wikimedia.org: *Virgil Solis, Dialectica (Dialectics), NGA 10472.jpg*
—*Six Women as Allegories of the Sciences*, Stefano Della Bella ((1610-64), Pintrest.com: *pinterest.com/pin/188236459399809511/*

**LOGICAL FALLACY** *Sophistical Refutations*: Dialectic and Logic, after Rafael by Roman printmaker Giovanni Antonio da Brescia, 1511-20, Rijksmuseum, Amsterdam, Commons.Wikimedia.org: *Twee sibyllen en engel en putto Dialectica en Logica, RP-P-1913-855.jpg*
—*Dialectica in conversation with a philosopher*, Netherlandish engraving after Franz Floris (c.1565), The British Museum, London, BritishMuseum.org: *britishmuseum.org/collection/object/P_F-1-287*
—*Logica*, from *The Seven Liberal Arts*, by Netherlander Jacobsz Cornelis (1587-1605), Rijksmuseum, Commons.Wikimedia.org: *Logica De zeven vrije kunsten (serietitel), RP-P-BI-7177.jpg*

*Grammatica* from *The Seven Liberal Arts*,
By Hans Sebald Beham

# Philosophy Of Language
*Grammatica Speculativa*

### Augustine
I. *De Magistro* I-VII
II. *De Magistro* VIII-XIV
1–50

### Aristotle
III. *De Interpretatione* I
& Aquinas *In libros Peri hermeneia expositio* I.2
51–56

### Maimonides
IV. *Guide for the Perplexed* I.46 & 50-54
V. *Guide for the Perplexed* I.55-60
57–89

### Aquinas
VI. *Summa theologica* Ia 13.1-4

VII. *Summa theologica* Ia 13.5-6
& *In Metaphysicam Aristotelis* IV.2

VIII. *Summa theologica* Ia 13.12
& *Quaestiones disputatae de veritate* 1.2-3

IX. *Summa theologica* IaIIae 9.1
& *Quaestiones disputatae de veritate* 14.1-2

90–135

*St. Augustine in his Study,* by Sandro Botticelli

# Language I

## Augustine
## *De Magistro* I-VII [1]

*A Dialogue between Augustine and Adeodatus,*
*his son, aged fifteen year.*

### Chapter I

[1] *AUG:* What does it seem to you we want to do when we speak?

*Adeo:* As it strikes me now, either to tell[2] something or to learn something.

*AUG:* I see, and I agree to one of these, for it is clear that when we speak, we wish to tell something. But how do we learn something?

*Adeo:* How, if not by asking questions?

*AUG:* Even then, as I see it, we only wish to tell something, for do you ask a question for any other reason, I ask you, then to tell what you want to the one you are asking? —*Adeo:* That's true.

*AUG:* So, now you do see that by speaking we wish only to tell something.

*Adeo:* That is not clear to me, for if speaking is only expressing words, it is clear we do that when we sing. And since we often sing when we are alone with no one present to learn, it doesn't seem to me we wish to tell anything.

---

[1] Retranslated by J. Tomarchio from *Concerning the Teacher*, Tr. George G. Leckie (D. Appleton–Century Co., 1938).

[2] Literally "teach": *docere*.

*AUG:* Ah, but I think there is a certain kind of telling by way of reminding, indeed a very important kind, which will become clear in this discussion of ours. But if you don't think that we learn something when we remember things, and that the man does not tell something who reminds, I won't object. And now I pose two reasons for speaking: either that we may tell something, or that we may remind either others or ourselves; and that's what we do when we sing. Or doesn't it seem like that to you?

*Adeo:* Not exactly. For seldom do I sing to remind myself; it is usually only to give myself pleasure.

*AUG:* I see what you mean. But don't you see that what pleases you in singing is a certain modulation of sound. And since it can be added to or separated from words, isn't speaking one thing and singing another? For there are songs for flute as well as guitar, and birds sing, and occasionally we as well make sounds of music without words. This sound can be called singing, but it cannot be called speaking. Or do you have any objection against this? —*Adeo:* None that matters.

[2] *AUG:* You agree, then, that speaking is done only for the sake of reminding or of telling?

*Adeo:* It would seem so if I weren't concerned that while praying, we are certainly speaking, and yet it isn't right to believe that God is either told anything by us or reminded by us.

*AUG:* It seems as if you don't know that we have been told to pray in our private rooms [Matt. VI.6], by which the inmost part of our mind is meant, for the sole reason that God does not need to be reminded of or told anything by us speaking in order for him to fulfill our desires. For one who speaks gives a sign of his will by means of a spoken sound. But it is in the most silent places of the rational soul—which is called the *inner person*—that God should be sought and entreated; for he wanted this to be his temple. Haven't you read in the Apostle: *Do you not know that you are the temple of God and that God's Spirit dwells in you?* [I Cor. III.16]. And also: *Christ dwells in the inner person* [*in interiorem hominem*: εἰς τὸν ἔσω ἄνθρωπον: Eph. III.16]. And haven't you attended to the Psalm: *Converse with your own heart on your bed and* be still. *Offer the sacrifices of righteousness and put your trust in the Lord* [Psalm IV.5-6]. Where then is a sacrifice of righteousness made, if not in the temple of the mind and the rooms of the heart? And the place for sacrifice is also the place for prayer. Therefore, there is no need to speak with spoken words when we pray, unless perhaps for the sake of indicating what is in our minds, as priests do, not for God to hear but for men to hear, and by being reminded be lifted up to God by their assent. Or do you disagree? —*Adeo:* I entirely agree.

*AUG:* Does it not concern you that when our great teacher taught the disciples to pray, he taught them particular words? Such teaching seems only to have told how we should speak in prayer.

*Adeo:* That does not trouble me at all, since he did not teach them words, but rather by means of words things, so as to remind themselves to whom they should pray and for what purpose they should pray when they do in those inner sanctuaries of their mind.

*AUG:* You understand that right. For I believe that you as well realize that even when one is forming a statement, even though we utter no sound, we still speak within the mind because we think words. And so, in all speaking we are only reminding, since memory by going over the words which inhere in it makes come to mind the very things the words are signs of. —*Adeo:* I understand and concur.

## Chapter II

[3] *AUG:* Then we agree that words are signs? —*Adeo:* Yes, we agree.

*AUG:* But can a sign be a sign unless it signifies something? —*Adeo*: No, it can't.

*AUG:* How many words are in this line: *If it please heaven that nothing be left from so great a city ...* [*Aeneid* II.659]. —*Adeo:* Thirteen.

*AUG:* Then there are thirteen signs. —*Adeo:* Yes, there are.

*AUG:* I believe you understand the line. —*Adeo:* Very well, I think.

*AUG:* Then tell me what each word signifies.

*Adeo:* Well, I can see what *if* signifies, but I can't find another word to explain it.

*AUG:* Whatever might be signified by the word, you at least know where what it signifies is.

*Adeo:* It seems to me that *if* signifies doubt, and where is doubt if not in the mind?

*AUG:* I'll accept that for now. Go on with the others.

*Adeo:* What does *nothing* signify except what is not?

*AUG:* Perhaps you're right about that. But I can't agree with you because of your recent agreement that a sign is not a sign unless it signifies something, so that the second word in the line is not a sign on account of its not signifying anything—which would mean we agreed falsely that all words are signs, or that every sign signifies something.

*Adeo:* You're really pressing the point too hard. Any word we utter is utter nonsense if we don't say what we mean. But I believe that you are not uttering nonsense while you are speaking to me now, but rather that by each word from your lips you are giving me a sign in order for me to understand something. Therefore, you ought not to say the two syllables *nothing* when you speak if you aren't signifying anything by means of them. But if you see that they are needed in order to say something by means of them, and that when they strike the ear we are told or reminded of something, then you also see just what I want to say but can't explain.

*AUG:* What should we do, then? Since the mind doesn't see the thing, and discovers or thinks it discovers that it does not exist, can't we say that a certain state of mind is what is signified, rather than a thing that does not exist? —*Adeo:* Perhaps that is just what I was trying to explain.

*AUG:* Be that as it may, let's continue then, so that a very silly thing not happen to us. —*Adeo:* What?

*AUG:* That nothing detains us, yet we experience delay.

*Adeo:* That really is ridiculous; and yet, I see it can happen, although I don't know how. In fact, I clearly see that it has happened.

[4] *AUG:* God willing, this sort of confusion will be cleared up in due order. Now go back to the line and try as best you can to explain what the other words in it signify.

*Adeo:* The third is the preposition *from*, instead of which I think we can say *out of*.

*AUG:* I'm not asking you to replace one well known word with another equally well-known word that means the same thing—even granting that it does mean the same thing, which for now we'll allow. Surely, if the poet had not said *from such great a city* but rather *out of so great a city*, and if I asked you what *from* means, you might say *out of*, and we would then have several words or signs signifying the same one thing, as you think. But I am asking about that one thing itself, whatever it be, that is signified by these two prepositions.

*Adeo:* It seems to mean a kind of separation from a thing that something has been in, whether the thing no longer remains, as in this line: *Although the city was destroyed, perhaps a few Trojans were left from the city*; or whether the thing does remain, as when we say, *There are traders in Africa from the city of Rome*.

*AUG:* I accept that and would rather not list how many exceptions may be found to your rule. However, you do realize, don't you, that you have explained words with words, and signs with signs, and things well known by means of things as well known. However, if you can, I want you to show me the things themselves of which these are the signs.

## Chapter III

[5] *Adeo:* I'm amazed that you don't know, or pretend not to know, that what you want done can't be done by my answers as long as we are engaged in discussion, since while we are in the act of discussing I can't answer except with words. Moreover, you're seeking things that, whatever else they are, are not words, and yet are also asking me about

them with words. Ask me about them without the help of words first, and then I'll reply in the same way.

145 *AUG:* I admit that you are within your rights. But were I to ask you what the syllable *wall* means when said, couldn't you point it out with your finger so that I could see the very thing itself that the syllable is a sign of? You would be showing it to me, even though you wouldn't be using words

150 *Adeo:* I admit that it can be done, but only in the case of names,[3] by means of which bodies are signified, as long as the bodies themselves are present.

*AUG:* Do we not call color a certain quality of a body, rather than a body? —*Adeo:* That is so.

155 *AUG:* Then why can't this be shown by pointing a finger? Or are you including the qualities of bodies with bodies, since when colors are present, for example, they can be shown just as well without words?

*Adeo:* When I said bodies, I meant all bodily things, that is, all things that are sensed in bodies.

160 *AUG:* But think about it now. Shouldn't you make some exceptions?

*Adeo:* You're giving me good advice, since I shouldn't say all bodily things, but rather all visible things. For I acknowledge that sound, odor, taste, weight, and other things of the sort that pertain to other senses, cannot be shown by pointing a finger, even though they cannot
165 be sensed without bodies.

*AUG:* Haven't you seen men converse with the deaf, so to speak, by means of gestures, the deaf likewise using gestures? Don't they ask questions and reply, and tell and point out everything they want to, or at least very many things. They don't merely point out visible things

---

[3] The Latin word *nomen* can mean *name* in general, or *noun* in particular as a part of speech in grammar—compare this usage to a conventional definition of *noun* in English: *the name of a person, place, thing, or idea.*

when they gesture, but also sounds and tastes and other things of the sort. There are actors in the theater that present and exhibit entire dramas by means of pantomime for the most part, without using words.

*Adeo:* I have no objection to make except that neither I nor even a pantomime himself can show you without words what *from* signifies.

[6] *AUG:* Perhaps that is true. But let's imagine that he can. I think you don't doubt that whatever bodily movement the pantomime might use to show me the thing signified by the word, the movement will not be the thing itself but rather a sign. Therefore, the movement, although not a word indicating another word, will nevertheless be a sign indicating a sign: both the single syllable *from* and the gesture will both mean one and the same thing, which is what I want shown to me in some way other than by making a sign.

*Adeo:* Please tell me how what you're asking for can be done?

AUG: In the same way the wall was shown.

*Adeo:* Not even a wall can be shown without a sign, as far as I can see from our discussion to this point. For the pointing of the finger is certainly not the wall, but by means of it a sign is given for the wall to be looked at. I see nothing, then, which can be shown without signs.

*AUG:* What if I were to ask you what walking is, and you get up and walk. Wouldn't it be shown to me by the thing itself rather than by words, or would you use some other signs?

*Adeo:* I admit that, and I'm ashamed not to have seen so obvious a thing. From this, thousands of other things now occur to me that can be shown through themselves and not through signs, as eating, drinking, sitting, standing, shouting, and innumerable others.

*AUG:* Come, tell me: if, knowing absolutely nothing about the meaning of the word, I was to ask you what walking is while you were in the act of walking, how would you tell me?

*Adeo:* I would walk a little more quickly after your question so that your attention would be directed to something new, and I would still only be doing what was to be shown.

*AUG:* Do you know that walking is one thing and hurrying another? For one who walks need not hurry, and one who hurries doesn't necessarily walk, since we speak of hurrying with regard to writing and reading and innumerable other things. Hence, if after my question you were to do more quickly what you were doing already, I would think walking is merely hurrying. Hurrying would be the new thing added, and so I would be misled by that.

*Adeo:* I admit that we cannot show a thing without a sign if we are asked while we are in the act of doing it. For if we do nothing more, the questioner will think we don't want to show him and suppose that we keep doing what we're doing to make fun of him. But if he asks about things that we're able to do, but doesn't ask while we are in the act of doing them, then by doing what he asks about after his question we can show him what he is asking about by means of the thing itself rather than by a sign—unless the questioner were perhaps to ask me what speaking is while I am in the act of speaking, since it is necessary for me to speak when I say something to tell him the answer to his question. If this happens, then by adhering to the thing itself that he wants shown him—not reaching beyond the thing itself for some sign by which to indicate it—I'll be telling him until I make it clear to him what he wants to know.

## Chapter IV

[7] *AUG:* Very astute, indeed. Now, then, are we in agreement that things can be shown without signs that we are not doing when we are asked but can do right then, or else things that are themselves signs—as in speaking, since when we speak, we make signs, and this is called signifying. —*Adeo:* Agreed.

*AUG:* Certain signs, if asked about, can be shown by means of signs. But when things that are not signs are asked about, they can be shown after the question by doing them, if they can be done, or by giving signs by which they can be brought to attention. —*Adeo:* That is so.

AUG: In this threefold division let us first consider this, namely, that signs are shown by means of signs. For words are not the only signs, are they? —*Adeo:* No.

AUG: Now it seems to me that when speaking we signify either words themselves by words, or other signs. For instance, when we say *gesture* or *letter*, the things signified by the words *gesture or letter* are also signs; or else, when we say *stone*, we signify something else that is not a sign, for this word is a sign, because it signifies something, but what is signified in this case is not in turn a sign.

But this kind of sign—the kind where things that are not signs are signified by words—does not belong to the present part of our discussion. For we have begun to consider that kind where signs are shown by means of signs, and in it we have discovered two parts, since through signs we tell or call to mind either the same kind of signs or other kinds of signs. Or does it not seem to you? —Adeo: That's obvious.

[8] *AUG:* Then tell me to what sense pertain signs that are words. —*Adeo:* To hearing.

*AUG:* And gesture? —*Adeo:* To sight.

*AUG:* What do we find about written words? Are they not better understood as signs of words than as words? A word is that which is uttered in spoken sound with some meaning, but the voice can be perceived only by the sense of hearing. Thus, does it happen that when a word is read, a sign is made to the eyes by which the sign that pertains to the ears comes into the mind. —*Adeo:* I agree entirely.

*AUG:* I think you agree also when I say that the word *name* signifies something to us. —*Adeo:* Truly it does.

AUG: What?

*Adeo:* To be sure, what something is called, as 'Romulus', 'Rome', 'virtue', 'river', and innumerable other things.

265 AUG: Is there no difference between the names and the things which are signified by means of them? —*Adeo:* A great deal of difference.

AUG: I would like to hear from you what it is.

*Adeo:* In the first place, the former are signs, while the latter are not.

270 AUG: Can we agree to call the things that can be signified by means of signs but yet are not signs *signifiable* things, just as we call things that can be seen *visible*, so that we may discuss these things more conveniently in the right order? —*Adeo:* Quite agreeable.

AUG: Are the four signs that you mentioned signified by no other signs?

275 *Adeo:* I am surprised you think I have forgotten that we found that written things are related to things spoken as signs of signs.

AUG: Tell me why they differ.

*Adeo:* Because the former are visible, the latter audible. For why shouldn't we say audible if we say signifiable?

280 AUG: I agree, and I thank you. But again, I ask, can these four signs be signified by no other audible signs, as the visible signs can be, as you recall?

*Adeo:* I also recall that this was said earlier. I answered that *name* signifies something, and I included the above four [names] under its 285 signification; both it and these I understand to be audible, if they be uttered by the voice, of course.

AUG: Now what is the difference between an audible sign and audible things signified that are in turn signs?

*Adeo:* Between what we call 'a name' and the four [names] that we 290 put under its signification I see this difference, that *name* is an audible sign of audible signs, whereas those included under its signification are audible signs of things—some of which are intelligible things, such as *virtue*.

[9] *AUG:* I accept and approve. But you know that all things that are spoken with some signification are called *words*? —*Adeo:* I do

*AUG:* And so, *name* is a word, since we see that it is spoken with a certain signification. And when we say that an eloquent man uses fair words, he is using fair names; and when the slave in Terence's play said to the old lord, *I seek fair words*, he said many names. —*Adeo:* I agree.

*AUG:* You grant, then, that by the syllable we pronounce when we say *word*, *name* is also signified, and thus *word* is a sign of *name*.[4] —*Adeo:* I agree.

*AUG:* I also want you to answer this. Since *word* is a sign of *name*, and *name* is a sign of *river*, and *river* is a sign now of a thing that can be seen, there is a difference between [on one hand] the difference between that which can be seen and *river* which is its sign; and [on the other hand] between this sign and the name that you have said to be its sign—so, what do you think the difference is between the sign of *name*, which we have found to be *word*, and *name* itself, of which it is the sign?

*Adeo:* I understand the difference to be this: that those things which are signified by *name* are also signified by *word*, for as *name* is a word, so also is *river* a word. Yet not everything that is signified by a word is signified by a name. For both *'If'*, which appears at the beginning of the line you mentioned, and *'from'*, from discussing which we've been led by reasoning into these matters, are words but not names; and there are many others. Therefore, since all names are words but not all words are names, it seems to me evident what I think the difference is between *word* and *name*, that is, between the sign of a sign that in turn signifies other signs.

*AUG:* Do you grant that every horse is an animal, but that not every animal is a horse? —*Adeo:* Who doubts that?

---

[4] You grant, then, that by the syllable we pronounce when we say word [*verbum*], name [*nomen*] is also signified, and thus *word* is a sign of *name* [as well as of *noun* or *adjective* in grammar].

AUG: Then the difference between *name* and *word* is the same as the difference between *horse* and *animal*. But perhaps you are kept from agreeing because we speak of verbs as words, where it signifies words which are declined by tenses, and these words are obviously not names.[5]

Adeo: That is precisely the point that made me doubtful.

AUG: Do not let that concern you. For speaking in a general sense, we call all the things that signify something *signs* and words are included under this. We also say *military signs* or *banners*, which are properly called signs, but words do not belong to this kind of sign. And yet if I were to say that just as every horse is an animal but not every animal a horse, so likewise every word is a sign, but not every sign is a word, I think you would not doubt it.

Adeo: Now I understand and agree willingly that there is the same difference between *word* thus understood and *name* that there is between *animal* and *horse*.

[10] AUG: Do you also know that when we say *animal*, the three-syllable word that is spoken is one thing and what it signifies is another thing.

Adeo: I have already agreed to that concerning all signs and signifiables.

AUG: Do all signs seem to you to signify something other than what they are, as when we say *animal*, this three-syllable word in no way signifies what it itself is?

---

[5] This is a point about terms of Latin grammar: as *nomen* can mean either *name* in general or *noun* as one of the eight parts of speech in grammar, so *verbum* can mean *word* in general or *verb* in particular. So, more accurately translated: "But perhaps you are kept from agreeing because we speak of *verbum* [word] in another way, where it signifies words which are declined by tenses, and these words are obviously not *names* [or *nouns: nomina*]."

*Adeo:* Not at all, for when we say *'sign'* it signifies not only other signs, whatever they may be, but also signifies itself, since it is a word, and all words are certainly signs.

*AUG:* How so? When we say the syllable *'word'*, does not something like this happen? For if this single-syllable word signifies everything that is spoken with a signification, then it is also included in the genus. —*Adeo:* That is true.

*AUG:* Is that not also true of *noun*? For it signifies nouns of all sorts, and *noun* itself is a noun. For if I were to ask what part of speech a noun is, could you correctly answer anything but *noun*?[6] —*Adeo*: That is true.

*AUG:* Then there are signs which signify themselves along with the other things they signify. —*Adeo:* Yes, there are.

*AUG:* When we say *'conjunction'*, does it seem to you that this three-syllable word belongs to this kind?

*Adeo:* Not at all, for things which it signifies are not names, or nouns, yet it is a name.

## Chapter V

[11] *AUG:* You have been paying attention. Now see whether signs are to be found that signify each other mutually, so that in whatever way the one may be signified by the other, the other is likewise signified by it. For the three-syllable word *conjunction* and the things that are signified by it, for example, *if, or, for, since, except, therefore, whereas*, and the like, are not reciprocal, since the examples listed are signified by *conjunction*, but it is not in turn signified by any of them.

*Adeo*: I see, and I want to know what signs do signify each other mutually.

---

[6] For the sake of the grammatical point, I translate *nomen* as *noun* rather than *name*.

375 AUG: You do know that when we say *name* and *word*, we say two words. —Adeo: I know that.

AUG: Do you know that when we say *name* and *word*, we also say two *names*. —Adeo: I know that also.

AUG: Then you know that *name* is signified by means of a word, and
380 *word* by means of a name. Adeo: I agree

AUG: Can you say what is the difference between them, aside from the fact that they are written and pronounced differently?

*Adeo:* Maybe I can. I see that the difference is the same as that which I decided on above. For when we say *words*, we signify everything that
385 is voiced with some signification; hence, every name and *name* itself is a word. But not every word is a name, although *word* itself is a name.

[12] AUG: If anyone should assert and maintain that every name is a word and every word is a name, would you be able to find any difference between them except the differing sound of the letters?

390 *Adeo:* I could not, nor do I think there is a difference.

AUG: What if all things that are voiced with some significance are both words and names, but yet words for one reason and names for another. Will there be any difference between a name and a word?

*Adeo:* I do not understand how.

395 AUG: You understand this at least, that everything colored is visible, and everything visible is colored, although the two words signify it with a distinction and a difference.

*Adeo:* Yes, I do understand.

AUG: Well now, how about if every word is thus a name and every
400 name a word, although these two names, or two words, namely, *name* and *word*, have different significations?

*Adeo:* I now see that this can happen, but I want you to explain to me how it happens.

*AUG*: You observe, I think, that everything that is voiced with some signification both strikes the ear so that it can be sensed and is committed to memory so that it can be known. —Adeo: Yes, I do observe that.

*AUG:* Then two things happen when we speak with the voice. —Adeo: That is so.

*AUG:* What if words are called words for one reason and names called names for another, namely, words from *striking* the ear [*verba, verberando*], and names from 'knowing' [*nomina, noscendo*]? As the first is named with reference to the ears, should not the second be named in relation to the soul?

[13] *Adeo:* I shall agree when you have shown how all words may correctly be called names.

*AUG:* That is easy. For I believe you agree that a pronoun is so called because it stands for a noun and yet denotes a thing with less complete signification that does noun. For I think that the rule you learned in grammar gave the definition thus: *A pronoun is a part of speech which, put in place of a noun, signifies the same thing, although less fully.*

*Adeo:* I remember that and agree.

*AUG:* You see, therefore, that according to this definition, pronouns only serve as names or nouns and can be substituted in the place of these alone, as when we say *this one* for *the man*, *he himself* for *the ruler*, *she* for *woman*, *this* for *gold*, *that* for *silver*—*one, he, himself, she, this, that* are pronouns; and *man, king, woman, gold, silver* are names by which things are signified more fully than by pronouns. —Adeo: I see that and agree.

*AUG:* Now mention a few conjunctions, whichever you please. —Adeo: *And, but, or, both.*

*AUG:* Don't all of these that you have said seem to you to be names, or nouns? —Adeo: Not exactly.

*AUG:* Did I not speak correctly when I said, *All of "these" that you have said*?

*Adeo:* Yes, quite correctly. And I see with admiration that you've shown I did express names, for otherwise the [pronoun] phrase *All of these* could not have been correctly said of them. But, still, I fear that you seem to me to speak correctly because I don't deny that the four conjunctions are words, so that *All of these* is correctly said of them [as words]. But if you ask me what part of speech *words* is, I can only say a name. So perhaps the pronoun refers to this noun, and your statement is correct in this way.

[14] *AUG:* You are in fact acutely mistaken. So as to be deceived no longer, attend more closely to what I say, if I'm in fact able to say it as I wish to. For discussing words with words is as entangled as crossing and scratching fingers with fingers, where which fingers itch and which give relief to itching can scarcely be distinguished, except by that one who is doing it.

*Adeo:* Your example has in fact aroused my most acute attention.

*AUG:* Clearly, I pronounce words, and they consist in letters.
—*Adeo:* That is so.

*AUG:* And so, in the first place, to use that authority which is so dear to us, when the Apostle Paul said, *For the Son of God, Christ Jesus ...was not one who is true and not true, but what is true was in him"* (II Corinthians I.19). I don't think we should consider the two syllables we say when we say *is true* to be in Christ, but rather what is signified by these two syllables. —*Adeo:* That's true.

*AUG:* You understand, therefore, that he who said, *What is true was in him,* said only that what was in him is called *what is true.* Similarly, if he had said, *Power was in him,* he would be understood to have said only that what is in him is called power—we should not think that the two syllables expressed in saying *power* were in him, rather than what was signified by the two syllables.

—*Adeo:* I understand and follow.

*AUG:* Do you not also understand that it makes no difference whether one says, *is called power* or *is named power*? —*Adeo:* It is obvious.

*AUG:* Hence it is obvious in the same way that it makes no difference if one says, *What is in him is called true* or *What is in him is named true.*

*Adeo:* I see also that this makes no difference.

*AUG:* Do you now see what I want to show you? —*Adeo:* Not yet well enough.

*AUG:* But you do see that a name is that which something is called by. —*Adeo:* That is very clear.

*AUG:* Then you see that *what is true* is a name if what was in him is named *true.* —*Adeo:* I cannot deny it.

*AUG:* And if I should ask you what part of speech *is* is, I think you would not say it is a noun but a verb, although you have learned by reasoning that it is also a name, or noun. —*Adeo:* That's exactly what I would say.

*AUG:* Do you still doubt that other parts of speech are also names in the same way that has been shown? *Adeo:* I do not doubt it, since I admit that they signify something. But if you ask me what each of the things that they signify is called or named, I can't but name those very parts of speech that we do not call names, or nouns, but which have been shown to be called such.

[15] *AUG:* Are you not at all worried that someone might weaken this reasoning of ours by saying that to the Apostle we should ascribe power over things, but not power over words, and that, therefore, the foundation of this statement is not as firm as we think; it is possible that, although Paul lived and taught in righteousness, yet he spoke incorrectly when he said, *In him was what is true,*[7] especially since he

---

[7] Augustine's Latin: "Non erat in Christo *est* et *non*, sed *est* in illo erat" (II Corinthians 1:19). Paul's Greek: ὁ τοῦ θεοῦ γὰρ υἱὸς Χριστὸς Ἰησοῦς ... οὐκ ἐγένετο Ναί καὶ Οὔ, ἀλλὰ Ναί ἐν αὐτῷ γέγονεν ..." N.B.: Latin did not have a separate word for *yes*; one way to say *yes* was *est*: "[it] is [so]".

confessed that he was unskilled in speaking? How then could this be refuted?

*Adeo:* I have no objection to make, and I beg you to find someone whose prestige is recognized among those who are skilled in words, that by this authority you may more ably accomplish what you wish.

*AUG:* Indeed, does that reasoning seem less qualified because an authority is lacking by means of which we have shown that something is signified by every part of speech, and if signified, then called; if called, then named; if named, then surely named by a name, or noun. This can be easily determined by considering different languages. For anyone can see that if you ask, what do the Greeks call what we call *quis* [who], the answer is τίς; what do the Greeks call what we call *volo* [I want], the answer is θέλω; what do the Greeks call what we call *bene* [well], the answer is καλῶς; what do the Greeks call what we call *scriptum* [text], the answer is τὸ γεγραμμένον; what do the Greeks call what we call *et* [and], the answer is καί; what do the Greeks call what we call *ab* [from], the answer is ἀπό; what do the Greeks call what we call *heu* [alas], the answer is οἴ. And it seems that one who questions in this way speaks correctly, which would not be possible unless the above parts of speech were names, or nouns. And so, since we can maintain that Paul spoke correctly, even if the authority of all orators be absent, why is there a need to look for some individual by whom our decision may be substantiated?

[16] But some duller or less cautious person might not grant this, and might assert that it ought not to be granted without the authority of those who by general consensus are guardians of the rules of words; hence I ask, can there be anyone available who excels in the Latin language more than Cicero? But he, in those superb orations of his named *Verrine*, called the preposition *coram* a name—or in this case, perhaps an adverb.

And yet, since it is possible that I do not understand this context well enough and it can be explained in different ways either by myself or by another, it is, I think, a thing to which no answer may be made. Now the noble masters of argument teach that a complete sentence is made up of a noun and a verb, which may be either affirmed or denied.

Tullius in one place calls this a proposition. And when it is the third person of the verb, they say that the nominative case of the noun should accompany it, which is true, for if you consider with me as we say, *The man sits*, *The horse runs*, you will agree, I think, that they are two propositions. —*Adeo:* I do acknowledge that.

*AUG:* You see there is a noun in each: in the first, *man*, and in the second, *horse;* and there is a verb in each; in the first, *sits,* and in the second, *runs.* —*Adeo:* I do see.

*AUG:* Then if I were to say *sits* only or *runs* only, you would rightly ask me who or what, and I would answer *man* or *horse,* or *animal,* or anything else by which the noun can be restored to the verb and the proposition be completed, that is, the sentence which can be affirmed or denied. —*Adeo:* I understand.

*AUG:* But attend to the rest. Suppose we see something remote and are uncertain whether it be an animal or a stone or something else, and suppose I say to you, *Because it is a man, it is an animal.* Would I not speak rashly?

*Adeo:* Quite rashly, though not at all if you said, *If it is a man, then it is animal.*

*AUG:* That is true. And what pleases me in your statement is *if.* It pleases you too. But the *because* in my statement dissatisfies both of us. —*Adeo:* I agree.

*AUG:* Now see whether these two statements are complete propositions: *If* pleases; *because* displeases. —*Adeo:* They are.

*AUG:* Tell me, now, which are the verbs and which the nouns in those propositions.

*Adeo:* I see that *pleases* and *displeases* are the verbs, but what are the nouns if not *if* and *because*?[8]

---

[8] Since they are the subjects of the verbs, they function as nouns in the sentence, even though as parts of speech they are prepositions and not nouns.

AUG: Then it is sufficiently proven that the two conjunctions are also names, or nouns? —*Adeo:* Quite sufficiently.

AUG: Can you treat other parts of speech in such a way that they will fall under the same rule? —*Adeo:* I can.

## Chapter VI

[17] AUG: Then let us move on. Tell me, as we have found that all words [*verba*] are names [*nomina*] and all names words, do all names seem to you to be terms [*vocabula*] and all terms names?

*Adeo:* Clearly, I do not see what difference there is between them except in the sound of the syllables.

AUG: At present I raise no objection, although some make a distinction in regard to the meaning, but we need not consider their opinion now. You surely note, however, that we have now discovered those signs which mutually signify each other, differing only in sound, and which signify themselves as well as all the other parts of speech.

*Adeo:* I do not understand.

AUG: Do you not understand that a name [*nomen*] is signified by *term* [*vocabulum*] and a term by *name*, and that thus there is no difference between them beyond the sound of the letters in so far as *name* in the general sense is concerned; for we also say *name* [nomen] in that special sense in which it is one of the eight parts of speech [noun], so that it does not contain the other seven. —*Adeo:* I understand.

AUG: But this is what I said, namely, that *term* [*vocabulum*] and *name* [*nomen*] mutually signify each other.

[18] *Adeo:* I grasp that, but I ask why you said *Since they signify themselves as well as the other parts of speech*?

AUG: Did not our reasoning teach us that all parts of speech can be called names and terms, that is, can be signified by both *name* and *term*? —*Adeo:* That is so.

*AUG:* What about *name* itself, that is, that sound expressed by the two syllables [*nomen*]? If I ask what you call it, will you not correctly answer me with *a term*? —Adeo: Yes.

*AUG:* Does the sign which we express when we say the three syllables *conjunction* signify itself in this way? For this name cannot be numbered with those things which it signifies. —Adeo: I quite accept that.

*AUG:* That is because it has been said that *name* signifies itself along with the other things which it signifies, and this, you may discern for yourself, also holds for *term*.

*Adeo:* That is now easy. But is has just occurred to me that *name* [*nomen*] is said both in a general sense and in a special sense [noun], yet I do not take *term* to be among the eight parts of speech. It seems to me, therefore, that they differ in this respect, in addition to the difference of sound between them.

*AUG:* Do you think that *name* [*nomen*] and ὄνομα differ otherwise than by the sound through which the Latin and Greek languages are distinguished.

*Adeo:* Indeed, that is just what I understand.

*AUG:* Then we have discovered those signs (1) which signify themselves; (2) of which each is signified reciprocally by the other; (3) by which whatever is signified, is signified as well by the other; and (4) the sound of which is the only difference between them. Of these, only the fourth is a new discovery; for the three former are understood of *name* [*nomen*] and of *word* [*verbum*]. —*Adeo:* It is entirely clear.

## Chapter VII

[19] *AUG:* Now I wish to review what we have discovered by means of this discussion.

*Adeo:* I shall do it insofar as I can. I remember that first of all we asked for what reason we speak. And it was found that we speak for the sake of telling or reminding, since when we question we only do it so that he who is questioned may learn what we wish to hear; and that singing, which we seem to do for pleasure, is not properly speaking; and that in praying to God, whom we cannot suppose to be taught or reminded, words are for the purpose either of reminding ourselves, or else so that others may be taught or reminded through us.

Then, when it was clearly understood that words are only signs, you quoted a line in order that I might show what each word signified. And the line was: *If it please heaven that nothing be left from so great a city* .... Although the second word, *nothing,* was quite well known and very obvious, still I could not find what it means. And since it seemed to me that it is not used recklessly in discourse, but that we use it in order to teach the hearer something by it, you suggested that perhaps this word indicates a state of mind in which the mind seeks something and finds, or thinks it finds, that the something does not exist. Then, avoiding with a jest deep matters unknown to me, you put off the explanation until another time—and do not think that I have forgotten that you owe it me also.

Then, when I was overtaxed to explain the third word in the line, *of,* you urged me not to substitute another word with the same meaning, but rather to indicate the thing itself which is signified by means of the word. And when we understood that this cannot be done in the act of speaking, we came to those things which are shown to the questioner by pointing the finger. I thought that these included all corporeal things, but we found that they are only the visible things. From here we went on, I do not know just how, to deaf men and actors, who signify by gesture and without the use of words not only things that can be seen, but also many other things, and almost everything that we say. Still, we found that gestures themselves are signs.

Then again, we began to inquire how we can show without any signs the things themselves that are signified by the signs—since *wall* and *color* and everything visible that is shown by pointing the finger were all proved to be shown by a certain sign. I erred in having said that nothing of this sort could be found, and at length we agreed that those things can be shown without a sign which we are not in the act of doing when we are asked about them, and which we can do after being asked. But speaking does not belong to this genus. For if, while we are in the act of speaking, we are asked what speaking is, it is quite evident that it is easy to show it by means of itself.

[20] By this we were reminded that either signs show signs; or they show other things that are not signs; or else without a sign, things are shown which we can do after we are questioned. And we undertook to investigate and discuss the first of these three more thoroughly. In this discussion it was revealed that one part of those signs include those that cannot in turn be signified by means of those signs that they signify, as in the three-syllable word *conjunction*; and another part, those signs that can in turn be signified by means of those signs that they signify, as when we say *sign* we also signify *word*, and when we say *word* we also signify *sign*; for *sign* and *word* are both two signs and two words.

It was shown, moreover, that in this kind of sign in which signs signify each other mutually, some mean not as much, some mean just as much, and some mean exactly the same thing. For the single-syllable word *sign* signifies absolutely everything by means of which anything is signified. *Word* is not, however, a sign of all other signs, but only of those that are uttered by the articulate voice.

Consequently, it is clear that although *word* is signified by *sign* and *sign* by *word,* namely, the two former syllable by the latter and the latter syllable by the former, yet *sign* means more than *word*, for more things are signified by the former syllable than by the latter one. But *word* in general means just as much as *name* in general. For our reasoning taught us that all parts of speech are also names: for pronouns can be supplied to them; and it can be said of all of them that they name something; and there is none of them which cannot make a complete proposition when a verb is added to it.

However, although *word* and *name* mean the same number of things, because all things that are words are also names, yet they do not mean the same thing. It was argued, and with sufficient reason, that things are called words for one reason and names for another, since the former were found to be impressed by vibration on the ear, but the later on the memory of the mind. And this can be understood from the fact that in talking we correctly say *What is the name of this thing?* when we wish to commit it to memory, whereas we do not say *What is the word of this thing?* We found that *nomen* and ὄνομα [*name*] signify not only just as much, but also the same thing exactly, and that there is no difference between them except that of the differing sounds in letters.

I had forgotten that in the kind of sign in which signs signify each other mutually, we found no sign that does not signify itself as well as the other things which it signifies. I have recalled these things as best I could. Go ahead and see now, you whom I believe to have spoken always with knowledge and certainty in this discussion, whether I have set forth these things well and in good order.

French Engraving of Augustine in his study.

*Vision of St. Augustine,* by Vittore Carpaaccio

## Language II

### Augustine
### *De Magistro* VIII-XIV [9]

### Chapter VIII

[21] *AUG:* Now that you have recalled adequately all the things I desired, I admit to you that these distinctions seem much clearer to me than they were when we unearthed them from unknown hiding places. But it is difficult at this point to say just where I am striving to lead you by so many circumlocutions. For it may seem that we are quibbling and so diverting the mind from earnest matters with naïve questions, or that we are seeking after some petty advantage. Or, if you suspect that this investigation tends towards some worthy object, you desire to know now what it is we are striving after or at least you want it to be mentioned. But I want you to believe that I wish neither to have been playing in this discussion, even if not in a childish sense, nor to have labored for petty or unimportant ends.

Still, if I say that there is a blessed life, towards which I so much desire we may be led under God's guidance, *that is*, by Truth itself, through degrees suited to our weak progress, I fear to appear laughable, because I have set out on such a road by considering not the things themselves that are signified, but signs. But be patient with this preparation, since it is not for amusement, but in order to exercise the strength and keenness of the mind, by means of which we can not only bear the warmth and light of that region where the blessed life resides, but can also love the true.

*Adeo:* But do continue as you began, for I never think those things unimportant that you consider suitable to say or to do.

---

[9] Retranslated by J. Tomarchio, from *Concerning the Teacher*, Tr. George G. Leckie (D. Appleton–Century Co., 1938).

[22] *AUG*: Then come, let us consider that case in which signs signify not other signs, but those things that we call signifiable. First, however, tell me whether a human is a human [*utrum homo homo sit*].

*Adeo:* But now you do seem to me to be jesting. —*AUG:* Why so?

*Adeo:* As you think that I should be asked whether a human is anything other than a human.

*AUG:* I believe that you would also think that you were being bantered if I should ask whether the first syllable of the word "human" be other than "hu-" and the second other than "-man"? —*Adeo:* Indeed, I should.

*AUG:* But these two syllables conjoined are "human", or do you object? —*Adeo:* Who could object to that?

*AUG:* Now I ask whether you are these two conjoined syllables. —*Adeo*: Not at all, but your purpose is clear.

*AUG:* Then tell me, and do not think me abusive. —*Adeo:* I infer that you think that I am not a human.

*AUG:* Why did you not think that, when you granted the truth of all the former inferences from which this derived?

*Adeo:* I shall not tell you what I think until I first hear from you whether, when you asked if a human is a human, you were asking about the syllables or about the thing itself which it signifies.

*AUG:* Do you rather tell me in what reference you take my questions; for if the reference is ambiguous, you should have taken care not to answer me before making certain how I put the question.

*Adeo:* But how could the equivocation embarrass me, when I have answered both: for a human is simply a human, and the one syllable is only one syllable, and what they signify is nothing other than what it is.

*AUG:* Of course, you know this. But why have you construed only the phrase "a human" in two ways, and not also the other words we have spoken.

*Adeo:* I am not at all certain that the others should not have been construed in this way.

*AUG:* If you had construed my first question (not to mention the others) entirely in the sense in which the syllables sound, you would have made no answer, for I could not have seemed to ask anything. But just now when I pronounced the three words, one of which I reiterated in the center, saying, *whether a human is a human*, you did not construe the first and last words as signs, but in terms of the things that are signified by them, and this is evident from the fact that you thought at once with certainty and confidence that my question should be answered. —*Adeo:* That is true.

*AUG:* Then why did it seem to construe the one [word] I repeated both according to the way in which it sounded and according to the thing that it signified?

*Adeo:* Ah, well, I now construe it entirely in the sense in which something is signified, for I do agree with you that we cannot discuss at all unless, when we hear words, we direct the mind to the things of which they are the signs. So now show me how that inference deceived me so that I concluded that I am not a human.

*AUG:* No; rather, I shall question you again, so that you may discover your error. —*Adeo:* Excellent.

[23] *AUG:* I shall not ask my first questions over again, for you have answered those already. Now, consider more carefully whether the syllable "hu-" in "human" is only the syllable "hu-" and whether "-man" is only "-man". —*Adeo:* I do not see any difference.

*AUG:* See whether "human" is not made by joining "hu-" and "-man".

*Adeo:* I do not agree at all. For we decided, and rightly so, when a sign is expressed to attend to that which is signified, and from the consideration of that to deny or affirm what is said. It has also been granted that, since the syllables uttered separately are expressed without any signification, they are just as they sound.

*AUG:* It is agreed then and firmly established in your mind that answers ought to be made only to questions that are about things which are signified by words. —*Adeo:* It seems to me agreeable, if the words are only words.

*AUG:* Very well, but how would you refute that sophist we hear about, who asserted that when his opponent spoke, a lion issued from his mouth? For first the sophist asked whether what we express proceeds from the mouth, which his opponent could not deny. Next, he managed the conversation, which was easily done, so that his opponent pronounced *lion* in speaking. When his opponent had done this, the sophist began to badger and heckle him, because his opponent had admitted that whatever we say comes forth from the mouth; nor was his opponent able to deny that he had spoken *lion*, and the sophist asked the tormented victim if he who were seen to vomit such an enormous beast were not an evil fellow.

*Adeo:* It would be quite easy to refute this quibbler, for I should not admit that whatever we say proceeds from our mouth. For what we say we signify; and, in speaking, what issues from the mouth is not the thing itself that is signified, but the sign by means of which it is signified, except in that case in which signs themselves are signified, a genus which we previously discussed.

[24] *AUG:* Ah, in this way you would have held your own against him. Nevertheless, what will you say when I ask whether a human is a noun? —*Adeo:* What indeed, but that it is a noun?

*AUG:* And when I look at you, do I see a noun? —*Adeo:* No.

*AUG:* Do you wish me to say what follows?

*Adeo:* No, not at all, for I can answer myself that I am not that human that I have called a noun, when you ask whether a "human" is a name [noun]; for it has been agreed that we are to affirm or to deny what is said according to the thing that is signified.

*AUG:* But it seems to me not merely incidental that you made that answer, for your discrimination was ruled by the law of reason itself that has been placed within our minds. For if I should ask what man is, you would perhaps answer that he is an animal. But if I were to ask what part of speech *man* is, you could answer correctly only a noun. Accordingly, when *man* is found to be both a noun and an animal, the former is said in the sense in which it is a sign, the latter is said in the sense of the thing that is signified.

And so, when anyone asks whether "human" is a name [noun], I can only answer that it is, for the question thus put indicates clearly that the questioner wishes to be answered according to the sense in which "human" is a sign. But if he asks whether a human is an animal, I may assent much more readily, since if he asked only what a human is, and indicated nothing in regard to "human" and to "animal", my mind would fix itself according to the law of speaking on that which is signified by the two syllables "human", and the answer would be *animal* only, or I might even give the full definition, namely, *a rational, mortal animal*. Do you understand the matter in this way?

*Adeo:* I do entirely. But when we have granted that "a human" is a noun, how shall we avoid that absurd conclusion by which we are asserted not to be men?

*AUG:* How indeed except by pointing out that the conclusion does not follow from the sense in which we agreed with the questioner? Or if he confesses to mean it not as a thing-reference but as a sign-reference, we need not be apprehensive, for why should one fear to admit that a a human is not "a human", namely, that he is not made up of syllables.

*Adeo:* Very true. Why then is it offensive to us when it is said, *You, therefore, are not a human* [*homo*], since according to our discussion that is quite true.

*AUG:* Because one cannot help thinking that the conclusion bears a reference to that which is signified by the two syllables "human" [*homo*] as soon as the words are expressed, by virtue of that law which by nature is very strong, namely, that when signs are heard, the attention is turned towards the things signified. —*Adeo:* I accept what you say.

## Chapter IX

[25] *AUG:* Now then, I wish you to understand that things that are signified are more to be depended upon than signs. For whatever exists because of another must of necessity be inferior to that because of which it exists, unless you think otherwise.

*Adeo*: It seems to me that assent should not be given too hastily. For when we say *filth,* this noun, I think, is far superior to that which it signifies. What offends us when we hear it does not pertain to the sound of the word itself, since *coenum* [filth] is changed by a single letter to *coelum* [heaven]. But we do see what a great difference there is between the things signified by these nouns. Hence, I should not attribute to this sign what we so loathe in the thing signified. So, for this reason I consider the sign superior to the thing, for we hear the sign with greater complaisance than we perceive the thing by means of any sense.

*AUG:* Most watchful indeed. Is it false, therefore, that all things are to be considered superior to their signs? —*Adeo:* It seems so.

*AUG:* Then tell me what plan you think they followed who gave a name to this vile and despicable thing. Do you approve of them, or not? —*Adeo:* Indeed, how should I presume to approve or disapprove, for I do not know what plan they followed.

*AUG:* At least you can determine what plan you follow when you utter the name.

*Adeo:* Clearly, I can; for I wish to signify that which I think ought to be told or reminded in order to tell or to remind him with whom I am speaking of the thing itself.

*AUG:* The telling or reminding, or the being told or being reminded, that you either express suitably by means of the name or that is expressed to you—ought that not to be held superior to the name itself?

*Adeo:* I grant that the knowledge itself that results from the sign should be considered superior to the sign, but not for that reason, I think, the thing also.

[26] *AUG:* In this argument of ours, therefore, although it be false that all things ought to be considered superior to their signs, yet it is not false that everything that exists because of another is inferior to that because of which it exists. Surely, the recognition [*cognitio*] of filth, for the sake of which the name *filth* was determined, ought to be considered superior to the name itself, which we found to be superior to filth itself. For the recognition is considered superior to the sign we spoke of for the sole reason that it's proved conclusively that the sign exists for the sake of the recognition and not the recognition because of the sign.

Since, for example, when a certain glutton and servant of the belly, as the Apostle calls him, said that he lived in order to eat, the temperate man who heard him chided him and said, *Would it not be better to eat in order to live?* This was clearly said in conformity with the rule that inferiors exist for the sake of superiors. And the Apostle was displeased only because the glutton's life should be of so little worth to him that he would have it degraded by the passion of gluttony as indicated by his saying that he lived for the sake of feasting. And this should be praised because the Apostle taught in these two distinctions that what ought to be done for the sake of something is that which should be subject to it, for it is understood that it is preferable to eat in order to live.

Similarly, you as well as other men who judge matters suitably would reply to a garrulous word-lover who said *I teach in order to talk* with *Man, why not rather speak in order to teach?* For if these things are true, as you know they are, you truly see how much less words are to be esteemed than that for the sake of which we use words, since the use of words is superior to the words. For words exist in order that they may be used, and in addition we use them in order to teach. As teaching is superior to talking, in like degree is speech better than words. So, of course the teachings are far superior to words. But I wish to hear whatever objections you have to offer.

[27] *Adeo:* I agree indeed that the teachings are superior to words. But whether the rule that everything which exists for the sake of something else is inferior to that for the sake of which it exists has no exceptions is more than I am able to say.

*AUG:* We shall discuss that more conveniently and more thoroughly at another time. For the present, what you have granted is enough to prove what I now wish. For you grant that the recognition of things is superior to the signs of things. Consequently, the recognition of things that are signified is to be preferred to the recognition of signs by which they are signified. Do you agree?

*Adeo:* Did I admit that the recognition of things is superior to the recognition of signs, and not just to signs themselves? Then I fear that I am not in agreement with you on this point. For if the name *filth* is better than the thing it signifies, then the recognition of the name ought also to be preferred to the recognition of the thing, even if the name itself be inferior to recognition. Indeed, there are four considerations involved: 1) the name; 2) the thing; 3) the recognition of the name; 4) the recognition of the thing. Since the first is more excellent than the second, why is not the third better than the fourth? But if it is not better, must it therefore be considered as inferior?

[28] *AUG:* I see that you have very admirably retained what you conceded and understood what you thought. But you understand, I think, that the one-syllable word *vice* is better than what it signifies, though the recognition of the name itself is far inferior to the knowledge of vices. Granted that you thus arrange and consider the four distinctions—1) name; 2) thing; 3) recognition of name; 4) recognition of thing—we correctly place the first before the second. For the name being placed in the verse where Persius says, *But he is drunk with vice*, not only does not vitiate the verse but adds a certain ornament. But when the thing itself that is signified by this name is in anything, it does vitiate it. Thus, we see that the third does not excel the fourth, but the fourth the third. For the recognition of the noun *vice* exists for the sake of the recognition of vices.

*Adeo:* Do you think that the recognition of vices is preferable even though it makes men more wretched? For among all the afflictions which man suffers, devised by the cruelty or cupidity of tyrants, this same Persius ranks first that torture which results when men are forced to acknowledge vices that they cannot avoid.

*AUG:* Reasoning in this way, you can also deny that recognition of virtues is preferable to the recognition of the word *virtue.* Because to see virtue but not to possess it is torture, and it was by this means that the satirist wished tyrants to be punished. [*Satyricon* 3:35-38].

*Adeo:* May God avert such madness. Now I do see that the recognitions by which learning instructs the soul is not to be held as culpable, but that those men are to be judged the most pitiable of all, as I think Persius judged them, who are infected by such a malady that there is no remedy for it.

*AUG:* You understand quite well. But then of what real moment is the opinion of Persius, the satirist, since in problems of the sort before us we are not subject to the authority of satirists? Well, if in some way one recognition is to be preferred to another, still that point is not easily explained just now. I am satisfied that it has been shown that the recognition of the thing that a sign signifies is more powerful that the sign itself, even if it is not superior to the recognition of a sign. Hence, let us discuss more thoroughly what the genus is of those things which we said can be shown through themselves [*per se*] without signs, as speaking, walking, sitting, throwing, etc. —*Adeo:* I recall now what you speak of.

## Chapter X

[29] *AUG:* Does it seem to you that anything that may be immediately done when one asks a question about it can be shown without a sign, or do you see some exception?

*Adeo:* Running through the items of this whole genus time and again, I do not indeed find anything in it which can be taught without some sign, except perhaps speaking and also possibly teaching. For I see that whatever I do after his question in order that he may learn, the questioner does not learn from the thing itself that he desires to have shown to him. For if I am asked what walking is when I am still, or doing something else, and if I, by walking immediately, try to teach without a sign what has been asked—all of which has been discussed earlier—then how shall I avoid having the asker think that walking consists in walking only so far as I walked? And if he did think that, he would be misinformed, for if someone walked not so far or farther than I did, the questioner would think that this individual had not walked. And what I have said about this one word will be true of all the others that we thought could be shown without a sign, except the ones we excluded [talking and teaching].

[30] *AUG:* I accept that, in truth; but does it not seem to you that speaking is one thing and teaching another?

*Adeo:* Surely it does, for if they were the same, none would teach without speaking, and since we teach many things by means of signs that are not words, who can doubt there is a difference?

*AUG:* Are teaching and signifying the same or do they differ in some way? —*Adeo:* I think that they are the same.

*AUG:* Is it not true that we signify in order to teach? —*Adeo:* That is true.

*AUG:* What if it be said that we teach in order to signify? Is the assertion not easily refuted by the former statement? —*Adeo:* That is so.

*AUG:* If then we signify that we may teach and do not teach in order to signify, teaching is one thing, signifying another.

*Adeo:* That is true, nor did I answer correctly that both are the same.

*AUG:* Now tell me if he who teaches what teaching is does it by signifying or in some other way. —*Adeo:* I do not see that there is any other way.

*AUG:* Therefore, what you said a while ago is false, namely, that when someone asks what teaching is, the thing itself can be taught without signs, since we see that not even this can be done without signifying. For you have granted that signifying is one thing, teaching another. And if, as it seems, they are different, and teaching is only by means of signifying, then teaching is not shown through itself [*per se*], as you thought. Consequently, nothing has yet been found that can be shown through itself excepting speaking, which also signifies itself as well as other things. Yet since this is a sign also, it is still not entirely clear what things can be taught without the aid of signs.

*Adeo:* I have no reason for disagreeing with you.

[31] *AUG:* It has been proved, therefore, that nothing is taught without signs, and recognition itself should be dearer to us than the signs by means of which we recognize, although all things that are signified cannot be greater than their signs. —*Adeo:* It seems so.

*AUG:* Do you recall by what great circumlocutions we at length reached this slight point? For since we began this interchange of words which has occupied us for some time, we have labored to discover the following three points: 1) whether anything can be taught without signs; 2) whether certain signs ought to be preferred to the things which they signify; 3) whether the recognition of things is superior to their signs. But there is a fourth point I wish to know briefly from you, namely, 4) whether you think that these points are so clear and distinct that you cannot doubt them.

*Adeo:* I wish indeed to have arrived at certainty after such great doubts and complications, but your question disturbs me, although I do not know why, and keeps me from agreeing. For I see that you would not have asked me about this, if you did not have some objection to raise, and the problem is such a labyrinth that I am not able to explore it thoroughly or to answer with assurance, for I am disquieted lest something lie hidden in these wonders which evades the keenness of my mind.

*AUG:* I commend your hesitation. For it indicates a mind that is cautious, and this is the greatest safeguard to equanimity. It is very difficult not to be perturbed when things we consider easily and readily provable are shaken by contrary arguments and, as it were, are wrenched from our hands. For just as it is proper to assent to things well explored and perused, so it is perilous to consider things known which are not known. Because there is a danger, when those things are often upset which we supposed would stand firmly and endure, lest we fall into such distrust and hatred of reason that it might seem that confidence in evident truth itself is not warranted.

[32] But come, let us consider more diligently whether you think any of the points should be doubted. For consider, if someone unskilled in the art of bird-catching, which is done with reeds and birdlime, should happen upon a fowler, carrying his instruments as he walked along, though not fowling at the time, he would hasten to follow and in wonderment he would reflect and ask himself, as indeed he might, what the man's equipment meant. Now if the fowler, seeing himself watched, were to exhibit his art, and skillfully employ the reed, and then noting a little bird nearby, if he were to charm, approach, and capture it with his reed and hawk, would the fowler not teach his observer without the use of signification, but rather by means of the thing itself that the observer desired to know?

*Adeo:* I fear this observer of bird-catching is like the man whom I referred to above, who inquires about walking; for it does not seem that in this case the entire art of fowling is exhibited.

*AUG:* It is easy to free you from that worry. For I suggest that an observer might be intelligent enough to recognize the whole complexity of the art from what he saw. It is enough for our purpose if certain men can be taught without signs about some things, if indeed not about all things.

*Adeo:* To that I can add that if the learner be very intelligent, he will know what walking is fully when it has been shown by a few steps.

*AUG:* That is agreeable. And I do not only not object, but I approve of your statement. For you see that the conclusion has been reached by both of us, namely, that some men can be taught certain things without signs, and that what we thought awhile back are false, that is, that there is nothing at all that can be shown without signs. For now, not only one thing or another of that sort, but thousands of things occur to the mind that may be shown through themselves when no sign has been given. Why then do we hesitate, I pray you? For passing over the innumerable spectacles of men in every theater where things are shown through themselves without signs, surely the sun and this light bathing and clothing all things, the moon and the other stars, the lands and the seas, and all things were are generated in them without number, are all exhibited and shown through themselves by God and nature to those who perceive them.

[33] If we consider this more carefully, then perhaps you may find that there is nothing that is learned by means of signs. For when a sign is given me, if it finds me not knowing of what thing it is a sign, it can teach me nothing, but if it finds me knowing the thing of which it is the sign, what do I learn from the sign? For the word does not show me the thing that it signifies when I read: *And their saraballae are not changed* [Daniel, III.94]). For if head-coverings of some sort are called by this name *saraballae*, when I have heard it, have I learned either what a head is or what coverings are? I know these before, and it is not when someone names them, but when they are seen by me that knowledge of them is achieved for me.

And indeed, when the syllable *head* was first expressed to me, I knew as little what it meant as when I first heard or read *saraballae*. But when *head* was repeated over and over, as I observed and noticed when it was said, I found it to be the word of a thing that was already well known to me by sight. Before I discovered this, the word was only a sound to me, and I learned that it is a sign when I discovered of what thing it is a sign—which thing, indeed, I had learned, as I said above, not through its signification, but by the sight of it. Therefore, that the sign is learned after the thing is recognized is rather more the case than that the thing itself is learned after the sign is given.

[34] That you may understand this more exactly, let us suppose that we hear for the first time the word *head*, and not knowing whether it is merely a meaningless sound or whether something is signified, we ask what a head is. (Remember, we want to have knowledge of the sign itself, and not of the thing that it signifies, which knowledge we certainly lack as long as we do not know of what it is a sign.) And if, when we inquire, the thing itself is shown to us by means of pointing the finger, when we have seen the thing, we learn the sign that we had only heard before without knowing it. Since, however, two factors are

involved with the sign, namely, sound and signification, we surely perceive the sound not through the sign, but through the vibration when the ear is struck, while we learn the signification when the thing itself is shown.

For the pointing of the finger can signify only that towards which the finger is pointed, but it was pointed not at the sign but at the member that is called the head; consequently, I have not learned by means of the pointing what the thing is, for I know that already; nor did I learn the sign in that way, since the pointed was not directed at the sign. But I do not wish to place too much emphasis on the pointing of the finger, because it seems to me that it is rather a sign of the demonstration itself rather than of the things demonstrated; as in the case of the adverb *There!* [*ecce!*], for we are accustomed to point the finger with this adverb, lest one sign of demonstration be not enough. And if I can, I shall try to prove to you above all that we learn nothing through those signs that are termed words. For it is more correct, as I have said, that we learn the meaning of the word, that is, the signification that is hidden in the sound, when the thing itself that it signifies has been recognized, than that we perceive the thing through signification.

[35]   And what I have said about *head* I should say too of *coverings* and of innumerable other things. And though I already know these, yet *saraballae* I do not know in the least. If someone were to indicate them by gesture or sketch them for me or show me something to which they are similar, I do not say that he would not teach me (which I could maintain if I wished to speak a little more fully). But I do say what is quite relevant to the point being discussed, namely that he would not have taught me by means of words.

If someone, seeing these *saraballae* while I was near should bring them to my attention, saying, *Look at the saraballae!* I would learn something unknown not through the words that were spoken, but through its appearance, by means of which I was made to know and to retain the meaning of the name. For when I learned the thing itself, I was not indebted to the words of others but to my eyes; yet perhaps I accepted their words in order to attend, that is, in order that I might find what was to be seen.

## Chapter XI

[36] To give them as much credit as possible, words possess only sufficient efficacy to remind us in order that we may seek things, but not to exhibit the things so that we may know them.

He teaches me something, moreover, who presents to my eyes or to any other bodily sense or even to my mind itself those things that I wish to know. By means of words, therefore, we learn only words, or rather the sound and vibration of words, for if those things that are not signs cannot be words, even though I have heard a word, I do not know that it is a word until I know what it signifies.

So, when things are known, the recognition of the words is also effected, but not by means of hearing words are they learned. For we do not learn the words that we know, nor can we say that we learn words we do not know, unless their signification has been perceived; and this happens not by means of hearing words that are pronounced, but by means of a recognition of the things signified. For it is the truest reasoning and most correctly said that when words are uttered, we either know already what they signify, or we do not know; if we know, then we remember rather than learn, but if we do not know, then we do not even remember, though perhaps we may be prompted to ask.

[37] If you say that, unless we see them, we cannot know the *saraballae* of which the name is only a sound to us; and that we cannot know the name itself more fully except by knowing the things themselves—and yet we accept the [biblical] story that boys triumphed over king and fires by faith and religion, that they sang praises to God, and that they won honor even from their enemies, and has this been transmitted to us by other means than by words?

I answer that everything signified by these words was already in our knowledge. For I already grasp what three boys are, and what a furnace is, and fire, and a king, what unhurt by fire is, and every other thing signified by those words. However, Ananias and Azariah and Misael [exhorted in a psalm to praise God] are as unknown to me as the *saraballae*; these names do not help me at all to know these men, nor can they help me.

I confess, moreover, that I believe rather than know that the things in that story were done at that time as has been written; and those whom we are believing knew the difference between believing and knowing. For the Prophet says, *If you will not believe, you will not understand.* Surely, he would not have said that, had he not thought that believing and understanding are different.

Therefore, what I understand I also believe, but I do not understand everything that I believe; for all that I understand I know, but I do not know all that I believe. Yet I am not unmindful of the usefulness of believing the many things that are not known. I include in this usefulness the story about the three youths. And though the majority of things must remain unknown to me, yet I do know what the usefulness of believing is.

[38] However, with reference to all the things that we understand, we consult not the speaker who utters words, but rather the guardian truth within the mind itself, perchance because we have been reminded by the words to do so. The One who is consulted teaches, for the one who is said to reside in the inner person is Christ, who is the unchangeable excellence of God, and his everlasting wisdom, which every rational soul in truth consults.

However, there is shown to each one as much as he can apprehend, according as his wish is more or less complete. And if sometimes one is deceived, this is not due to a defect in the truth that he has consulted, any more than it is a defect of external light that the eyes of the body are often deceived. Rather, we confess that we consult this external light about visible things, in order that it may show them to us so far as we have the power to perceive.

## Chapter XII

[39] If we consult light concerning color and other things that we sense through the body; if we consult elements of this world and the bodies that we sense; if we consult the senses themselves, which the mind uses as interpreters in recognizing things of this kind; and if we also consult the inner truth, by means of reason, about things that are

understood: then what can be said to indicate that we learn anything by means of words beyond that sound that strikes the ear?

For all the things that we perceive are perceived either through a sense power of the body or by means of the mind. We call the former sensibles, the latter intelligibles; or to speak in the manner of our scriptural authorities, the former are *carnal,* the latter *spiritual.* If we are asked about sensibles that are at hand, we answer when questioned as when we are questioned while gazing at the new moon about where it is or what it is like. If the one who asks is not seeing it, he believes words, and sometimes he does not believe. However, he does not learn anything unless he also sees what is mentioned. If he does learn, he learns by means of the things themselves and from his own senses, and not through spoken words. For the same words are heard by the man who sees for himself and by the man who does not see.

However, if a question is asked not about things sensed immediately, but about things that we have sensed in the past, then in this case we speak not of the things themselves but of images impressed by the things on the mind and committed to memory. I don't know at all how we can mistake these as true while we are seeing that they are false, unless it be because we do not speak of what we are seeing or sensing, but rather of what we have seen and have sensed. We thus carry these images in the recesses of the memory as records of things sensed before.

When contemplating these things in the mind, we say nothing that is false if we speak with good attention. But these records of things are our own, and he who hears of them, if he has been in their presence and sensed them, learns nothing from my words, but rather recalls to mind what is spoken of through the images hidden in himself. But if he has never perceived the things that are being spoken of, then it is clear that he believes rather than learns through words.

[40] Indeed, when things are discussed that we perceive through the mind, by means namely of intellect and reason, these are said to be things that we see immediately in that inner light of truth by virtue of which what is called the inner person is illumined, and upon this

depends his joy. But then our hearer, if he himself also sees those things with his inner and pure eye, knows what I am speaking about by means of his own contemplation, but not through any words.

Accordingly, even though I speak true things, I still do not teach him who beholds true things, for he is taught not through my words, but by means of the things themselves that God shows within the soul. Hence if he is questioned, he can answer about them. What could be more absurd than to think that he is taught by means of my speaking, when even before I speak, he can express those very things if questioned?

Now, if it often happens that one who is being questioned first denies something, and then is driven by other questions to affirm what he has denied, this happens because of a defect in his discernment, insofar as he cannot consult that light about the whole matter. He is directed to do it part by part, when he is questioned step by step about the parts themselves of which the whole consists, which he is unable to grasp in its entirety. Even if he is guided in this case by the words of the questioner, nevertheless he does not manage to grasp the whole by means of verbal instruction, but rather by means of questions put in such a way that he who is being questioned is able to teach himself through his inner power according to the measure of his ability.

An apt example is found in our recent procedure, for when I asked you whether anything can be taught by words, the question at first seemed absurd to you, because you did not have a comprehensive view of the problem. Thus, it was appropriate for me to formulate my questions in such a way that your powers might be brought under the direction of the inner Teacher. I would thus say things which, when I spoke them to you, you would admit being true, of which you would be certain, and about which you would declare that you had knowledge. From what source would you learn these things?

You would perhaps answer that I had taught them to you. To that I would reply, *What if I were to say that I had seen a man flying?* Would my words carry the same certitude as if you were to hear that wise men are superior to fools? You would immediately answer the negative and assert that you do not believe the former statement, or if you do believe it, that you do not know it to be true, but that you do know the latter statement with great certainty. From this discussion you would understand clearly that you did not learn anything from me through words, either about a man flying, of which you knew nothing, even though I stated it, nor about the relative worth of wise men and fools, which you did know quite well. If in addition you were also questioned about each word, you would state on oath that the latter is well known to you, while the former is not known. Then indeed you would admit all that you had denied, as you knew with clarity and certainty the things in which it consists.

Whenever we say anything, either the hearer does not know whether what is said is false or true, or knows that it is false, or knows that it is true. In the first case, he will either believe (that is, accept with good confidence), or he will form an opinion, or he will doubt. In the second case, he will resist the statement and reject it. In the third case, he merely confirms. In none of these three cases does the hearer learn anything from what is heard. For all three—he who does not know about the thing we have spoken about, he who knows that what we said is false, and he who would be able when asked to state things without having heard them from us—have been shown to have learned nothing through words.

## Chapter XIII

[41] From what has been said it follows, therefore, that in the case of those things that are grasped by the mind, anyone who is unable to grasp them hears to no purpose the words of him who does discern them; though we may make an exception in regard to the fact that where such things are unknown, there is a certain utility in believing them until they are known. On the other hand, whoever can discern those things that are grasped by the mind is inwardly a pupil of truth and outwardly a judge of the speaker, or rather of his statements. For often he knows what has been said, though the speaker himself does not know; as if, for example, someone who is a follower of Epicurus and so thinks that the soul is mortal should receive the arguments on the soul's immortality expounded by men of greater wisdom. If someone who is versed in spiritual things hears the speaker state the argument for the immortality of the soul, he will judge that true things

have been said, but the speaker does not know that they are true; for, to the contrary, he thinks that they are quite false. Can he be understood as teaching what he does not know? He does use, however, the very same words that one who understood would use.

[42] Now, therefore, not even this is left to words, namely, that at any rate they express the mind of the speaker, since a speaker may indeed not know the things he speaks about. Consider also lying and deceiving, and you will easily understand from both of them that words not only do not disclose the true intention of the mind, but that they may serve to conceal it. For I by no means doubt that by words truthful men try and to some extent do contrive to disclose their minds, which would be accomplished, as all agree, if liars were not allowed to speak. And yet we have had the experience both in ourselves and in others of words being expressed that were not about the thing being thought.

It seems to me that this can happen in two ways: (1) either when something that has been committed to memory and often repeated is expressed by one who is preoccupied with other things, as often happens to us when we sing a hymn; (2) or when against our will we make a slip in speech, for in this case, too, signs are expressed which are not of the things that we have in mind. For indeed those who lie also think of the things they express, so that, although we do not know whether they tell the truth, we do yet know that they have in mind what they are saying, if they do not do one of the two things cited above. If anyone contends that this only happens now and then, and is apparent when it happens, I do not object, though frequently it is not observed and has often deceived me.

[43] But among these there is another genus of words, one that is very prevalent and the cause of countless disagreements and battles, namely, the kind of words involved when one who speaks signifies the thing he is thinking, but for the most part only to himself and certain others, while he does not signify the same thing to the one he is speaking to or to some others. For if someone were to say in our presence that man is surpassed in power by large animals, we would not be able to brook such a statement; we would deny this false and repugnant assertion with vehemence, though perhaps the speaker

meant by *power* bodily strength. He may have expressed by the word what he had in mind, neither lying, not making a mistake about the thing, nor linking together memorized words while turning other things over in his mind, nor saying by a slip of the tongue what he did not intend to say. He merely calls the thing about which he was thinking by a name that is different from the one by which we call it. We would agree with him at once if we could read his mind and see directly the thought that he was unable to express by the words spoken the statement made.

They say that definition can cure this error, so that in this case, if the speaker were to define what virtue [*virtus*] is, it would be clear than the controversy is not about the thing but about the word. Now I may grant that this is so, but how often is it possible to find good definers? And yet many things have been charged against the science of defining, which are not approved by me in all respects, but it is not suitable to discuss this at present.

[44] I pass over the fact that we hear many things imperfectly and yet wrangle long and forcefully as if we had heard perfectly; for example, you were saying but some time ago that you had heard that *piety* is signified by a certain Punic word which I had called *mercy*, and you had heard this from those who know the language well. But I objected and insisted that you had forgotten what you had heard, for you seemed to me to say *faith* rather than *piety*, though you were sitting near me and the two words are by no means deceptive to the ear because of a similarity in sound. Yet for a long time I thought that you did not know what had been said to you, whereas it was I who did not know what you had said. If I had heard you well, it would not have seemed at all absurd to me that in Punic *piety* and *mercy* are called by one word.

These things happen now and then, but, as I said, we shall overlook them lest I seem to bring false witness against words because of the negligence of the hearer or even because of human defects. The points enumerated above are more distressing where, though we speak the same language as the speaker and the words are clearly heard and are Latin, we still are not able to understand the speaker.

[45] But witness: I now relent and admit that when words are perceived in the hearing of him to whom they are known, the hearer may rest assured that the speaker has thought about the things that they signify. But we are now asking if for that reason he learns whether the speaker has told the truth?

**Chapter XIV**

For do teachers profess that it is their thoughts that are perceived and grasped by the students, and not the sciences themselves that they convey through speaking? For who is so stupidly curious as to send his son to school in order that he may learn what the teacher thinks? But all those sciences that they profess to teach, and the science of virtue itself and wisdom, teachers explain through words. Then those who are called pupils consider within themselves whether what has been explained has been said truly; looking of course to that inner truth, to the extent each is able.

Thus, they learn, and when the inner truth makes known to them that true things have been said, they applaud, but without knowing that instead of applauding teachers they are applauding learners, if indeed their teachers know what they are saying. But men are mistaken, so that they call those teachers who are not, merely because for the most part there is no delay between the time of speaking and the time of recognition. And since after the speaker has reminded them, the pupils quickly learn within, they think that they have been taught outwardly by him who prompts them.

[46] But we shall, God willing, inquire at some other time about the utility of words, which if it is well considered is no mean matter. For the present, I have warned you that we should not attribute more to words than is proper. So that now we may not only believe but also begin to understand that it has truly been written on divine authority that we are not allowed to call anyone on earth our master because *there is only one Master of all, who is in heaven* [Matt. xxiii.8]. But what *in heaven* means He Himself will advertise to us by means of men, through signs and outwardly, so that we may by turning inwardly to Him be made wise; whom to know and to love is the blessed life

which, though all claim to seek it, few indeed may rejoice that they have found.

But now pray tell me what you think about this long disquisition of mine. For if you know that what I have said is true, then had you been questioned about each statement, you would have said that you did know it. You see, therefore, from whom you have learned these matters. Surely, not from me to whom you would have given the correct answer if questioned. However, if you do not know that they are true, neither the inner person nor I have taught you; not I, because I can never teach; not the inner person, because you have it not yet in you to learn.

*Adeo:* But I have learned by being reminded by your words that the human being is only prompted by words to learn, and it is clear that only a very small measure of what a speaker thinks is expressed in his words. And whether he who speaks from without is saying true things, only he who dwells withing can advise, whom I shall love the more ardently, he himself supporting, as I progress in understanding.

Nevertheless, I am most grateful to you for the discourse you delivered without breaking the thread of your thought, because it anticipated and dissolved all the objections that occurred to me, and nothing that was causing me doubt has been overlooked by you, nor is there anything answered by your words that the inner oracle is not likewise responding.

Adam tells Eve his names for the animals,
*Dictionnaire raisonné universel d'histoire naturelle.*

# LANGUAGE III

### Aristotle
*De interpretatione* Chapter I [10]

[i] Ἔστι μὲν οὖν τὰ ἐν τῇ φωνῇ τῶν ἐν τῇ ψυχῇ παθημάτων σύμβολα, καὶ τὰ γραφόμενα τῶν ἐν τῇ φωνῇ.

[ii] καὶ ὥσπερ οὐδὲ γράμματα πᾶσι τὰ αὐτά, οὐδὲ φωναὶ αἱ αὐταί·

[iii] ὧν μέντοι ταῦτα σημεῖα πρώτως, ταὐτὰ πᾶσι παθήματα τῆς ψυχῆς, καὶ ὧν ταῦτα ὁμοιώματα, πράγματα ἤδη ταὐτά. [iv] περὶ μὲν οὖν τούτων εἴρηται ἐν τοῖς περὶ ψυχῆς· ἄλλης γὰρ πραγματείας.

[v] Ἔστι δ', ὥσπερ ἐν τῇ ψυχῇ ὁτὲ μὲν νόημα ἄνευ τοῦ ἀληθεύειν ἢ ψεύδεσθαι, ὁτὲ δὲ ἤδη ᾧ ἀνάγκη τούτων ὑπάρχειν θάτερον, οὕτω καὶ ἐν τῇ φωνῇ·

[i] What is in speech are symbols of affections in the soul, and what is written down [are symbols] of what is in speech.

[ii] And just as what is written down is not the same for all human beings, neither are spoken sounds.

[iii] However, what these are signs of primarily, affections of soul, these are the same for all, and what these affections are likenesses of, the things, are also the same.

[iv] But these matters are spoken of in my writings on soul; what is to be done here is different.

[v] Now just as there are times when there is a conception in the soul without its being true or being false, but also times when of necessity one or the other of these obtains, so too in speech.

---

[10] Tr. J. Tomarchio, from *In Aristotelis libros Peri hermeneias* (Marietti, 1955); Greek text of the Loeb Classical Library, *The Categories of Interpretation* (Harvard University Press, 1938).

[vi] περὶ γὰρ σύνθεσιν καὶ διαίρεσίν ἐστι τὸ ψεῦδος καὶ τὸ ἀληθές.

[vii] τὰ μὲν οὖν ὀνόματα αὐτὰ καὶ τὰ ῥήματα ἔοικε τῷ ἄνευ συνθέσεως καὶ διαιρέσεως νοήματι, οἷον τὸ ἄνθρωπος ἢ τὸ λευκόν, ὅταν μὴ προστεθῇ τι· [viii] οὔτε γὰρ ψεῦδος οὔτε ἀληθές πω.

[vi] For false and true is about combination and separation.

[vii] But names themselves and verbs seem to belong to conception without combination or separation, such as *man* or *white*, whenever nothing else is enunciated. [viii] For there is not yet either what is false or what is true.

## Aquinas
### *In libros Peri hermeneia expositio*
Liber I, Lectio 2

... He states that things are understood from writing, spoken sounds, and affections of soul. Since an affection[11] is from some agent's affecting, affections of soul have their origin from things themselves. And if the human being were in fact a naturally solitary animal, the affections of soul by which they are conformed to things would suffice for them to have awareness of them within themselves. But since the human being is a naturally political and social animal, it was necessary that the conceptions of one human being be made known to others, which comes about through speech; and so significant sounds were needed in order for human beings to live together. It is for this reason that individuals of different languages are not able to live together well.

---

[11] *Passio* is the noun formed from the participle of the deponent verb *pati*, meaning *be affected, undergo, suffer, experience*; it is sometimes used to refer to the category that Aristotle names with the infinitive παθεῖν in his lists of categories in the *Categories, Topics,* and *Metaphysics*.

Moreover, if the human being made use only of sense knowledge, which looks only to the here and now, significant sound would be enough for him to live together with others, just as it is for animals, which by means of certain sounds manifest their conceptions to one another. But since the human being also makes use of intellectual knowledge, which abstracts from the here and now, a care attends them not only for the things that are there before them in time and place, but also for the things that are distant in place and future in time. So, in order for human beings to manifest their conceptions even of the things that are distant in place and the things that are to happen in future time, use of things written down was necessary.

But since Logic is directed to acquiring knowledge of things, the signification of words that is directly related to the conceptions themselves of understanding pertains to what it principally considers, but the signification of things written down, as more remote, does not pertain to what it considers, but rather to what grammarians consider. Thus, in showing the order among signifiers, he does not begin with written things but with spoken sounds, the significance of which he shows first, saying: *what is in speech are marks—or signs—of the affections that are in soul*. ...

Concerning what he says about the affections that are in soul, we should notice that usually only sense affections of desire are generally called *affections* of soul, such as anger, delight, and other things of the sort, as is said in *Ethics* 2. Now it is true that there are certain sounds of human beings that naturally signify affections of this sort, such as the groans of the sick and of other animals, as is said in *Politics* 1. But the present discourse is about sounds that are significant by human convention; and so, by *affections of soul* here must be understood conceptions of understanding, which nouns and verbs and sentences signify immediately, in Aristotle's opinion.

For it cannot be that they signify the things themselves immediately, which is clear from their way of signifying, since this name *human being* signifies human nature in abstraction from singulars, so it cannot be that it immediately signifies a singular human being. And for this reason, Platonists asserted that it signifies the separate idea itself of human being. But since in Aristotle's opinion this thing does not really exist independently but exists only in understanding, it was thus necessary for Aristotle to say that spoken sounds signify conceptions of understanding immediately and, with them mediating, things.

And since it is not usual for Aristotle to name conceptions of understanding *affections*, Andronicus stated that this book is not Aristotle's. But one clearly finds him in *De anima* 1 calling all operations of soul *affections*. So even a conception itself of understanding can be called an affection, either because our understanding never occurs without imagination, which never occurs without a bodily affection, for which reason the philosopher calls imaginative power *receptive understanding* in *De anima* 3; or else because by an extension of the name *affection* to every reception, even an act of understanding of potential understanding is a certain *being affected*, as is said in *De anima* 3.

Moreover, he makes use of the name affections rather than perceptions, either because it is from some affection of soul, such as from love or hate, that it comes about that a human being wants to signify to another in speech what is conceived within; or also because the signification of spoken sounds is directed to a conception of understanding insofar as it arises from things by way of a certain affecting or impressing....

Next, he shows that affections of soul exist naturally, just as things do, based on the fact that that they are the same among all human beings: *Just as affections of soul are the same for all human beings,* he writes, *of which primary things*—or primary affections—*these* spoken sounds *are marks,* or signs (because affections of soul are related to spoken sounds as primary to secondary, since spoken sounds are brought about only to express inner affections of soul), *so also are things the same* among all human beings, *of which* things *these* affections of soul *are likenesses.*[12]

---

[12] Aquinas is interpolating words into the quotation by way of glossing or explication.

Now it should be noted that he had said that things written down are marks, or signs, of spoken sounds, and spoken sounds likewise of affections of soul. But now he says that affections of soul are likenesses of things. He says this because things are only known by soul though some likeness of theirs existing either in sense or in understanding. However, written things are signs of spoken sounds and sounds of affections in such a way that there is not present in them any characteristic of likeness, but only the characteristic of a convention, as in the case of many other signs, as a trumpet is a sign of war. In the case of affections of soul, however, one must take note of the characteristic of likeness in order for them to express things, since they designate them naturally, and not by convention.

However, some object to this and want to bring evidence against his assertion that the affections of soul that spoken sounds signify are the same for all human beings: primarily, [they say] those different human beings have different opinions about things, so that all affections of soul do not seem to be the same among all human beings. To this objection Boethius responds that Aristotle is here calling *affections of soul* the conceptions of understanding that is never deceived: its conceptions must be the same among human beings, because if someone really disagrees, he does not understand.

For there can be what is false in understanding insofar as it combines or separates, but not insofar as it knows *what something is*, or the thing's essence, as is said in De anima 3; this must be understood to refer to the simple conceptions of understanding that uncompounded words signify, which are the same among all human beings, because if someone really understands *what a human being is* as anything in any way other than any human being he may apprehend, he does not understand *human being*. Now such simple conceptions of understanding are what spoken sounds signify primarily. For this reason, is it said in Metaphysics 4 that *the characteristic a name means is a definition*.[13] And thus does he say distinctly *of which primary things* these are marks, to refer to the primary conceptions primarily signified by spoken sounds.

---

[13] An alternative translation: *the meaning that a name signifies is a limit.*

A manuscript of *The Guide for The Perplexed*.
Hebrew translation made by Samuel Ibn Tibbon,,
written in a cursive Spanish hand and adorned with illuminations.

# LANGUAGE IV

## Moses Maimonides
### *The Guide for the Perplexed* Part I Ch. 35–54 [14]

### Chapter 35

Do not think that what we have laid down in the preceding chapters on the importance, obscurity, and difficulty of the subject, and its unsuitableness for communication to ordinary persons, includes the doctrine of God's incorporeality and His exemption from all affections (πάθη). This is not the case. For in the same way as all people must be informed, and even children must be trained in the belief that God is One, and that none besides Him is to be worshipped, so must all be taught by simple authority that God is incorporeal; that there is no similarity in any way whatsoever between Him and His creatures: that His existence is not like the existence of His creatures, His life not like that of any living being, His wisdom not like the wisdom of the wisest of men; and that the difference between Him and His creatures is not merely quantitative, but absolute [as between two individuals of two different classes]: I mean to say that all must understand that our wisdom and His, or our power and His do not differ quantitatively or qualitatively, or in a similar manner; for two things, of which the one is strong and the other weak, are necessarily similar, belong to the same class, and can be included in one definition. The same is the case with any other comparisons: they can only be made between two things belonging to the same class, as has been shown in works on Natural Science. Anything predicated of God is totally different from our attributes; no definition can comprehend both; therefore, His existence and that of any other being totally differ from each other, and the term existence is applied to both equivocally, as I shall explain.

---

[14] Tr. Michael Friedlander (George Routledge & Sons, London; E.P. Dutton & Co., New York, 1904), emended for pedagogical purposes.

This suffices for the guidance of children and of ordinary persons who must believe that there is a Being existing, perfect, incorporeal, not inherent in a body as a force in it—God, who is above all kinds of deficiency, above all affections. But the question concerning the attributes of God, their inadmissibility, and the meaning of those attributes which are ascribed to Him; concerning the Creation, His Providence, in providing for everything; concerning His will, His perception, His knowledge of everything; concerning prophecy and its various degrees: concerning the meaning of His names which imply the idea of unity, though they are more than one; all these things are very difficult problems, the true "Secrets of the Law", the "secrets" mentioned so frequently in the books of the Prophets, and in the words of our Teachers, the subjects of which we should only mention in the headings of the chapters, as we have already stated, and only in the presence of a person satisfying the above-named conditions....

## Chapter 50

... If, however, you have a desire to rise to a higher state, viz., that of reflection, and truly to hold the conviction that God is One and possesses true unity, without admitting plurality or divisibility in any sense whatever, you must understand that God has no essential attribute in any form or in any sense whatever, and that the rejection of corporeality implies the rejection of essential attributes.

Those who believe that God is One, and that He has many attributes, declare the unity with their lips, and assume plurality in their thoughts. This is like the doctrine of the Christians, who say that He is one and He is three, and that the three are one. Of the same character is the doctrine of those who say that God is One, but that He has many attributes; and that He with His attributes is One, although they deny corporeality and affirm His most absolute freedom from matter; as if our object were to seek forms of expression, not subjects of belief.

For belief is only possible after the apprehension of a thing; it consists in the conviction that the thing apprehended has its existence beyond the mind [in reality] exactly as it is conceived in the mind....

## Chapter 51

There are many things whose existence is manifest and obvious; some of these are innate notions or objects of sensation, others are nearly so: and, in fact, they would require no proof if man had been left in his primitive state. Such are the existence of motion, of man's free will, of phases of production and destruction, and of the natural properties perceived by the senses, e.g., the heat of fire, the coldness of water, and many other similar things. False notions, however, may be spread either by a person laboring under error, or by one who has some particular end in view, and who establishes theories contrary to the real nature of things, by denying the existence of things perceived by the senses, or by affirming the existence of what does not exist. Philosophers are thus required to establish by proof things which are self-evident, and to disprove the existence of things which only exist in man's imagination. Thus, Aristotle gives a proof for the existence of motion, because it had been denied: he disproves the reality of atoms, because it had been asserted.

To the same class belongs the rejection of essential attributes in reference to God. For it is a self-evident truth that the attribute is not inherent in the object to which it is ascribed, but it is superadded to its essence, and is consequently an accident; if the attribute denoted the essence [τὸ τί ἦν εἶναι] of the object, it would be either mere tautology, as if, e.g., one would say "man is man," or the explanation of a name, as, e.g., "man is a speaking animal"; for the words "speaking animal" include the true essence of man, and there is no third element besides life and speech in the definition of man; when he, therefore, is described by the attributes of life and speech, these are nothing but an explanation of the name "man," that is to say, that the thing which is called man, consists of life and speech.

It will now be clear that the attribute must be one of two things, either the essence of the object described—in that case it is a mere explanation of a name, and on that account we might admit the attribute in reference to God, but we reject it from another cause as will be shown—or the attribute is something different from the object described, some extraneous superadded element; in that case the attribute would be an accident, and he who merely rejects the appellation "accidents" in reference to the attributes of God, does not thereby alter their character: for everything superadded to the essence of an object joins it without forming part of its essential properties, and that constitutes an accident.

Add to this the logical consequence of admitting many attributes, viz., the existence of many eternal beings. There cannot be any belief in the unity of God except by admitting that He is one simple substance, without any composition or plurality of elements: one from whatever side you view it, and by whatever test you examine it: not divisible into two parts in any way and by any cause, nor capable of any form of plurality either objectively or subjectively, as will be proved in this treatise.

Some thinkers have gone so far as to say that the attributes of God are neither His essence nor anything extraneous to His essence. This is like the assertion of some theorists, that the ideals, i.e., the *universalia*, are neither existing nor non-existent, and like the views of others, that the atom does not fill a definite place, but keeps an atom of space occupied; that man has no freedom of action at all, but has acquirement. Such things are only said: they exist only in words, not in thought, much less in reality.

But as you know, and as all know who do not delude themselves, these theories are preserved by a multitude of words, by misleading similes sustained by declamation and invective, and by numerous methods borrowed both from dialectics and sophistry. If after uttering them and supporting them by such words, a man were to examine for himself his own belief on this subject, he would see nothing but confusion and stupidity in an endeavor to prove the existence of things which do not exist, or to find a mean between two opposites that have no mean. Or is there a mean between existence and non-existence, or between the identity and non-identity of two things? But, as we said, to such absurdities men were forced by the great license given to the imagination, and by the fact that every existing material thing is necessarily imagined as a certain substance possessing several attributes; for nothing has ever been found that consists of one simple substance without any attribute.

Guided by such imaginations, men thought that God was also composed of many different elements, viz., of His essence and of the attributes superadded to His essence. Following up this comparison, some believed that God was corporeal, and that He possessed attributes: others, abandoning this theory, denied the corporeality, but retained the attributes. The adherence to the literal sense of the text of Holy Writ is the source of all this error, as I shall show in some of the chapters devoted to this theme.

## Chapter 52

Every description of an object by an affirmative attribute, which includes the assertion that an object is of a certain kind, must be made in one of the following five ways:—

First. The object is described by its definition, as e.g., man is described as a being that lives and has reason; such a description, containing the true essence of the object, is, as we have already shown, nothing else but the explanation of a name. All agree that this kind of description cannot be given of God; for there are no previous causes to His existence, by which He could be defined: and on that account it is a well-known principle, received by all the philosophers, who are precise in their statements, that no definition can be given of God.

Secondly. An object is described by part of its definition, as when, e.g., man is described as a living being or as a rational being. This kind of description includes the necessary connection [of the two ideas]; for when we say that every man is rational, we mean by it that every being which has the characteristics of man must also have reason. All agree that this kind of description is inappropriate in reference to God; for if we were to speak of a portion of His essence, we should consider His essence to be a compound. The inappropriateness of this kind of description in reference to God is the same as that of the preceding kind.

Thirdly. An object is described by something different from its true essence, by something that does not complement or establish the essence of the object. The description, therefore, relates to a quality; but quality, in its most general sense, is an accident. If God could be described in this way, He would be the substratum of accidents—a sufficient reason for rejecting the idea that He possesses quality, since it diverges from the true conception of his essence. It is surprising how those who admit the application of attributes to God can reject, in reference to Him, comparison and qualification. For when they say, "He cannot be qualified," they can only mean that He possess no quality; and yet every positive essential attribute of an object either constitutes its essence—and in that case it is identical with the essence—or it contains a quality of the object....

Consequently, these three classes of attributes, describing the essence of a thing, or part of the essence, or a quality of it, are clearly inadmissible in reference to God, for they imply composition, which, as we shall prove, is out of the question as regards the Creator. We say, with regard to this latter, point, that He is absolutely One.

Fourthly. A thing is described by its relation to another thing, e.g., to time, to space, or to a different individual; thus, we say, Zaid, the father of A or the partner of G, or who dwells at a certain place, or who lived at a stated time. This kind of attribute does not necessarily imply plurality or change in the essence of the object described ....

At first thought, it would seem that they may be employed in reference to God, but after careful and thorough consideration we are convinced of their inadmissibility. It is quite clear that there is no relation between God and time or space. For time is an accident connected with motion ... and since motion is one of the conditions to which only material bodies are subject, and God is immaterial, there can be no relation between Him and time. Similarly, there is no relation between Him and space.

But what we have to investigate and to examine is this: whether some real relation exists between God and any of the substances created by Him, by which He could be described? That there is no correlation between Him and any of His creatures can easily be seen; for the characteristic of two objects correlative to each other is the equality of their reciprocal relation. Now, as God has absolute existence, while all other beings have only possible existence, as we shall show, there consequently cannot be any correlation [between God and His creatures].

That a certain kind of relation does exist between them is by some considered possible, but wrongly. It is impossible to imagine a relation between intellect and sight, although, as we believe, the same kind of existence is common to both; how, then could a relation be imagined between any creature and God, who has nothing in common with any other being; for even the term existence is applied to Him and other things, according to our opinion, only by way of pure equivocity. Consequently, there is no relation whatever between Him and any other being. For whenever we speak of a relation between two things, these belong to the same kind; but when two things belong to different kinds though of the same class, there is no relation between them.... How, then, could there be a relation between God and His creatures, considering the important difference between them in respect to true existence, the greatest of all differences.

Besides, if any relation existed between them, God would be subject to the accident of relation; and although that would not be an accident to the essence of God, it would still be, to some extent, a kind of accident. You would, therefore, be wrong if you applied affirmative attributes in their literal sense to God, though they contained only relations; these, however are the most appropriate of all attributes to be employed, in a less strict sense, in reference to God, because they do not imply that a plurality of eternal things exists, or that any change takes place in the essence of God, when those things change to which God is in relation.

Fifthly. A thing is described by its actions; I do not mean by its actions the inherent capacity for a certain work, as is expressed in *carpenter, painter, or smith*—for these belong to the class of qualities which have been mentioned above—but I mean the action the latter has performed—we speak, e.g., of Zaid, who made this door, built that wall, wove that garment. This kind of attribute is separate from the essences of the thing described, and, therefore, appropriate to be employed in describing the Creator, especially since we know that these different actions do not imply that different elements must be contained in the substance of the agent, by which the different actions are produced, as will be explained. On the contrary, all the actions of God emanate from His essence, not from any extraneous thing superadded to His essence, as we have shown.

What we have explained in the present chapter is this: that God is one in every respect, containing no plurality or any element superadded to His essence, and that the many attributes of different significations applied in Scripture to God, originate in the multitude of His actions, not in a plurality existing in His essence, and are partly employed with the object of conveying to us some notion of His perfection, in accordance with what we consider perfection, as has been explained by us. The possibility of one simple substance excluding plurality, though accomplishing different actions, will be illustrated by examples in the next chapter.

## Chapter 53

The circumstance which caused men to believe in the existence of divine attributes is similar to that which caused others to believe in the corporeality of God. The latter have not arrived at that belief by speculation, but by following the literal sense of certain passages in the Bible. The same is the case with the attributes; when in the books of the Prophets and of the Law, God is described by attributes, such passages are taken in their literal sense, and it is then believed that God possesses attributes—as if He were to be exalted above corporeality, and not above things connected with corporeality ....

We apply to all such passages the principle, "The Torah speaks in the language of the sons of man," and say that the object of all these terms is to describe God as the most perfect being, not as possessing those qualities which are only perfections in relation to created living beings. Many of the attributes express different acts of God, but that difference does not necessitate any difference as regards Him from whom the acts proceed. This fact, viz., that from one agency different effects may result, although that agency has not free will, and much more so if it has free will, I will illustrate by an instance taken from our own sphere.

Fire melts certain things and makes others hard, it boils and burns, it bleaches and blackens. If we described the fire as bleaching, blackening, burning, boiling, hardening and melting, we should be correct, and yet he who does not know the nature of fire, would think that it included six different elements, one by which it blackens, another by which it bleaches, a third by which it boils, a fourth by which it consumes, a fifth by which it melts, a sixth by which it hardens things—actions which are opposed to one another, and of which each has its peculiar property. He, however, who knows the nature of fire, will know that by virtue of one quality in action, namely, by heat, it produces all these effects.

If this is the case with that which is done by nature, how much more is it the case with regard to God, who is above all description. If we, therefore, perceive in God certain relations of various kinds—for wisdom in us is different from power, and power from will—it does by no means follow that different elements are really contained in Him, that He contains one element by which He knows, another by which He wills, and another by which He exercises power, as is, in fact, the signification of the attributes of God according to the attributes....

There still remains one difficulty which led them to that error, and which I am now going to mention. Those who assert the existence of the attributes do not found their opinion on the variety of God's actions; they say it is true that one substance can be the source of various effects, but His essential attributes cannot be qualifications of His actions, because it is impossible to imagine that the Creator created Himself. They vary with regard to the so-called essential attributes—I mean as regards their number—according to the text of the Scripture which each of them follows. I will enumerate those on which all agree, and the knowledge of which they believe that they have derived from reasoning, not from some words of the Prophets, namely, the following four: life, power, wisdom, and will. They believe that these are four different things, and such perfections as cannot possibly be absent from the Creator, and that these cannot be qualifications of His actions. This is their opinion.

But you must know that wisdom and life in reference to God are not different from each other; for in every being that is conscious of itself, life and wisdom are the same thing, that is to say, if by wisdom we understand the consciousness of self. Besides, the subject and the object of that consciousness are undoubtedly identical [as regards God]; for according to our opinion, He is not composed of an element that apprehends, and another that does not apprehend; He is not like man, who is a combination of a conscious soul and an unconscious body. If, therefore, by *wisdom* we mean the faculty of self-consciousness, wisdom and life are one and the same thing. They, however, do not speak of wisdom in this sense, but of His power to apprehend His creatures.

There is also no doubt that power and will do not exist in God in reference to Himself; for He cannot have power or will as regards Himself; we cannot imagine such a thing. They take these attributes as different relations between God and His creatures, signifying that He has power in creating things, will in giving to things existence as He desires, and wisdom in knowing what He created. Consequently, these attributes do not refer to the essence of God, but express relations between Him and His creatures.

Therefore, we who truly believe in the Unity of God, declare, that as we do not believe that some element is included in His essence by which He created the heavens, another by which He created the [four] elements, a third by which He created the ideals, in the same way we reject the idea that His essence contains an element by which He has power, another element by which He has will, and a third by which He has a knowledge of His creatures. On the contrary, He is a simple essence, without any additional element whatever; He created the universe, and knows it, but not by an extraneous force. There is no difference whether these various attributes refer to His actions or to relations between Him and His works; in fact, these relations, as we have also shown, exist only in the thoughts of men. This is what we must believe concerning the attributes occurring in the books of the Prophets; some may also be taken as expressive of the perfection of God by way of comparison with what we consider as perfections in us, as we shall explain.

## Chapter 54

The wisest man, our Teacher Moses, asked two things of God, and received a reply respecting both. The one thing he asked was, that God should let him know His true essence: the other, which in fact he asked first, that God should let him know His attributes.

In answer to both these petitions God promised that He would let him know all His attributes, and that these were nothing but His actions. He also told him that His true essence could not be perceived, and pointed out a method by which he could obtain the utmost knowledge of God possible for man to acquire. The knowledge obtained by Moses has not been possessed by any human being before him or after him. His petition to know the attributes of God is contained in the following words: "Show me now thy way, that I may know thee, that I may find grace in thy sight" (Exod. xxxiii. 13).

Consider how many excellent ideas found expression in the words, "Show me thy way, that I may know thee." We learn from them that God is known by His attributes, for Moses believed that he knew Him, when he was shown the way of God. The words "That I may find grace in thy sight," imply that he who knows God finds grace in His eyes. Not only is he acceptable and welcome to God who fasts and prays, but everyone who knows Him. He who has no knowledge of God is the object of His wrath and displeasure. The pleasure and the displeasure of God, the approach to Him and the withdrawal from Him are proportional to the amount of man's knowledge or ignorance concerning the Creator. We have already gone too far away from our subject, let us now return to it.

Moses prayed to God to grant him knowledge of His attributes, and also pardon for His people; when the latter had been granted, he continued to pray for the knowledge of God's essence in the words, "Show me thy glory" (*ibid.* 18), and then received, respecting his first request, "Show me thy way," the following favorable reply, "I will make all my goodness to pass before thee" (*ibid.* 19); as regards the second request, however, he was told, "Thou canst not see my face" (*ibid.* 20).

The words "all my goodness" imply that God promised to show him the whole creation, concerning which it has been stated, "And God saw everything that he had made, and, behold, it was very good" (Gen. i. 31); when I say "to show him the whole creation," I mean to imply that God promised to make him comprehend the nature of all things, their relation to each other, and the way they are governed by God both in reference to the universe as a whole and to each creature in particular. This knowledge is referred to when we are told of Moses, "he is firmly established in all mine house" (Num. xii. 7); that is, "his knowledge of all the creatures in My universe is correct and firmly established"; for false opinions are not firmly established. Consequently, the knowledge of the works of God is the knowledge of His attributes, by which He can be known.

The fact that God promised Moses to give him a knowledge of His works, may be inferred from the circumstance that God taught him such attributes as refer exclusively to His works, viz., "merciful and gracious, longsuffering and abundant in goodness," etc., (Exod. xxxiv. 6). It is therefore clear that the ways which Moses wished to know, and which God taught him, are the actions emanating from God.

Our Sages call them *middot* (qualities) and speak of the thirteen *middoth* of God (Talm. B. Rosh ha-shanah, p. 17b). They used the term also in reference to man; compare, "There are four different *middoth* (characters) among those who go to the house of learning"; and, "There are four different *middoth* (characters) among those who give charity" (Mishnah Abot, v. 13, 14). They do not mean to say that God really possesses *middot* (qualities), but that He performs actions similar to such of our actions as originate in certain qualities, i.e., in certain psychical dispositions, not that God has really such dispositions. Although Moses was shown "all His goodness," i.e., all His works, only the thirteen *middot* are mentioned, because they include those acts of God which refer to the creation and the government of mankind, and to know these acts was the principal object of the prayer of Moses. This is shown by the conclusion of his prayer, "that I may know thee, that I may find grace in thy sight, and consider that this nation is thy people" (Exod. xxxiii. 16), that is to say, the people whom I have to rule by certain acts in the performance of which I must be guided by Thy own acts in governing them. We have thus shown that "the ways" used in the Bible and *middot* used in the Mishnah are identical, denoting the acts emanating from God in reference to the universe.

Whenever any one of His actions is perceived by us, we ascribe to God that emotion which is the source of the act when performed by ourselves, and we call Him by an epithet which is formed from the verb expressing that emotion. We see, e.g., how well He provides for the life of the embryo of living beings; how He endows with certain faculties both the embryo itself and those who have to rear it after its birth, in order that it may be protected from death and destruction, guarded against all harm, and assisted in the performance of all that is required [for its development]. Similar acts, when performed by us, are due to a certain emotion and tenderness called mercy and pity. God is, therefore, said to be merciful: e.g., "Like as a father is merciful to his children, so the Lord is merciful to them that fear Him" (Ps. ciii. 13); "And I will spare them, as a man spareth (*yahamol*) his own son that serveth him" (Mal. iii. 17).

Such instances do not imply that God is influenced by a feeling of mercy, but that acts similar to those which a father performs for his son, out of pity, mercy and real affection, emanate from God solely for the benefit of His pious men, and are by no means the result of any impression or change [produced in God]. When we give something to a person who has no claim upon us, we perform an act of grace, e.g., "Grant them graciously unto us" (Judges xxi. 22). [The same term is used in reference to God, e.g.] "which God hath graciously given" (Gen. xxxiii. 5); "Because God hath dealt graciously with me" (*ibid.* 11). Instances of this kind are numerous. God creates and guides beings who have no claim upon Him to be created and guided by Him; He is therefore called gracious (*ḥannun*).

His actions towards mankind also include great calamities, which overtake individuals and bring death to them, or affect whole families and even entire regions, spread death, destroy generation after generation, and spare nothing whatsoever. Hence there occur inundations, earthquakes, destructive storms, expeditions of one nation against the other for the sake of destroying it with the sword and blotting out its memory, and many other evils of the same kind. Whenever such evils are caused by us to any person, they originate in great anger, violent jealousy, or a desire for revenge. God is therefore called, because of these acts, "jealous," "revengeful," "wrathful," and "keeping anger" (Nah. i. 2) that is to say, He performs acts similar to those which, when performed by us, originate in certain psychical dispositions, in jealousy, desire for retaliation, revenge, or anger: they are in accordance with the guilt of those who are to be punished, and not the result of any emotion: for He is above all defect!

The same is the case with all divine acts: though resembling those acts which emanate from our passions and psychical dispositions, they are not due to anything superadded to His essence. The governor of a country, if he is a prophet, should conform to these attributes. Acts [of punishment] must be performed by him moderately and in accordance with justice, not merely as an outlet of his passion. He must not let loose his anger, nor allow his passion to overcome him: for all passions are bad, and they must be guarded against as far as it lies in man's power. At times and towards some persons he must be merciful and gracious, not only from motives of mercy and compassion, but according to their merits: at other times and towards other persons he must evince anger, revenge, and wrath in proportion to their guilt, but not from motives of passion. He must be able to condemn a person to death by fire without anger, passion, or loathing against him, and must exclusively be guided by what he perceives of the guilt of the person, and by a sense of the great benefit which a large number will derive from such a sentence.

You have, no doubt, noticed in the Torah how the commandment to annihilate the seven nations, and "to save alive nothing that breatheth" (Deut. xx. 16) is followed immediately by the words, "That they teach you not to do after all their abominations, which they have done unto their gods: so should you sin against the Lord your God" (*ibid.* 18); that is to say, you shall not think that this commandment implies an act of cruelty or of retaliation; it is an act demanded by the tendency of man to remove everything that might turn him away from the right path, and to clear away all obstacles in the road to perfection, that is, to the knowledge of God.

Nevertheless, acts of mercy, pardon, pity, and grace should more frequently be performed by the governor of a country than acts of punishment; seeing that all the thirteen *middoth* of God are attributes of mercy with only one exception, namely, "visiting the iniquity of the fathers upon the children" (Exod. xxxiv. 7); for the meaning of the preceding attribute (in the original *ve-nakkeh lo yenakkeh*) is "and he will not utterly destroy"; (and not "He will by no means clear the guilty"); compare, "And she will be utterly destroyed (*ve-nikketah*), she shall sit upon the ground" (Isa. iii. 26).

When it is said that God is visiting the iniquity of the fathers upon the children, this refers exclusively to the sin of idolatry, and to no other sin. That this is the case may be inferred from what is said in the ten commandments, "upon the third and fourth generation of my enemies" (Exod. xx. 5), none except idolaters being called "enemy"; compare also, "Every abomination to the Lord, which he hates" (Deut. xii. 31). It was, however, considered sufficient to extend the punishment to the fourth generation, because the fourth generation is the utmost a man can see of his posterity; and when, therefore, the idolaters of a place are destroyed, the old man worshipping idols is killed, his son, his grandson, and his great-grandson, that is, the fourth generation. By the mention of this attribute we are, as it were, told that His commandments, undoubtedly in harmony with His acts, include the death even of the little children of idolaters because of the sin of their fathers and grandfathers. This principle we find frequently applied in the Law, as, e.g., we read concerning the city that has been led astray to idolatry, "destroy it utterly, and all that is therein" (Deut. xiii. 15). All this has been ordained in order that every vestige of that which would lead to great injury should he blotted out, as we have explained.

We have gone too far away from the subject of this chapter, but we have shown why it has been considered sufficient to mention only these (thirteen) out of all His acts: namely, because they are required for the good government of a country; for the chief aim of man should be to make himself, as far as possible, similar to God: that is to say, to make his acts similar to the acts of God, or as our Sages expressed it in explaining the verse, "Ye shall be holy" (Lev. xxi. 2): "He is gracious, so be you also gracious: He is merciful, so be you also merciful."

The principal object of this chapter was to show that all attributes ascribed to God are attributes of His acts, and do not imply that God has any qualities.

Detail of Illuminated Manuscript of the Guide:
*Maimonides teaching the measure of men.*

# LANGUAGE V

## Moses Maimonides
### *The Guide for the Perplexed* Part I Ch. 55–60 [15]

### Chapter 55

We have already, on several occasions, shown in this treatise that everything that implies corporeality or passiveness, is to be negated in reference to God, for all passiveness implies change: and the agent producing that state is undoubtedly different from the thing affected by it; and if God could be affected in any way whatever, another being beside Him would act on Him and cause change in Him.

All kinds of non-existence must likewise be negated in reference to Him: no perfection whatever can therefore be imagined to be at one time absent from Him, and at another present in Him: for if this were the case, He would [at a certain time] only be potentially perfect. Potentiality always implies non-existence, and when anything has to pass from potentiality into reality, another thing that exists in reality is required to effect that transition. Hence it follows that all perfections must really exist in God, and none of them must in any way be a mere potentiality.

Another thing likewise to be denied in reference to God, is similarity to any existing being. This has been generally accepted, and is also mentioned in the books of the Prophets: e.g., "To whom, then, will you liken me?" (Isa. xl. 25); "To whom, then, will you liken God?" (*ibid.* 18); "There is none like unto Thee" (Jer. x. 6). Instances of this kind are frequent. In short, it is necessary to demonstrate by proof that nothing can be predicated of God that implies any of these four things: corporeality, emotion or change, nonexistence—e.g., that something

---

[15] Tr. Michael Friedlander (George Routledge & Sons, London; E.P. Dutton & Co., New York, 1904), emended for pedagogical purposes.

would be potential at one time and real at another--and similarity with any of His creatures.

In this respect our knowledge of God is aided by the study of Natural Science. For he who is ignorant of the latter cannot understand the defect implied in emotions, the difference between potentiality and reality, the non-existence implied in all potentiality, the inferiority of a thing that exists in potency to that which moves in order to cause its transition from potentiality into reality, and the inferiority of that which moves for this purpose compared with its condition when the transition has been effected. He who knows these things, but without their proofs, does not know the details which logically result from these general propositions: and therefore he cannot prove that God exists, or that the [four] things mentioned above are inadmissible in reference to God.

Having premised these remarks, I shall explain in the next chapter the error of those who believe that God has essential attributes: those who have some knowledge of Logic and Natural Science will understand it.

## Chapter 56

Similarity is based on a certain relation between two things; if between two things no relation can be found, there can be no similarity between them, and there is no relation between two things that have no similarity to each other; e.g., we do not say this heat is similar to that color, or this voice is similar to that sweetness. This is self-evident. Since the existence of a relation between God and man, or between Him and other beings has been denied, similarity must likewise be denied.

You must know that two things of the same kind—i.e., whose essential properties are the same, and which are distinguished from each other by greatness and smallness, strength and weakness, etc.— are necessarily similar, though different in this one way; e.g., a grain of mustard and the sphere of the fixed stars are similar as regards the three dimensions, although the one is exceedingly great, the other exceeding small, the property of having [three] dimensions is the same in both; or the heat of wax melted by the sun and the heat of the element of fire, are similar as regards heat; although the heat is exceedingly great in the one case, and exceedingly small in the other, the existence of that quality (heat) is the same in both.

Thus, those who believe in the presence of essential attributes in God, viz., Existence, Life, Power, Wisdom, and Will, should know that these attributes, when applied to God, have not the same meaning as when applied to us, and that the difference does not only consist in magnitude, or in the degree of perfection, stability, and durability. It cannot be said, as they practically believe, that His existence is only more stable, His life more permanent, His power greater, His wisdom more perfect, and His will more general than ours, and that the same definition applies to both.

This is in no way admissible, for the expression *more than* is used in comparing two things as regards a certain attribute predicated of both of them in exactly the same sense, and consequently implied similarity [between God and His creatures]. When they ascribe to God essential attributes, these so-called essential attributes should not have any similarity to the attributes of other things, and according to their own opinion should not be included in one and the same definition, just as there is not similarity between the essence of God and that of other beings. They do not follow this principle, for they hold that one definition may include them, and that, nevertheless, there is no similarity between them.

Those who are familiar with the meaning of similarity will certainly understand that the term existence, when applied to God and to other beings, is perfectly equivocal. In like manner, the terms Wisdom, Power, Will, and Life are applied to God and to other beings by way of perfect equivocity, admitting of no comparison whatever. Nor must you think that these attributes are employed as compound terms; for compound terms are such as are applied to two things which have a similarity to each other in respect to a certain property which is in both of them an accident, not an essential, constituent element. The attributes of God, however, are not considered as accidental by an intelligent person, while all attributes applied to man are accidents, according to the Mutakallemim.

I am therefore at a loss to see how they can find any similarity [between the attributes of God and those of man]; how their definitions can be identical and their significations the same! This is a decisive proof that there is, in no way or sense, anything common to the attributes predicated of God, and those used in reference to ourselves; they have only the same names, and nothing else is common to them.

Such being the case, it is not proper to believe, on account of the use of the same attributes, that there is in God something additional to His essence, in the same way as attributes are joined to our essence. This is most important, for those who understand it. Keep it in memory, and study it thoroughly, in order to be well prepared for that which I am going to explain to you.

**Chapter 57**

ON ATTRIBUTES. Remarks more recondite than the preceding.

It is known that existence is an accident appertaining to all things, and therefore an element superadded to their essence. This must evidently be the case as regards everything the existence of which is due to some cause: its existence is an element superadded to its essence. But as regards a being whose existence is not due to any cause--God alone is that being, for His existence, as we have said, is absolute--existence and essence are perfectly identical. He is not a substance to which existence is joined as an accident, as an additional element. His existence is always absolute and has never been a new element or an accident in Him. Consequently, God exists without possessing the attribute of existence.

Similarly, He lives, without possessing the attribute of life; knows, without possessing the attribute of knowledge; is omnipotent without possessing the attribute of omnipotence; is wise, without possessing the attribute of wisdom: all this reduces itself to one and the same entity; there is no plurality in Him, as will be shown.

It is further necessary to consider that unity and plurality are accidents supervening to a thing according as it consists of many elements or of one. This is fully explained in the book called Metaphysics. In the same way as number is not the substance of the things numbered, so is unity not the substance of the thing which has the attribute of unity, for unity and plurality are accidents belonging to the category of discrete quantity and supervening to such things as are capable of receiving them. To that being, however, which has truly simple, absolute existence, and in which composition is inconceivable, the accident of unity is as inadmissible as the accident of plurality; that is to say, God's unity is not an element superadded, but He is One without possessing the attribute of unity.

The investigation of this subject, which is almost too subtle for our understanding, must not be based on current expressions employed in describing it, for these are the great source of error. It would be extremely difficult for us to find, in any language whatsoever, words adequate to this subject, and we can only employ inadequate language. In our endeavor to show that God does not include a plurality, we can only say "He is one," although "one" and "many" are both terms which serve to distinguish quantity. We therefore make the subject clearer and show to the understanding the way of truth by saying He is one but does not possess the attribute of unity.

The same is the case when we say God is the First (*Kadmon*), to express that He has not been created; the term "First" is decidedly inaccurate, for it can in its true sense only be applied to a being that is subject to the relation of time; the latter, however, is an accident to motion which again is connected with a body. Besides the attribute "first" is a relative term, being in regard to time the same as the terms "long" and "short" are in regard to a line. Both expressions, "first" and "created," are equally inadmissible in reference to any being to which the attribute of time is not applicable, just as we do not say "crooked" or "straight" in reference to taste, "salted" or "insipid" in reference to the voice.

These subjects are not unknown to those who have accustomed themselves to seek a true understanding of the things, and to establish their properties in accordance with the abstract notions which the mind has formed of them, and who are not misled by the inaccuracy of the words employed. All attributes, such as "the First," "the Last," occurring in the Scriptures in reference to God, are as metaphorical as the expressions "ear" and "eye." They simply signify that God is not subject to any change or innovation whatever; they do not imply that God can be described by time, or that there is any comparison between Him and any other being as regards time, and that He is called on that account "the first" and "the last." In short, all similar expressions are borrowed from the language commonly used among the people. In the same way we use "One" in reference to God, to express that there is nothing similar to Him, but we do not mean to say that an attribute of unity is added to His essence.

## Chapter 58

This chapter is even more recondite than the preceding. Know that the negative attributes of God are the true attributes: they do not include any incorrect notions or any deficiency whatever in reference to God, while positive attributes imply polytheism, and are inadequate, as we have already shown. It is now necessary to explain how negative expressions can in a certain sense be employed as attributes, and how they are distinguished from positive attributes. Then I shall show that we cannot describe the Creator by any means except by negative attributes.

An attribute does not exclusively belong to the one thing to which it is related; while qualifying one thing, it can also be employed to qualify other things, and is in that case not peculiar to that one thing. For example, if you see a thing from a distance, and on enquiring what it is, are told that it is a living being, you have certainly learnt an attribute of the thing seen, and although that attribute does not exclusively belong to the thing perceived, it expresses that the thing is not a plant or a mineral. Again, if a man is in a certain house, and you know that something is in the house, but not exactly what, you ask what is in that house, and you are told, not a plant nor a mineral. You have thereby obtained some special knowledge of the thing; you have learnt that it is a living being, although you do not yet know what kind of a living being it is.

The negative attributes have this in common with the positive, that they necessarily circumscribe the thing to some extent, although such circumscription consists only in the exclusion of what otherwise would not be excluded. In the following point, however, the negative attributes are distinguished from the positive. The positive attributes, although not peculiar to one thing, describe a portion of what we desire to know, either some part of its essence or some of its accidents; the negative attributes, on the other hand, do not as regards the essence of the thing we desire to know in any way tell us what it is, except it be indirectly, as has been shown in the instance given by us.

After this introduction, I would observe that—as has already been shown—God's existence is absolute, that it includes no composition, as will be proved, and that we comprehend only the fact that He exists, not His essence. Consequently it is a false assumption to hold that He has any positive attribute; for He does not possess existence in addition to His essence; it therefore cannot be said that the one may be described as an attribute [of the other]; much less has He [in addition to His existence] a compound essence, consisting of two constituent elements to which the attribute could refer; still less has He accidents, which could be described by an attribute. Hence it is clear that He has no positive attribute whatever.

The negative attributes, however, are those which are necessary to direct the mind to the truths which we must believe concerning God; for, on the one hand, they do not imply any plurality, and, on the other, they convey to man the highest possible knowledge of God; e.g., it has been established by proof that some being must exist besides those things which can be perceived by the senses, or apprehended by the mind; when we say of this being, that it exists, we mean that its non-existence is impossible. We then perceive that such a being is not, for instance, like the four elements, which are inanimate, and we therefore say that it is living, expressing thereby that it is not dead. We call such a being incorporeal, because we notice that it is unlike the heavens, which are living, but material. Seeing that it is also different from the intellect, which, though incorporeal and living, owes its existence to some cause, we say it is the first, expressing thereby that its existence is not due to any cause.

We further notice, that the existence, that is the essence, of this being is not limited to its own existence; many existences emanate from it, and its influence is not like that of the fire in producing heat, or that of the sun in sending forth light, but consists in constantly giving them stability and order by well-established rule, as we shall show: we say, on that account, it has power, wisdom, and will, i.e., it is not feeble or ignorant, or hasty, and does not abandon its creatures; when we say that it is not feeble, we mean that its existence is capable of producing the existence of many other things; by saying that it is not ignorant, we mean *it perceives* or *it lives*—for everything that perceives is living—by saying, "It is not hasty, and does not abandon its creatures," we mean that all these creatures preserve a certain order and arrangement; they are not left to themselves; they are not produced aimlessly, but whatever condition they receive from that being is given with design and intention. We thus learn that there is no other being like unto God, and we say that He is One, i.e., there are not more Gods than one.

It has thus been shown that every attribute predicated of God either denotes the quality of an action, or—when the attribute is intended to convey some idea of the Divine Being itself, and not of His actions—the negation of the opposite. Even these negative attributes must not be formed and applied to God, except in the way in which, as you know, sometimes an attribute is negative in reference to a thing, although that attribute can naturally never be applied to it in the same sense, as, e.g., we say, "This wall does not see."

Those who read the present work are aware that, notwithstanding all the efforts of the mind, we can obtain no knowledge of the essence of the heavens—a revolving substance which has been measured by us in spans and cubits, and examined even as regards the proportions of the several spheres to each other and respecting most of their motions—although we know that they must consist of matter and form; but the matter not being the same as sublunary matter, we can only describe the heavens in terms expressing negative properties, but not in terms denoting positive qualities. Thus, we say that the heavens are not light, not heavy, not passive and therefore not subject to impressions, and that they do not possess the sensations of taste and smell; or we use similar negative attributes. All this we do, because we do not know their substance.

What, then, can be the result of our efforts, when we try to obtain a knowledge of a Being that is free from substance, that is most simple, whose existence is absolute, and not due to any cause, to whose perfect essence nothing can be superadded, and whose perfection consists, as we have shown, in the absence of all defects. All we understand is the fact that He exists, that He is a Being to whom none of His creatures is similar, who has nothing in common with them, who does not include plurality, who is never too feeble to produce other beings, and whose relation to the universe is that of a steersman to a boat; and even this is not a real relation, a real simile, but serves only to convey to us the idea that God rules the universe; that is, that He give it duration, and preserves its necessary arrangement.

This subject will be treated more fully. Praised be He! In the contemplation of His essence, our comprehension and knowledge prove insufficient; in the examination of His works, how they necessarily result from His will, our knowledge proves to be ignorance, and in the endeavor to extol Him in words, all our efforts in speech are mere weakness and failure!

## Chapter 59

The following question might perhaps be asked: since there is no possibility of obtaining a knowledge of the true essence of God, and since it has also been proved that the only thing that man can apprehend of Him is the fact that He exists, and that all positive attributes are inadmissible, as has been shown; what is the difference among those who have obtained a knowledge of God? Must not the knowledge obtained by our teacher Moses, and by Solomon, be the same as that obtained by any one of the lowest class of philosophers, since there can be no addition to this knowledge?

But, on the other hand, it is generally accepted among theologians and also among philosophers, that there can be a great difference between two persons as regards the knowledge of God obtained by them. Know that this is really the case, that those who have obtained knowledge of God differ greatly from each other; for in the same way as by each additional attribute a thing is more specified, and is brought nearer to the true apprehension of the observer, so by each additional negative attribute you advance toward the knowledge of God, and you are nearer to it than he who does not negative, in reference to God, those qualities which you are convinced by proof must be negatived.

There may thus be a man who after having earnestly devoted many years to the pursuit of one science, and to the true understanding of its principles till he is fully convinced of its truths, has obtained as the sole result of this study the conviction that a certain quality must be negatived in reference to God, and the capacity of demonstrating that it is impossible to apply it to Him. Superficial thinkers will have no proof for this, will doubtfully ask, "Is that thing existing in the Creator, or not?" And those who are deprived of sight will positively ascribe it to God, although it has been clearly shown that He does not possess it.

For example, while I show that God is incorporeal, another doubts and is not certain whether He is corporeal or incorporeal; others even positively declare that He is corporeal and appear before the Lord with that belief. Now see how great the difference is between these three men; the first is undoubtedly nearest to the Almighty; the second is remote, and the third still more distant from Him. If there be a fourth person who holds himself convinced by proof that emotions are impossible in God, while the first who rejects the corporeality, is not convinced of that impossibility, that fourth person is undoubtedly nearer the knowledge of God than the first, and so on, so that a person who, convinced by proof, negatives a number of things in reference to God, which according to our belief may possibly be in Him or emanate from Him, is undoubtedly a more perfect man than we are, and would surpass us still more if we positively believed these things to be properties of God.

It will now be clear to you, that every time you establish by proof the negation of a thing in reference to God, you become more perfect, while with every additional positive assertion you follow your imagination and recede from the true knowledge of God, and by such researches and studies as would show us the inapplicability of what is inadmissible as regards the Creator, not by such methods as would prove the necessity of ascribing to Him anything extraneous to His essence, or asserting that He has a certain perfection, when we find it to be a perfection in relation to us. The perfections are all to some extent acquired properties, and a property which must be acquired does not exist in everything capable of making such acquisition.

You must bear in mind, that by affirming anything of God, you are removed from Him in two respects; first, whatever you affirm, is only a perfection in relation to us; secondly, He does not possess anything superadded to this essence; His essence includes all His perfections, as we have shown. Since it is a well-known fact that even that knowledge of God which is accessible to man cannot be attained except by negations, and that negations do not convey a true idea of the being to which they refer, all people, both of past and present generations, declared that God cannot be the object of human comprehension, that none but Himself comprehends what He is, and that our knowledge consists in knowing, that we are unable truly to comprehend Him. All philosophers say, "He has overpowered us by His grace, and is invisible to us through the intensity of His light," like the sun which cannot be perceived by eyes which are too weak to bear its rays.

Much more has been said on this topic, but it is useless to repeat it here. The idea is best expressed in the book of Psalms, "Silence is praise to Thee" (LXV.2). It is a very expressive remark on this subject; for whatever we utter with the intention of extolling and of praising Him, contains something that cannot be applied to God, and includes derogatory expressions; it is therefore more becoming to be silent, and to be content with intellectual reflection, as has been recommended by men of the highest culture, in the words, "Commune with your own heart upon your bed, and be still" (Ps. IV.4)....

There is no necessity at all for you to use positive attributes of God with the view of magnifying Him in your thoughts, or to go beyond the limits which the men of the Great Synagogue have introduced in the prayers and in the blessings, for this is sufficient for all purposes, and even more than sufficient, as Rabbi Haninah said. Other attributes, such as occur in the books of the Prophets, may be uttered when we meet with them in reading those books; but we must bear in mind what has already been explained, that they are either attributes of God's actions, or expressions implying the negation of the opposite. This likewise should not be divulged to the multitude; but a reflection of this kind is fitted for the few only who believe that the glorification of God does not consist in uttering that which is not be uttered, but in reflecting on that on which man should reflect.... Solomon has already given us sufficient instruction on this subject by saying, "For God is in heaven, and thou upon earth; therefore, let thy words be few" (Eccles. V.2).

## Chapter 60

I will give you in this chapter some illustrations, in order that you may better understand the propriety of forming as many negative attributes as possible, and the impropriety of ascribing to God any positive attributes.

A person may know for certain that a "ship" is in existence, but he may not know to what thing that name is applied, whether to a substance or to an accident: a second person then learns that the ship is not an accident; a third, that it is not a mineral; a fourth, that it is not a plant growing in the earth; a fifth, that it is not a body whose parts are joined together by nature; a sixth, that it is not a flat thing like boards or doors; a seventh, that it is not a sphere; an eighth, that it is not pointed; a ninth, that it is not round-shaped; nor equilateral; a tenth, that it is not solid. It is clear that this tenth person has almost arrived at the correct notion of a "ship" by the foregoing negative attributes, as if he had exactly the same notion as those have who imagine it to be a wooden substance which is hollow, long, and composed of many pieces of wood, that is to say, who know it by positive attributes. Of the other persons in our illustration, each one is more remote from the correct notion of a ship than the next mentioned, so that the first knows nothing about it but the name.

In the same manner you will come nearer to the knowledge and comprehension of God by the negative attributes. But you must be careful, in what you negative, to negative by proof, not by mere words, for each time you ascertain by proof that a certain thing, believed to exist in the Creator, must be negatived, you have undoubtedly come one step nearer to the knowledge of God. It is in this sense that some men come very near to God, and others remain exceedingly remote from Him, not in the sense of those who are deprived of vision, and believe that God occupies a place, which man can physically approach or from which he can recede. Examine this well, know it, and be content with it. The way which will bring you nearer to God has been clearly shown to you; walk in it, if you have the desire.

On the other hand, there is a great danger in applying positive attributes to God. For it has been shown that every perfection we could imagine, even if existing in God in accordance with the opinion of those who assert the existence of attributes, would in reality not be of the same kind as that imagined by us, but would only be called by the same name, according to our explanation; it would in fact amount to a negation.

Suppose, e.g., you say He has knowledge, and that knowledge, which admits of no change and of no plurality, embraces many changeable things; His knowledge remains unaltered, while new things are constantly formed, and His knowledge of a thing before it exists, while it exists, and when it has ceased to exist, is the same without the least change: you would thereby declare that His knowledge is not like ours: and similarly that His existence is not like ours. You thus necessarily arrive at some negation, without obtaining a true conception of an essential attribute: on the contrary, you are led to assume that there is a plurality in God, and to believe that He, though one essence, has several unknown attributes.

For if you intend to affirm them, you cannot compare them with those attributes known by us, and they are consequently not of the same kind. You are, as it were, brought by the belief in the reality of the attributes, to say that God is one subject of which several things are predicated: though the subject is not like ordinary subjects, and the predicates are not like ordinary predicates. This belief would ultimately lead us to associate other things with God, and not to believe that He is One. For of every subject certain things can undoubtedly be predicated, and although in reality subject and predicate are combined in one thing, by the actual definition they consist of two elements, the notion contained in the subject not being the same as that contained in the predicate. In the course of this treatise, it will be proved to you that God cannot be a compound, and that He is simple in the strictest sense of the word.

I do not merely declare that he who affirms attributes of God has not sufficient knowledge concerning the Creator, admits some association with God, or conceives Him to be different from what He is: but I say that he unconsciously loses his belief in God. For he whose knowledge concerning a thing is insufficient, understands one part of it while he is ignorant of the other, as, e.g., a person who knows that man possesses life, but does not know that man possesses understanding: but in reference to God, in whose real existence there is no plurality, it is impossible that one thing should be known, and another unknown.

Similarly, he who associates a thing with [the properties of] another thing, conceives a true and correct notion of the one thing and applies that notion also to the other; while those who admit the attributes of God, do not consider them as identical with His essence, but as extraneous elements. Again, he who conceives an incorrect notion of a thing, must necessarily have a correct idea of the thing to some extent, he, however, who says that taste belongs to the category of quantity has not, according to my opinion, an incorrect notion of taste, but is entirely ignorant of its nature, for he does not know to what thing the term "taste" is to be applied. This is a very difficult subject: consider it well.

According to this explanation you will understand that those who do not recognize in reference to God the negation of things, which others negate by clear proof, are deficient in the knowledge of God, and are remote from comprehending Him. Consequently, the smaller the number of things is which a person can negate in relation to God, the less he knows of Him as has been explained in the beginning of this chapter; but the man who affirms an attribute of God, knows nothing but the same: for the thing to which, in his imagination, he applies that name, does not exist; it is a mere fiction and invention, as if he applied that name to a non-existing being, for there is, in reality, no such thing.

For example, someone has heard of the elephant, and knows that it is an animal, and wishes to know its form and nature. A person, who is either misled or misleading, tells him it is an animal with one leg, three wings, lives in the depth of the sea, has a transparent body: its face is wide like that of a man, has the same form and shape, speaks like a man, flies sometimes in the air, and sometimes swims like a fish. I should not say, that he described the elephant incorrectly, or that he has an insufficient knowledge of the elephant, but I would say that the thing thus described is an invention and fiction, and that in reality there exists nothing like it: it is a non-existing being, called by the name of a really existing being, and like the griffin, the centaur, and similar imaginary combinations for which simple and compound names have been borrowed from real things.

The present case is analogous: namely, God, praised be His name, exists, and His existence has been proved to be absolute and perfectly simple, as I shall explain. If such a simple, absolutely existing essence were said to have attributes, as has been contended, and were combined with extraneous elements, it would in no way be an existing thing, as has been proved by us; and when we say that that essence, which is called "God," is a substance with many properties by which it can be described, we apply that name to a thing which does not at all exist. Consider, therefore, what are the consequences of affirming attributes to God! As to those attributes of God which occur in the Pentateuch, or in the books of the Prophets, we must assume that they are exclusively employed, as has been stated by us, to convey to us some notion of the perfections of the Creator, or to express qualities of actions emanating from Him.

Title page of *Moreh nevukhim* (The Guide for the Perplexed), 1553

# THOMAS AQUINAS

# LANGUAGE DAYS VI–IX

*Summa theologica*
Prima pars Question 13 Articles 1-5 & 12
Prima secundae Question 9 Article 1

*Quaestiones disputatae de veritate*
Question 1 Articles 1-3
Question 14 Articles 1-2

## On Disputed Question Format

In the prologue of SUMMA THEOLOGICA, Aquinas says that he offers readers a synthesis of sacred doctrine to facilitate teaching it to beginners. He aims to make his presentation as succinct and lucid as the subject allows, in an order suited to learning. Is his effort thus to systematize the elements of Christian teaching like Euclid's effort to systematize the elements of geometry?

Aquinas also argues in his first question that sacred doctrine is scientific in that it reasons from its first principles to its conclusions to give reasons for them. Yet rather than presenting propositions to be proven in due order, Aquinas presents questions to be asked in due order. He prefaces each of his replies to his questions with arguments opposite his position, and he follows each with responses to those opposing arguments.

This disputed question format represents a significant choice on Aquinas' part. In his earlier SUMMA CONTRA GENTILES, he offers as much a reasoned account of Christian beliefs as can be given without appeal to sacred scripture, with a view to debating with those who do not accept Christian revelation. In this earlier *Summa* of apologetic theology, he employs a syllogistic way of arguing not unlike Aristotle's. In contrast, the dialectical format of the disputed questions used in his *Summa* of sacred theology is taken from the teaching practices of the medieval university.

The elements of the disputed question are discernable in the medieval university's three modes of teaching: *lectio, quaestio, disputatio*. The Master of Theology had bachelor assistants read the texts of the official reading list to students, accompanied by line-by-line explication of their "literal" meaning. The texts naturally posed questions of textual interpretation that the Master himself took up in lectures on the texts. Such textual questions naturally led in turn to theoretical questions about the things themselves. Such theoretical questions were taken up in classroom debates.

Over the course of a semester, a Master proposed for debate points of inquiry on a theme, such as "On Truth" or "On the Power of God." In such a classroom disputation, the Master's bachelor represented his position and students urged arguments of opponents, bygone, contemporary, or putative, referencing texts and offering arguments "from reason." The order of inquiry followed the lead of the question itself; citations of text were employed to parse the theoretical elements of questions and solutions. The Master recapitulated his classroom debates in edited publications, presenting his own replies to the disputed questions in the dialectical context of both received and ongoing controversy about them.

Most of Aquinas's *Quaestiones disputatae* are the fruits of this regular classroom activity. However, most of the *Summa theologica* is not. Not unlike Plato's dialogues, it is rather an imitation of such live dialectic, a literary genre of *pro et contra* that Aquinas chose as the vehicle of his thought. We do well then to keep asking as we read these disputed questions of the *Summa* why Aquinas presents what he does, in the order that he does, with the objections that he does.

*Allegory of Theology and Metaphysics,*
by Giovanni Antonio da Brescia

# LANGUAGE VI

## AQUINAS
*Summa theologica* Ia 4.3 Corpus & 13.1-4 [16]

---

### *Summa* Ia 4.3 Corpus
*Whether any creature could be like God.*

*I reply:* What needs to be said is that since likeness is attendant on a matching of or sharing in form, likeness is of many kinds following upon many ways of sharing in form. Now some things are said to be alike which share in a same form according to a same characteristic and in a same way,[17] and these things are called, not only alike, but equally alike, as two equally white things are said to be alike in their whiteness.

In another way, things are said to be alike which share in a form according to a same characteristic but not in a same way, rather more and less, as something less white is said to be like something more white. This is an incomplete likeness.

In a third way, some things are said to be alike which share in a same form, but not according to the same characteristic, as is clear with non-univocal agents. For since every agent effects something like itself to the extent that it is an agent, and each acts according to its own form, it is necessary that there be in an effect a likeness of the form of its agent. Therefore, if the agent is contained within a same species with its effect, there will be a likeness in form between what makes and what is made according to a same species characteristic—for example, a human being generates a human being.

---

[16] Tr. J. Tomarchio, from the Leonine text, *Summa theologiae* (Marietti, 1952).

[17] Note how Aquinas again distinguishes between a form's *ratio* and its *modus*, i.e., its formal *characteristic* and its *way* of existing. He made this distinction above to account for a sameness in the forms in the knower and in the known; here for such sameness in a cause and its effects.

If, however, the agent is not contained within the same species, there will be a likeness, but not according to the same species characteristic; for example, what are generated from the power of the sun do indeed approach to some likeness of the sun, however not so that they receive the sun's form according to a likeness of species, but according to a likeness of genus.[18]

Therefore, if there is some agent that is not contained within any genus, its effects would approach to a likeness of the agent's form even more remotely, however not so as to participate in the likeness of the agent's form according to a same characteristic of species or genus, but according to an analogy, as existing itself is common to everything. In this way, things that are from God, to the extent that they are beings, are likened to him as the primary and universal principle of all existing.

### Question 13: *De divines nominibus*

Having considered what pertains to our knowledge of God, we need to consider names for God, for each thing is named by us according to the way we know it.[19]

### *Summa* Ia 13.1
*Whether there is any name applicable to God.*

*Argument 1:* Dionysius says in Ch. 1 of *De divinis nominibus*, *There is neither a name for him nor a notion of him;* and in Proverbs 30 it says, *What is his name, and what is his son's name, if you know it?*

*Argument 2:* Every word means something either in an abstract way or in a concrete way. Words that signify in a concrete way are not applicable to God because he is simple; but nor are words that signify in an abstract way applicable, since they do not signify some complete independently existing thing. Therefore, there is no name to call God.

---

[18] Thus mineral, vegetable, and animal bodies receive the heat of the sun's body, not only to different degrees, but in different ways, effecting different characteristics in each accordingly.

[19] *On Names for God.* The word *nomen* is transliterated as *name* because it has no equivalent in English, being the Latin term for both nouns and adjectives as a part of speech (see Arg. 3 of *Prima* 13.1). Thus the question concerns nouns and adjectives we use to name God.

*Argument 3:* Names signify a substance together with its quality; verbs and participles signify it together with time; and pronouns with a demonstrative or relative reference. None of these are applicable to God, since he is without a quality, without any attribute, and without time; and since he cannot be sensed, he cannot be pointed at; and thus, he cannot be signified with a relative, since relative pronouns refer to antecedents, which are names, participles, or demonstrative pronouns. Therefore, there is no way that God can be named by us.

*To the contrary:* It says in Exodus 15, *The Lord is like a fighting man, his name is the Almighty.*

*I reply:* What needs to be said is that, as the philosopher says, *spoken sounds are signs of perceptions, and perceptions likenesses of things.* Thus, is it clear that spoken sounds relate to things signified with a conception of understanding mediating. Therefore, something can be named by us according to the way in which it can be known by us with understanding. But it was shown above that although God cannot be seen by us in this life in his essence, he can be known by us from creatures according to his relation to them as their principle, either by means of a superlative or by means of an exclusion. Therefore, he can be named by us from his creatures, though not in such a way that a name signifying him expresses his essence as *what it is*, in the way that the name *human being* in its signification does express the essence of a human being as *what it is*: for it signifies a definition that discloses its essence, since *the characteristic that its name signifies is its definition.*[20]

*To the first argument it should be said:* The reason that God is said not to have a name or to be beyond naming is that his essence is above what we can understand of God and signify in speech.

---

[20] This could also be translated, *For the meaning that a name signifies is a limit.* It refers to *Metaphysics* 1012 a23-25: ὁ γὰρ λόγος οὗ τὸ ὄνομα σημεῖον ὁρισμὸς ἔσται (in Aquinas's paraphrase, **ratio** *enim quam significat* **nomen** *est* **definitio**). Aristotle is explaining how to answer someone who challenges the principle of non-contradiction: he says that as long as the challenger names some one thing, the *logos* that the name is a sign of becomes an ὁρισμός (a limit or definition); Aquinas, in speaking of how no name can delimit God's essence, says that the *ratio* which a name signifies is a *definitio* (limit or definition). Both are playing on the fact that ὁρισμός and *definitio* have the ordinary meaning of *limit* or *boundary*.

***To the second it should be said:*** Since we come to the knowledge of God through creatures and name him from them, the names we attribute to God signify him in a way proper to the material creatures whose knowledge is natural to us, as said above. Now among creatures of this sort, those things that are complete and independent are composite, but a form that is in them is not some complete independent thing, but rather that because of which a thing is something. For this reason, all the names applied by us to signify some complete independent thing signify it in a concrete way, in the way proper to composites; but names applied to signify simple forms signify something not as independent, but rather as that because of which a thing is something, just as *whiteness* signifies it as that because of which some thing is white. Since therefore God is simple and God is independent, we attribute abstract names to him to signify his simplicity, and concrete names to signify his independence and completeness—although both names fall short of his way of being, as our understanding does not in this way of life know him as he is.[21]

***To the third it should be said:*** To signify a substance together with its quality is to signify an individual together with the nature or the determined form in which it stands. For this reason, since, as has been said, there are things said of God in a concrete way to signify his independence and completeness, names signifying a subject together with its quality are said of God in this way.— Verbs and participles which connote time are said of him in that eternity includes all time, for just as we are only able to apprehend and signify the simple substances[22] in the way we do composites, likewise we can only understand simple eternity and express it in speech in the way we do temporal things; this is because of our understanding's natural relation to things composite and temporal.— Demonstrative pronouns are said of God insofar as they point to what is thought, not to what is sensed: for he is included

---

[21] For example, it is said both that God is good and that God is goodness itself; that God is loving and that God is love.

[22] Aquinas has in mind Aristotle's *first movers* or *intelligences*, which he understands to be independently existing immaterial forms, and so *separate substances* (i.e., beings existing 'separate' from matter); he identifies them with the angels of biblical revelation.

under what can be pointed at insofar as he can be understood by us. And in the way that names, participles, and demonstrative pronouns are said of God, so also can he be signified with relative pronouns.

LEXICOLOGICAL NOTES

**Understanding: *intellectus*.** The word *intellectus* can name acts and expressions of understanding as well as the capacity to understand. It is used in the plural and translated *perceptions* in the first sentence of the Reply, and used in the singular in the second sentence, where Thomas in effect says that it is clear (in Latin) that *intellections* involve *intellect*: "Spoken sounds are signs of perceptions [*intellectus*], and perceptions likenesses of things. Thus, it is clear that spoken sounds relate to things signified with a conception of understanding [*intellectus*] mediating." A traditional transliteration is *intellect*, but the English word *understanding* operates in English more as *intellectus* does in Latin, both in its resonating with the verb *to understand* and in its naming acts and expressions as well as the capacity of understanding.

**Essence: *essentia*.** In *De ente et essentia* 1, Aquinas defines *essence* as that according to which [*per*] and by means of which [*in*] a being has existing. He says that it is properly said only of what is in things, and not of what is only in mind, so that blindness and baldness, for example, do not have essences, properly speaking. What *essence* names also goes by three other names: "It is also called *form* insofar as *form signifies the fixity of each thing*, as Avicenna says in his *Metaphysics*. …But the name *nature* seems to have been taken up to signify the essence of a thing insofar as it has direction to its own activity, since there is no thing bereft of an activity of its own. The name *kind* [*quidditas*] is taken from what is signified by its definition. However, it is called *essence* insofar as according to and by means of it a being has existing."

Cicero coined the word *essentia* to imitate the etymology of *ousia*, boasting he would teach Aristotle to speak Latin! Like *ousia*, *essentia* is formed from the present participle of the verb *to be* [*esse*] and a feminine abstract noun ending; transliterated etymologically into English, *beingness*. In *Summa theologica* Ia 29.2, Aquinas says that he thinks *essentia* gives in Latin the proper meaning of *ousia* for Greeks: "According to the philosopher in *Metaphysics* V, *substance* is meant in two ways. In one way, *substance* means the thing's kind [*quidditas*], which its definition signifies, as when we say that *its definition signifies a thing's substance;* the Greeks call this sense of *substance ousia*, and this sense we can call *essence*. In another way, *substance* means *the subject or individual thing that stands in the category of substance* [in Greek, ὑπόστασις]."

**Characteristic: *ratio*.** Like *logos*, *ratio* originally comes from the verb *to reckon* and meant *a reckoning*. Like *idea*, it can name the discernable and articulable type, look, or characteristic of a thing. Thus, *ratio* variously names: the power of thinking (i.e., reason); the act of thinking (i.e., reasoning); the object of thinking, i.e., its defining characteristic or the reason it is what it is; and such expressions of thinking as *meaning, idea, conception, formulation, account, argument, rationale*.

Aquinas says in *De veritate* 24.8 that for knowledge to occur, there must be the same *ratio* in the known's form that makes it what it is and in the form in knowers by which they recognize what it is: "[F]or understanding to understand what anything is, there must come to be in it a likeness of characteristic that is the same in species even if it does not have the same way of existing. For the form existing in understanding or sense is not a principle of knowing according to the way of existing [*modus essendi*] that it has in them, but rather according to the characteristic [*ratio*] by which it unites with the exterior thing." Thus, the *ratio* is the selfsame characteristic common to the many forms of being, thinking, and speaking something: the identifying characteristic that is one and the same in the essential forms in virtue of which Socrates, Plato, and Diotima are each human; in the cognitive forms in virtue of which knowers recognize them as human; and in the definitional forms we form to define what it is to be human.

## *Summa* Ia 13.2
### *Whether any name is said of God substantively.* [23]

It seems that no name may be said of God substantively. For Damascene says:

*Argument 1:* Each of the things that are said of God must not signify what his substance is, but rather show either what it is not, or a certain relation, or something of what follows upon his nature or action.

*Argument 2:* Dionysius says in the first chapter of *De divinis nominibus, You will find that every hymn of sacred theologians divides the names that manifest and praise God according to the Godhead's emanations of good*. The meaning of this is that the names that sacred teachers adopt for divine praise are distinguished according to emanations of God himself. But what signifies something's emanation signifies nothing

---

[23] *substantialiter*, i.e., as signifying his essence or nature, rather than his actions or relations. Keep in mind that Aquinas has already stated that in naming his essence we do not signify it as *what it is*. In his earlier treatment of the infinity of God's essence (Ia.12), he argued that no finite intellect can comprehensively grasp of an infinite nature *what it is*. In other words, we can conceive, name, and speak of a thing's essence without having grasped its essential characteristic. Such is by no means unique to God; Aquinas observes in *De ente et essentia* 1 that for most things we know and name, we substitute for the essential characteristic we have not managed to grasp the attributes caused by its essence, its proper accidents or properties.

pertaining to its essence. Therefore, names said of God are not said of him in a substantive way.

*Argument 3:* Moreover, anything named by us is named according as it is understood by us. But God is not understood by us in this life according to his substance. Nor therefore is any name applied by us said of God according to his substance.

*To the contrary:* Augustine says in Bk VI of *De trinitate, For God to be is for him to be strong and to be wise, and anything else you might say about his simplicity is something by which his substance is signified.* Therefore, all names of this sort signify God's substance.

*I reply:* What needs to be said is that it is clear that names that are said of God negatively, or that signify his relation to the creature, in no way signify his substance, but signify rather an exclusion of something from him, or a relation of him to something, or of something to him. But as for names of the type *good* and *wise*, which are said of God unqualifiedly and affirmatively, there have been various opinions.

There are some who have said that although all such names are said of God affirmatively, nevertheless they were made use of more to exclude something from God than to affirm something in him. Thus, they say that when we say that God is *living*, we mean that God does not exist in the way that inanimate things exist; and other such names should be taken likewise. Rabbi Moses argued this. But others say that all such names are used to signify his relation to created things, as if when we say *God is good* the sense is *God is the cause of goodness in things.* And the account of other such names is the same.

But each of those accounts seems to be inadequate for three reasons. First of all, from neither of these positions can a reason be given why some names are said of God more than others. God is the cause of bodies as he is of good things, so if nothing more is signified when it is said *God is good* than *God is the cause of good things*, it could likewise be said that *God is a body* because he is the cause of bodies; moreover, in thus saying that he is a body there will also excluded from him his being a being only in potency, like prime matter.

Secondly, it would follow that all names said of God are said of him in a secondary sense, as *health* is said in a secondary sense of medicine, in that it only signifies that it is a cause of health in the living thing, which is called *healthy* in the primary sense.

Thirdly, this account is contrary to the intention of those who speak of God. For when they say *God is living*, they mean to say something other than that he is the cause of our life or that he differs from inanimate bodies.

And so, another account must be given, namely that names of this sort signify the divine substance and are predicated of God substantively but fall short of a manifestation of it. This becomes clear as follows. Names signify God according to the way in which our understanding knows him. Now since our understanding knows God from creatures, it knows him in the way that creatures manifest him. Now it was shown above that God possesses originally in himself all perfections of creatures, being simply and in every way complete. So, any creature manifests him and is like him only to that degree that it has some perfection; however it does not manifest him as something of its same species or genus, but rather as an excelling principle whose effects fall short of its form, but whose effects nevertheless attain to a certain likeness of it, just as the forms of lower bodies manifest the sun's power. (This was explained above where divine perfection is treated.) In this way, therefore, the sort of names cited do signify the divine substance, but they do so incompletely, just as creatures manifest it incompletely.

Therefore, when it is said *God is good*, the meaning is not *God is the cause of goodness*, nor *God is not evil*; rather the meaning is *what we call goodness in creatures preexists in God*, and indeed in a higher way. And so, from this it does not follow that being good belongs to God insofar as he causes goodness, but on the contrary, because he is good he infuses goodness into things, as Augustine says in *On Christian doctrine*, *Insofar as he is good are we so*.

**To the first argument it should be said**: Damascene says that these names do not signify what God is, because what God is, is expressed by none of those names completely; but each of them does signify him incompletely, just as creatures manifest him incompletely.

***To the second it should be said:*** Sometimes in the signification of names the reason why the name is used of things is different than what the name is used to signify, e.g., the name *fly* is used of the thing because it flies, however it is not used to signify that it flies, but rather to signify a certain species of insect; otherwise, all flying things would be *flies*. Accordingly it must be said that divine names of this sort are indeed used because of the emanations of divinity, since creatures do manifest God according to diverse emanations of perfection, even if incompletely. Nevertheless, these names are not used to signify those emanations themselves, as if when it is said *God is living* the meaning is *life emanates from him*; but rather to signify him as the principle itself of things insofar as life preexists in him, although in a more eminent way than is understood or signified.

***To the third:*** we cannot know the essence of God in this life as it is in itself, but we do know it as it is manifested in the perfections of creatures. The names used by us signify it accordingly.

A LEXICOLOGICAL NOTE

PERFECTION: *perfectio.* This abstract noun is formed from the passive participle of the verb *perficio*, to complete, finish, or accomplish. The verb *perficio* is formed from the intensive prefix *per-*, thoroughly or completely, and the verb *facio*, to do, make, or make happen, so that to *perfect* something is to do, make, or effect it completely; and to be *perfect* or *perfected* is to be all done, made, or finished; and a *perfection* is a completion, complement, or accomplishment. Something *imperfect* or done *imperfectly* is in Latin not so much flawed or defective as incomplete or limited; in the above translation these words have been rendered as *incomplete* and *incompletely*: In this way, therefore, the sort of names cited above do signify the divine substance, but they do so incompletely *[imperfecte]* just as creatures manifest it incompletely. Aquinas says in *Prima* 4.2 that the perfections of all things pertain to the perfection of existing because for them to be perfected is for them to have existing in some way. On this account, a *perfection* is a "complement" of existing, and a being is *perfected* when it has the complement of existing proper to its nature.

## *Summa* Ia 13.3

*Whether any name is said of God in its proper sense.*

Thus, the inquiry proceeds to the third question. It seems that no name is said of God in a proper sense.

*Argument 1:* All the names that we say of God are taken from creatures, as has been said. But the names of creatures are said of God metaphorically, as when it is said *God is a rock,* or *a lion,* or something of this sort. Therefore, all names said of God are said metaphorically.

*Argument 2:* Moreover, no name is said of anything in a proper sense if it is truer to exclude it than to predicate it. But all such names as *good, wise,* etc., are more truly excluded from God than predicated of him, as is clear in the second chapter of Dionysius' *De divinis hierarchiis.* Therefore, none of those names is said of God in a proper sense.

*Argument 3:* Moreover, names for bodies are only said of God metaphorically, since he is incorporeal. But all such names imply certain corporeal conditions, since they consign time, and composition, and other things of this sort, which are conditions of bodies. Therefore, all such names are said of God metaphorically.

*To the contrary,* Ambrose says in Book II of *On Faith: There are some names which clearly show what is proper to divinity, and some which express the perspicuous truth of divine majesty; but there are others that are said of God by a transference based on similarity.* Therefore, not all names are said of God metaphorically, but some are said in a proper sense.

*I reply:* What needs to be said is that, as has been said, we know God from perfections that emanate from him into creatures, though these perfections are in God in a more eminent way than in creatures. Now our understanding perceives them in the way in which they are in creatures, and as it perceives them, so does it signify them with names. Therefore, we must consider two things in names that we attribute to God, namely, the perfections themselves that they signify, such as *goodness, life,* and the sort, and their way of signifying them. Therefore, with respect to what names of this sort signify, they apply in a proper sense to God, and more properly even than to creatures, and are said of him in a prior way. But as for their way of signifying, they are not said of God in a proper sense, since they have a way of signifying that applies to creatures.

***To the first argument it should be said:*** some names signify such perfections that emanate from God into created things in such a way that the incomplete way in which divine perfection is participated in by the creature is included in the very meaning of the name, in the way *rock* signifies a being that exists materially; such names can only be attributed to God metaphorically. However, some names signify the perfections themselves simply, without including in their signification any way of participating, as do *being, good, living,* and others of this sort; and such as these are said of God in their proper sense.

***To the second it should be said:*** Dionysius thus says that names of this sort are denied of God because what is signified by the name does not apply to him in the way that the name signifies it, but rather in a more excellent way. For this reason, in the same place Dionysius says that God is *beyond every substance and life.*

***To the third it must be said:*** Those names that are said of God in a proper sense connote corporeal conditions not in the very meaning of the name, but with respect to its way of signifying. But things said of God metaphorically connote a bodily condition in its very meaning.

### A Lexicological Note

**WHAT IS SIGNIFIED–WAY OF SIGNIFYING:** *res significata–modus significandi.*
This distinction is between *what* is signified and *how* it is signified. Aquinas refers to this distinction in Article 1 when he notes the difference between concrete and abstract names such as *white* and *whiteness* or *rational* and *rationality*, stating that concrete names apply to things having forms and abstract names to the forms they have. The *what* here translates the Latin word *res*, which has an even wider extension of meaning than *thing*, typically used to translate it: *res* can have the concrete sense of *some thing* or the more general sense of *something*. The adjective *realis* and adverb *realiter* come from *res*, as do *real* and *really*. The common meaning is existing among or in things, and not in thought only. Aquinas distinguishes in *De veritate* 21.1 between three types of predicate. The predicate in *Socrates is white* adds to the subject something *real* and *really* distinct from it, i.e., something in the thing that is not the thing itself. The predicate in *Socrates is bald* adds nothing *real* in the thing, but only a negation of reason. The predicate in Socrates is *rational* adds a determination of reason *based on* something real *in*, though not really distinct *from*, the thing: *rational* does not name something in Socrates that is other than Socrates himself, but rather a characterization of him based in his substantial form.

## *Summa* Ia 13.4
### *Whether the names said of God are synonymous names.*

Thus, we come to the fourth point. It seems that the names said of God are synonymous names.

*Argument 1:* Names are called synonymous that signify what is altogether the same. But the names said of God signify altogether the same thing in God, since the goodness of God is his essence, as is likewise his wisdom. Therefore, these names are altogether synonyms.

*Argument 2:* If it should be said that the names signify what is the same, not with respect to a thing, but with respect to diverse characteristics—on the contrary: a characteristic to which nothing corresponds in the thing is useless; so, if those characteristics are many and the thing is one, it seems that those characteristics are useless.

*Argument 3:* What is one thing with one characteristic is more one than what is one thing with many a characteristic. But God is most one. Therefore, it seems that he is not one thing with many a characteristic. So, names said of God do not signify diverse characteristics, and thus are synonyms.

*To the contrary,* all synonyms when joined to one another lead to nonsense, as would saying *clothing clothes*. Therefore, if all names said of God are synonyms, it could not appropriately be said *good God,* or anything else of the kind; however, it is written in Jeremiah 32:18: *O most strong, great, and powerful, your name is Lord of hosts.*

*I reply:* It must be said that such names said of God are not synonyms. Now this would be easy to see were we to say that such names are introduced to exclude something, or to designate a causal relation with respect to creatures, because then there would be diverse characteristics of these names according to diverse things denied or according to diverse effects co-signified. But just as we have said that such names signify the divine substance, although incompletely, it is also clear from what we said that they have diverse characteristics. For the characteristic that the name signifies is the understanding's conception about the thing signified by the name.

Now since our understanding knows God from creatures, to understand God it forms conceptions proportioned to the perfections emanating from God into creatures. And the perfections that preexist in God in unity and simplicity are received in creatures in division and multiplicity. For this reason, there corresponds to the diverse perfections of creatures one simple principle that is manifested by the diverse perfections of creatures in variety and multiplicity; and so, to the various and multiple conceptions of our understanding there corresponds an altogether simple one that is incompletely understood in such conceptions. Thus, although names attributed to God signify one thing, nevertheless, because they signify it under multiple and diverse characteristics, they are not synonyms.

***Thus, the solution to the first argument is clear***, because names are called synonyms when they signify what is one with respect to one characteristic. Names that signify the diverse characteristics of one thing do not signify what is primarily and properly one, since a name only ever signifies a thing with a concept of understanding mediating, as has been said.

***To the second it should be said***: the many characteristics of these names are not empty and useless, since there corresponds to them something one and simple manifested incompletely and in many ways through all such things.

***To the third it should be said***: it pertains to God's perfect unity that all things that are multiple and divided in others are in him simply and unitedly. Thus, does it come about that as a thing he is one and yet many in characteristic, because our understanding perceives him in many ways just as things manifest him in many ways.

## Analogical Predication

*Same meaning? Different meanings? Related Meanings?*

The man is *healthy*.
His heart is *healthy*.
His blood pressure is *healthy*.
His urine is *healthy*.
His diet is *healthy*.
His habits are *healthy*.
His attitude is *healthy*.

*medical* knowledge
*medical* text
*medical* skill
*medical* practitioner
*medical* personnel
*medical* instruments
*medical* procedure
*medical* advice
*medical* assistance

*final* goal
*final* result
*final* stage
*final* decision
*final* determination
*final* cause

a *heart* is an organ
a *heart* is a pump
his *heart* is enlarged
he has a big *heart*
he has a broken *heart*
he has hardened his *heart*
the *heart* has *reasons* of which *reason* knows not
the *heart* of man is an abyss
the *heart* of the matter

# LANGUAGE VII

## AQUINAS
*Summa theologica* Prima pars Question 13 Article 5-6 [24]
*In Metaphysicam Aristotelis* Book IV Chapter 2 [25]

---

### *Summa* Ia 13.5

*Whether things said of God and creatures are said of them univocally.* [26]

Thus, we come to the fifth point of inquiry. It seems that things said of God and creatures are said of them univocally.

***Argument 1:*** Every equivocal term traces back to a univocal term, as every many traces back to a one. For if the name *dipper* is said equivocally of a thing one dips and of a constellation, it must be because it is said univocally of some things, e.g., all things that dip, otherwise it would go on forever. Now some agents are univocal agents that match their effects in both name and definition, as when a man generates a man; but some are equivocal agents, as when the sun's fire causes heat, however only equivocally.[27] Therefore it seems that the first agent to which all agents trace back is a univocal agent. And thus, what is said of God and creatures is predicated univocally.

***Argument 2:*** Moreover, there is no similarity attendant on equivocal terms. Therefore, since there is some similarity of the creature to God, as is said in Genesis 1, *Let us make man in our image and likeness*, it seems that there is something univocally said of God and creatures.

---

[24] Tr. J. Tomarchio, from *Summa theologiae* (Marietti, 1952).

[25] Tr. J. Tomarchio, from *In Metaphysicam Aristotelis Commentaria*, (Marietti, 1953).

[26] The terms to be used are *univoce, aequivoce,* and *analogice,* here transliterated, but less literally, *in the same sense, in different senses,* and *in related senses, e.g., animal* is said of a man and a dog *univocally; dipper* of a utensil and a constellation *equivocally;* and *healthy* of a man and his diet in related senses, or *analogically*.

[27] That is, a rock heated by the sun is not hot in the way the sun's fire is hot.

***Argument 3:*** Moreover, a measure is of like genus as what is measured, as is said in *Metaphysics* 10. But God is the first measure of all beings, as is said in the same place. Therefore, God is of like genus with creatures, and thus something can be said univocally of God and creatures.

***To the contrary:*** Whatever is predicated of several things with the same name but not with the same characteristic is predicated of them equivocally. But no name is applicable to God with the characteristic according to which it is said of a creature: for example, wisdom in a creature is a quality, but not in God; and if the genus changes, so does the characteristic, since it is part of its definition. And the same reason obtains in other cases. Therefore, whatever is said of God and creatures is said equivocally.

Moreover, God is more distant from creatures than is any creature from any other. Yet on account of the distance among various creatures, it turns out that nothing can be said of them univocally, as things that do not share in any genus. Much less, then, can anything be predicated of God and creatures univocally; rather everything is predicated equivocally.

***I reply:*** What needs to be said is that it is impossible that anything be predicated of God and creatures univocally. Since every effect that is not equal to the power of its agent-cause receives the agent's likeness not according to the same characteristic but incompletely, what is in the effects in a partial and multiple way is in the cause in a way simple and the same—as the sun for example by one power produces manifold and various forms in things that are lower. In the same way, as was said above, all the perfections of things that are in created things in a partial and multiple way preexist in God unitedly.

Now when any name that pertains to a perfection is said of a creature, it signifies that perfection as distinct from others with respect to the characteristic of the definition: for example, when the name *wise* is said of a human being, we signify some perfection distinct from the essence of a human being, and from his power, and from his existing, and from all such things. But when we say this name of God, we do not mean to signify something distinct from his essence or power or existing. And so, when this name *wise* is said of a human being, it in a way circumscribes and encompasses what is signified; but not when it is said of God, rather it leaves the thing signified uncontained and exceeding the signification of the name.

But neither can the words be said purely equivocally, as some have said. For on this account, nothing could be known about God from creatures, nor demonstrated. But this is as opposed to philosophers, who prove many things about God demonstratively, as to the Apostle, who says in Romans 1:20, *The invisible things of God are clearly seen through the things that he has made when understood.*

It must therefore be said that such names are said of God and creatures according to an analogy, that is, a relation. But this occurs in two ways with words: either because several senses have relation to one, as *health* is said of medicine and of urine insofar as each has a connection and relation to the living thing's health, of which the one is a sign and the other a cause; or because one has a relation to the other, as *health* is said of medicine and of a living thing insofar as medicine is the cause of the health that is in the living thing. It is in this second way that things are said of God and of creatures analogically, and not purely equivocally nor univocally. For we can only name God from creatures, as was said above, and so whatever is said of God and creatures is said insofar as there is some connection of the creature to God as to its principle and the cause in which all the perfections of things preexist eminently.

This kind of commonality is in between pure equivocation and unqualified univocity. For there is not one characteristic in the case of words that are said analogically, as there are in words said univocally, but neither are there totally diverse ones, as in words said equivocally; rather, a name that is said in many ways signifies diverse relations to something one: as *health* said of urine signifies a sign of a living thing's health, but said of medicine it signifies the cause of that same health.

***To the first argument it should be said:*** Although equivocal predicates must be traced back to univocal ones, nevertheless a non-univocal agent is of necessity prior to a univocal agent. For a non-univocal agent is the cause of the whole universal species, as the sun is the cause of the generation of all human beings. But a univocal agent is not the agent cause of the whole universal species (otherwise it would be the cause of itself, since it is contained in the species), rather it is the cause of the particular, with respect to the individual that it brings to participate in the species. Therefore, the universal cause of the entire species is not a univocal agent. Rather the universal cause is prior to the particular one.

However, this universal agent, even if not univocal, is nevertheless not altogether equivocal, since otherwise it would not make something similar to itself. However, it can be called an analogical agent, just as all univocal predicates trace back to a first one that is not univocal but analogical, which is *being*.[28]

***To the second argument:*** The likeness of the creature to God is incomplete, because it does not even represent what is the same in genus, as said above.

***To the third argument:*** God is not a measure proportionate to the measured. So, it is not necessary that God and creatures be contained under one genus. And what was said *to the contrary* argues for the conclusion that such names are predicated of God and creatures in a non-univocal way, however not in an equivocal way.

### A Lexicological Note

**ENCOMPASS:** *comprehendit.* In its ordinary sense, this verb means to grasp physically; in an extended sense, to grasp in thought; and in a technical sense, to grasp the essential difference of a thing's essence so as to know comprehensively *what* it is. Aquinas calls such a grasp *quidditative* knowledge (from the Latin adverb *quid*, meaning *what*— knowledge of *what* its essence is). As noted above, Aquinas thinks that it is rare for us to

---

[28] *That is:* A human parent is the particular and univocal cause of an individual human being, but not of human nature as such; the sun as a universal cause of all species of physical life is an analogical cause not only of human beings but of human nature as well; as the universal cause of all species of being and all beings, God is the analogical cause of every nature and every being.

succeed in grasping created essences in this way, and impossible for us to grasp God's infinite essence in this way, who alone *encompasses* his own essence in understanding himself.

## *Summa* Ia 13.6
### *Whether names are meant of creatures in a prior way than of God.*

*Argument 1:* We name a thing according to the way in which we know it, because names, according to the philosopher, are signs of perceptions. But we know the creature in a way prior to the way we know God. Therefore, the names applied by us apply to creatures in a way prior to the way they do to God.

*Argument 2:* Moreover, according to Dionysius in the book *De divinis nominibus*, we name God from creatures. But names transferred from creatures to God are said in a prior way of creatures than of God, for example, *lion, rock*, and the sort. Therefore, all names that are said of God and of creatures are said of creatures in a way prior to the way they are of God.

*Argument 3:* Moreover, all names that are said in common of God and creatures are said of God as the cause of all things, as Dionysius says. But what is said of anything by way of its cause is said of it in a posterior way; thus, a living thing is called healthy in a prior way than is medicine, which is a cause of health. Therefore, names of this sort are said of creatures in a way prior to the way they are of God.

**To the contrary** is what is said in Ephesians 3:14-15: *I bend my knees to the Father of our Lord Jesus, from whom is named all fatherhood in heaven and on earth*. And the same characteristic is seen in other names that are said of God and creatures. Therefore, names of this sort are said of God in a way prior to the way they are of creatures.

*I reply:* What needs to be said is that in all names that are said of several things analogically, it is necessary that they all be said with a view to one, so that the one must be placed in the definition of all. And since the characteristic that the name signifies is its definition, as is said in *Metaphysics* IV [1012a21-24], it is necessary that that name be said in a prior way of that which is placed in the definition of the others, and in a posterior way of the others, according to the order in which they approach that one more or less—as *health* that is said of a living thing enters into the definition of *health* that is said of medicine, which is called *healthy* insofar as it causes health *in a living thing;* and into the definition of *health* that is said of urine, which is called *healthy* insofar as it is a sign of the health *of a living thing.*

In this way therefore, all names that are said of God metaphorically are said of creatures in a way prior to that of God, since said of God they signify nothing but similarities to such creatures. Thus, just as *weeping* said of a willow means nothing but that the branches of the tree are disposed to droop in a way similar to that in which the face of a man who weeps does[29]—according to a similarity of proportion—so too the name *lion* said of God signifies nothing but that God is disposed to act with strength in his actions, as a lion in its.

Now the same characteristic would hold of the other names that are said of God non-metaphorically if they were said of God only causally, as some have maintained. In this way, then, when it is said *God is good*, it would be nothing, but *God is the cause of the goodness of the creature,* and so the name *good* said of God would include the goodness of the creature in the understanding of it, and for this reason *good* would be said of the creature in way prior to that of God. But it was shown above that names of this sort are said of God not only causally but essentially, since when it is said *God is good* or *wise*, it does not only signify that he is the cause of wisdom or of goodness, but that these preexist in him in a more excellent way.

For this reason, then, what must be said is that as far as what is signified by a name goes, they are said of God in a way prior to that of creatures, because perfections of this sort flow from God into creatures. But as far as the application of the name goes, they are applied by us in a prior way to creatures, which we know prior to God. For this reason, they have a *way* of signifying that suits creatures, as was said above.

---

[29] I give an English example; Aquinas speaks of a meadow in bloom as 'laughing' like a man.

***To the first, therefore, it should be said:*** the objection goes as far as the application of the name goes.

170 ***To the second it should be said***: the relation in the case of names said of God metaphorically and other names is not the same, as said.

***To the third it should be said***: the objection would follow if names of this sort we said of God causally but not essentially, as *healthy* is said of medicine.

---

## *In Metaphysicam Aristotelis*
### Aristotle, *Metaphysics* IV.2 [30]

[i] τὸ δὲ ὂν λέγεται μὲν πολλαχῶς, ἀλλὰ πρὸς ἓν καὶ μίαν τινὰ φύσιν καὶ οὐχ ὁμωνύμως, ἀλλ' ὥσπερ καὶ τὸ ὑγιεινὸν ἅπαν πρὸς ὑγίειαν, τὸ μὲν τῷ φυλάττειν, τὸ δὲ τῷ ποιεῖν, τὸ δὲ τῷ σημεῖον εἶναι τῆς ὑγιείας, τὸ δ' ὅτι δεκτικὸν αὐτῆς,

[ii] καὶ τὸ ἰατρικὸν πρὸς ἰατρικήν· τὸ μὲν γὰρ τῷ ἔχειν ἰατρικὴν λέγεται ἰατρικόν, τὸ δὲ τῷ εὐφυὲς εἶναι πρὸς αὐτήν, τὸ δὲ τῷ ἔργον εἶναι τῆς ἰατρικῆς, ὁμοιοτρόπως δὲ καὶ ἄλλα ληψόμεθα λεγόμενα τούτοις.

[i] Now *being* is said[31] in many ways, but in relation to one thing and one kind of thing, not equivocally, but in just the way that what is *healthy* is always said in relation to *health*: either as preserving it, or as causing it, or as being a sign of health, or because receptive of it.

[ii] So too what is *medical* is in relation to *medical skill*, since what is for possessing medical skill is called medical, and what is suitable for it, and what is for an act of medical skill, and we shall find still others said in a similar way as these.

---

[30] Tr. J. Tomarchio, Greek from the Loeb, *The Metaphysics* (Harvard University Press, 1933).

[31] Both λέγεται in Greek and *loquitur* in Latin can mean *is said* in the passive voice and *means* in the middle voice: "Now being *is meant* in many ways ..."

[iii] οὕτω δὲ καὶ τὸ ὂν λέγεται πολλαχῶς μὲν ἀλλ' ἅπαν πρὸς μίαν ἀρχήν:

[iv] τὰ μὲν γὰρ ὅτι οὐσίαι, ὄντα λέγεται, τὰ δ' ὅτι πάθη οὐσίας, τὰ δ' ὅτι ὁδὸς εἰς οὐσίαν ἢ φθοραὶ ἢ στερήσεις ἢ ποιότητες ἢ ποιητικὰ ἢ γεννητικὰ οὐσίας ἢ τῶν πρὸς τὴν οὐσίαν λεγομένων, ἢ τούτων τινὸς ἀποφάσεις ἢ οὐσίας: [v] διὸ καὶ τὸ μὴ ὂν εἶναι μὴ ὂν φαμεν.

[vi] καθάπερ οὖν καὶ τῶν ὑγιεινῶν ἁπάντων μία ἐπιστήμη ἔστιν, ὁμοίως τοῦτο καὶ ἐπὶ τῶν ἄλλων. [vii] οὐ γὰρ μόνον τῶν καθ' ἓν λεγομένων ἐπιστήμης ἐστὶ θεωρῆσαι μιᾶς ἀλλὰ καὶ τῶν πρὸς μίαν λεγομένων φύσιν: καὶ γὰρ ταῦτα τρόπον τινὰ λέγονται καθ' ἕν.

[iii] And so also *being* is said in many ways, but always in relation to one principle: [iv] for some are called beings because they are substances, some because they are effects in substance, some because they are a process toward substance, or destructions, or privations, or qualities, or productive or generative of substance, or said about substance—or negations of one of these or of substance. [v] For this reason we even say that what is not a being *is* not one.

[vi] Accordingly, just as there is one science of all healthy things, this is likewise the case for the others too. [vii] For it is not only studying what is said in one way that belongs to one science, but also what is said in relation to one nature. For even these are in a certain sense said in one way.

### *In Metaphysicam Aristotelis Commentaria*
### Liber IV, Lectio 1

175    He says first that *being*, or what exists, is said in many ways. But one needs to know that when something is predicated of diverse things in many ways, it is sometimes according to characteristics in every way the same, in which case it is said to be predicated of them univocally, for example *animal* said of *horse* and *cow*.

However sometimes it is according to characteristics in every way diverse, and then it is said to be predicated of them equivocally, for example *dipper* said of a constellation and a utensil.[32]

And sometimes it is said according to characteristics that are partly diverse and partly not diverse: although diverse in that they entail different relations, still one in that these diverse relations relate to something one and the same. This is said to be predicated analogically, that is, proportionally, depending on how each is related to that one according to its own relation.

One also needs to know that with analogical names the one to which the diverse relations are related is one in number, and not just in characteristic like the one that a univocal name designates. And so, he says that although *being* is said in many ways, it is still not said equivocally, but rather with a view to a one, though not to a one that is one only in characteristic, but that is one as some one nature. And this is clear in the examples given below.

He first gives an example of when many contribute to a one that is an end, as is clear in the name *healthful* or *healthy*. For *healthy* is not said univocally of diet, medicine, urine, and an animal. For the characteristic of what is healthy as said of diet is because of its preserving health; and as said of medicine, because of its causing health; but it is said of urine in that it is a sign of health. However as said of an animal, the characteristic of it is that it is receptive of or subject to health. In this way therefore every healthful or healthy thing is said of one and the same health. For it is the same health that the animal is subject of, the urine signifies, the medicine causes, and the diet preserves.

Secondly, he gives an example of when many contribute to a one that is an efficient principle. For there is something called *medical* as having the art of medicine, such as a trained medical practitioner; and something because it has a natural aptitude for having the art of medicine, such as people who are talented at easily acquiring the art of medicine; and it also happens that certain medicinals act by native

---

[32] I substitute this example for Latin *canis* (dog) said of a *star* and an *animal*.

properties. There is also something called medical or medicinal because the practice of medicine is done by means of it, for example instruments used by medical practitioners can be called medical, as well as the medications used by medical practitioners to heal. Likewise, other things called *medical* in various ways can be understood in a way similar to these.

And just as in the above cases, so too *being* is said in many ways, but each one is said in relation to a first one. However, the first is not an end or an agency, as in the above examples, but a subject. For some are called *beings* or *existing* because of their existing on their own, such as substances, which are called beings principally and in a prior way. But others are called so because they are effects in or properties of substance, such as the attributes proper to each substance.

However, some are called beings because they are a way to substance, such as natural formations and change. Yet others are called beings because they are degenerations of substance, since a degeneration is a way toward not existing, just as a formation is a way toward substance. And because destruction ends in privation, as formation does in form, the privations themselves of substantial forms are also correctly said to exist. Moreover, some qualities or attributes are called beings because they are enactive or formative of substance, or of what are said according to some relation of the above to substance, or according to any other relation. Likewise, negations of what have a relation to substance, or even of substance itself, are said to be, so that we say that what is not a being is not a being, which would not be said if existing did not in some way belong to negation.

One should know however that these ways of existing can be reduced to four. The one that is the weakest is the one that exists in reason alone, namely negation and privation, because reason deals with them as if dealing with particular beings when it affirms or denies anything about them. How negations and privation differ will be said later. Another one close to this in weakness is the way that natural formation and degeneration and change are called beings, since they have an admixture of privation and negation. For change is an incomplete act, as is said in *Physics* 3. However, there is a third one called *a being* that does not have an admixture of non-being, but does have a weak act of being, because it has it not on its own but in another, such as qualities, quantities, and properties of substance.

However, the fourth kind is what is most complete, precisely because it has an act of being by its nature without any admixture of privation and it has a firm and solid act of being by being that which exists on its own, such as substances. It is to this one as to the first and principal one that all the others are related. For qualities and quantities are said to exist insofar as they inhere in substance; and changes and natural formations insofar as they tend toward substance or toward some one of the above; privations and negations, however, insofar as they exclude one of the above three.

## A Lexicological Note

**Substance:** *substantia*. It is an abstract noun formed from the present participle of the verb *substo*, which in classical Latin meant *stand firm*, and was used to name a man's property as his "standing" in the commonwealth. Because *ousia* likewise had this meaning in ordinary Greek, *substantia* was at first used to translate *ousia*. When Cicero coined the Latin abstract noun *essentia* from participle *essens* to imitate the etymology of *ousia*, he initiated a bifurcated tradition of translation that has crossed over from Latin into English. Aquinas notes in several places that the twofold sense of *substantia* in Latin makes it an ambivalent translation of *ousia*, the primary sense of which Boethius thought best captured by *essentia*. But as in this commentary, Aquinas will use *substantia* both to speak of *an essence* and *a subject* of it, i.e., of *what* a man is (the human *essentia*) as well as of *an existing man* such as Socrates (who is a *suppositum* of the essence*)*.

The Latin verb *substo* also acquired the sense of *stand under* in addition to *stand firm*, in which sense it etymologically answers to the Greek noun ὑπόστασις; both words can name the logical subject of predications as well as the entitative subject of attributes. To complicate matters further, ὑπόστασις was also translated by the Latin word *suppositum*, from the verb *supponere*, meaning to set under or to subject, from the passive participle of which comes our noun *a subject*.

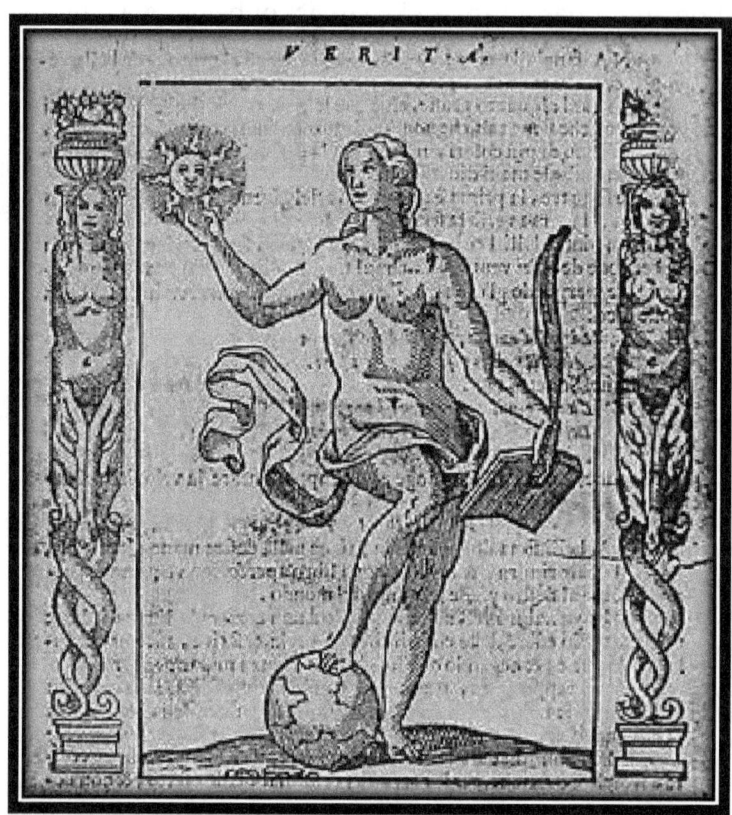

*Truth* by Cesare Ripa
*In Nova Iconologia*

# LANGUAGE VIII

### AQUINAS
*Summa theologica* Prima pars Question 13 Article 12 [33]
*Quaestiones disputatae de veritate* Question 1 Articles 1-3 [34]

---

### *Summa* Ia 13.12
*Whether affirmative propositions about God can be formulated.*

Thus, the inquiry proceeds to the twelfth point. It seems that affirmative propositions about God cannot be formulated.

*Argument 1:* Dionysius says in the 2nd chapter of *De caelestis hierarchiis*, Negations about God are true, but affirmations are not fit.

*Argument 2:* Moreover, Boethius says in his book *De trinitate*, A simple form cannot be a subject. But God is a simple form most of all, as shown above. Therefore, he cannot be a subject. But everything from which an affirmative proposition is formed is taken as a subject. Therefore, an affirmative proposition about God cannot be formed.

*Argument 3:* Moreover, any understanding that understands a thing other than it is, is false. But God has existence without any combination [of constitutive principles], as was proven above.[35] Therefore since any affirmative understanding understands what it understands by a combination, it seems that an affirmative proposition about God cannot be formulated with truth.

---

[33] Tr. J. Tomarchio, from the Leonine text in *Summa theologiae* (Marietti, 1948).

[34] Tr. J. Tomarchio from the Leonine text in *Quaestiones disputatae de veritate* (Marietti, 1953).

[35] The objection (and Reply) plays on entitative 'combinations' of principles of beings (such as soul and body) and logical 'combinations' of subjects and predicates (such 'rational' with 'animal' or 'wise' with 'man').

***To the contrary:*** There is nothing false present in faith. But there are some affirmative propositions present in the faith, such as that God is three and one and that he is omnipotent. Therefore, affirmative propositions about God can be formed with truth.

***I reply:*** It needs to be said that affirmative assertions about God can be formulated. To see this one must know that in every true affirmative assertion the predicate and the subject must in a way mean something the same in relation to an individual, and something different in relation to a characteristic. This is clear as much in assertions of an attributive predicate as in assertions of a substantive predicate. For it is evident [in the assertion, *the man is white*] that *man* and *white* are the same in subject but different in characteristic, since *man*'s characteristic is other than *white*'s characteristic. Likewise, when I say *the man is an animal*, the very one that is a man is in fact an animal, since in the same individual there is sentient nature for which he is called an animal, and rational nature for which he is called a man. So even in this case, the predicate and the subject are the same relative to the individual, but different relative to characteristic.

But even in assertions in which the same thing is predicated of itself this in some way obtains, insofar as what understanding asserts on the side of the subject it draws to the side of the individual, but what it asserts on the side of the predicate it draws to the nature of a form in the individual thing; thus is it said, *Predicates hold formally, and subjects materially*. To this diversity of characteristic there corresponds the plurality of predicate and subject, but through its combination understanding signifies their identity in the thing.

Now God, considered in himself, is altogether one and simple; nevertheless, our understanding knows him according to diverse conceptions, because it cannot see him as he is in himself. Nevertheless, although it understands him under diverse conceptions, it still knows that to all its conceptions there corresponds a thing absolutely one and the same. Therefore, it represents this plurality relative to characteristic through a plurality of predicate and subject, and it represents their unity through a combination.

***To the first argument:*** Dionysius says that affirmations about God are *not fit*, or in another translation *unfitting*, insofar as no name is applicable to God with respect to its way of signifying, as was said.

***To the second argument:*** Our understanding cannot grasp simple independently existing forms as they are in themselves, but rather grasps them in the way it does composites, in which there is something that serves as subject and something that is in it. And so, it grasps the simple form with the characteristic of a subject, and attributes something to it.[36]

***To the third argument:*** The assertion, *An understanding that understands a thing other than it is, is false*, is ambivalent, in that the adverb *other* can modify the verb *understands* on the part either of what is understood or on the part of what understands.

If the adverb modifies on the part of what is understood, then the assertion is true, and the meaning is: *Any understanding that understands a thing to be other than it is, is false.* But this has no place in what has been argued, since our understanding in formulating an assertion about God does not mean that he is composite, but simple.

But if the adverb modifies on the part of what understands, then the assertion is false. For the understanding's way in understanding is different than the thing's way in being. For it is evident that our understanding understands material things that exist below it immaterially: not that it understands them to be immaterial, but rather that it has an immaterial way in understanding them. Similarly, when it understands simple things that are above it, it understands them in its own way, namely by way of combining — although not so that it understands them to be combined. Thus, our understanding is not false when formulating a combination about God.

---

[36] Aquinas has in mind immaterial or angelic substances which he argues are natural forms subsisting on their own without individuating matter as substrate, so that each is an individual being unique to its species. Thus in using 'angel' as a common noun, one must not understand a nature common to individuals, but rather only a logical or grammatical subject of predication.

## De veritate 1.1 Corpus
### *The inquiry concerns truth.*
### *The first thing to ask is what truth is.*

*I reply:* What needs to be said is that, just as for things that can be demonstrated it is necessary to trace back to original principles known to understanding through themselves, so too in investigating what each thing is. In either case, otherwise, the inquiry would go on infinitely and so all knowledge and knowing of things be abolished.

Now that which understanding conceives of first of all as most known to it, and to which all its other conceptions reduce, is a being, as Avicenna says in the first book of his Metaphysics. From which it follows that all other conceptions of understanding are gotten by addition to that of a being. But there is not anything that can be added to the being as though extraneous to it, in the way a difference is added to a genus or an accident to a subject, for a nature is a being essentially. For this reason the Philosopher proves in *Metaphysics* III that there is no genus of being, but rather anything said to be added to the being does so as expressing a way of the being's a being that the name being does not.[37]

This happens in two ways, one of which is that the way of being expressed is one specific to the being. For there are diverse degrees of being a being according to which diverse ways of existing are grasped and diverse kinds of things understood in terms of these. For example, *substance* does not add onto a being any difference that designates a nature superadded to the being, but rather by the name *substance* is expressed its specific way of existing, namely its existing on its own; and similarly for other kinds of thing.[38]

---

[37] The Latin word *modus* is often transliterated 'mode', but it is the ordinary word for 'way' in Latin, the only extraordinary thing about it being how ubiquitous it is.

[38] Aquinas is distinguishing between our classing things according to predicamental kinds, such as animal, vegetable, mineral, or according to predicamental attributes such as color, shape, size, and categorizing kinds of beings according to the kind of being they have, or diverse ways of existing, such as substances, quantities, qualities, or relations. For example, to call Socrates a human being is to say what kind of being he is; to call him a substance is to say

In another way the way of being expressed may be understood as a general one that comes with every being. This way is itself understood in two respects: in one way, it comes with each being on its own; in the other, it comes with each being in relation to another.

The first way is itself twofold, as either affirmatively or negatively expressed of the being. Now nothing is understood to be affirmed of a being simply unless it be the essence according to which it is said to be existing. Accordingly is it given the name *something*, which differs from *a being* in this, namely, that a *being* is taken from its act of existing whereas the name *something* expresses the being's formal kind or essence—as Avicenna says in the first book of his *Metaphysics*. Then there is the negation that comes with every being simply, undividedness, and the name *one* expresses this undividedness, for to be one thing is nothing else but to be an undivided being.

If, however, a being's way of being is understood in the second way, namely in a relation of one to another, this is understood in two ways. In a first way, it is understood according to a division of one from another, and the expression *some thing* expresses this, for it is called *some thing* as *something other*. Accordingly, as a being is called one thing insofar as it is undivided in itself, so is it called some thing insofar as it is divided from others. A second way in which a way of being can be understood is according to a conformity of one being with another, and this cannot be unless there is something understood by its nature to conform with every being. Now this is soul, which is all things *in a certain way*, as said in *De anima* III.

Now in soul there is both cognitive power and appetitive. The name *good* expresses the conformity of a being to the appetitive, for which reason it is said in the *Ethics* Book I, *Good is what all things seek*. The name *true* expresses conformity of a being to understanding.

Now any knowing is accomplished by an assimilation of the thing knowing to the thing known, so that assimilation is called the

---

what kind of being he has, or his way of being a being, his way of existing. Now, what is meant by calling him a being, something, one thing, or a good thing?

cause of knowing—as vision knows color by its being configured according a species of color. So, the first relating of a being to understanding is that the being agree with the understanding of it, which agreement is called an *equaling* of understanding and thing, and it is in this way that the character of the true is formally achieved. This then is what *true* adds to *being*, namely conformity or equaling of thing and of understanding—upon which conformity there follows the knowing of the thing, as has been said.[39]

Therefore, the being of a thing precedes the character of truth, but knowing is an effect of its truth. Accordingly, truth or what is true is found defined in three ways:

*In one way*, definition is found according to what precedes the characteristic of truth and upon which what is true is based:
 —as Augustine in his *Soliloquies, What is true is what exists;*
 —and Avicenna in his *Metaphysics, The truth of each thing is the possession of its own existing that has been established for it;*
 —and by another author, *The true is the undividedness of existing and what is existing.*

*In another way*, it is defined according to that in which the characteristic of truth comes to completion formally:
 —and thus Isaac says that *truth is the equaling of thing and of understanding;*
 —and Anselm in his *De veritate, Truth is a rightness perceptible by mind alone.* Such rightness is according to a certain equaling, as says the Philosopher in Metaphysics IV, that *in determining what is true we say that it is when said to be, or is not when said not to be.*

In a third way what is true is defined according to the effect following upon it:
 —thus Hilary says that *what is true declares and displays what is;*
 —and Augustine in *True Religion, Truth is that by which what is, is shown;* and in the same book, *Truth is what we judge things below it by.*

---

[39] Aquinas has identified six names said of every and any being *as a being*: *ens* and *res, unum* and *aliquid, bonum* and *verum.* All these names are concrete substantives, not abstractions such as *being, unity, truth.* They have come to be called "transcendental properties of being", but Aquinas does not present them as properties; he calls them sundry names of a self-same subject.

## De veritate 1.2 Corpus
### To inquire whether truth is found more principally in understanding than in things.

*I reply:* What needs to be said is that in the case of what is said of many things in a prior and a posterior way, that which receives the common predicate in a prior way does not have to be the cause of the others, but rather that in which the characteristic of the common predicate is found complete, as healthy is said in a prior way of an animal in which the characteristic of health is first found complete, whereas medicine is called healthy as causing its health effectively. Likewise, since *true* is said of various things in prior and posterior ways, it must be in a prior way of that in which the characteristic of truth is found complete.

Now the completion of any movement is in its terminus and the moving of a cognitive power ends in the soul—since the known has to be in the knower in the knower's way—but the moving of an appetitive power ends in the thing. For this reason the philosopher in *De anima* 3 maintains there to be a kind of circle in acts of soul, in that the things that are outside the soul move understanding, and the thing understood moves desire, and then desire leads to our arriving at the thing from which the movement began.

Now as stated in the previous article, *the good* is meant in relation to desire and *the true* in relation to understanding. For this reason, the philosopher says in *Metaphysics* VI that good and evil are in things, and the true and the false in mind. Now a thing is called *true* only insofar as conformed to understanding, so that what is true is found in a posterior way in things and in a prior way in understanding.

But one needs to know that a thing is related with practical understanding differently than with theoretical understanding. Because practical understanding causes things, it is the measure of the things that come about through it, but because theoretical understanding accepts from things and is in a way moved by those things, the things thus measure it. From this is it clear that the natural things from which our understanding gets knowledge measure our understanding, as is said in *Metaphysics* X, however they are measured by the divine understanding in which they are all created, just as all artifacts are by their artisan's understanding. In this way, therefore, divine understanding is what measures as unmeasured; a natural thing is what measures as measured; and our understanding is what is measured [by] while not measuring natural things, at any rate, but only products of art.

Since therefore a natural thing is set between two kinds of understanding, it is called *true* depending on its conformity to each of them. It is called true in conformity to divine understanding insofar as it fulfils what it is directed to according to divine understanding ... but a thing is called true in conformity to human understanding insofar as it is meant by its nature to give a true impression of itself. On the other side, things are called false that are meant by their nature to seem to be what they are not or to be like what they are not, as is said in *Metaphysics* V.

Now the first characteristic of truth is in the thing in a way prior to the second, since its relation to the divine understanding is prior to that with the human; for this reason, even if there were no human understanding, things would still be called true as directed to divine understanding. But were it not impossible for both the one and other understanding to be thought removed, the characteristic of truth would in no way remain.

## *De veritate* 1.3 Corpus
### *To inquire whether truth is only in understanding combining and separating.*

*I reply:* What needs to be said is that just as what is true is found in understanding in a way prior to in things, so too it is found in an act of understanding combining and separating in a way prior to an act of understanding formulating essences. Now the characteristic of what is true consists in conformity of thing and of understanding, and since there is no conformity of a same thing to itself but conformity is rather of diverse things, the characteristic of truth will be found in understanding at the point when understanding first begins to have something of its own which the thing outside soul does not have, something corresponding to it on which conformity can attend.

Now when formulating kinds, understanding only has a likeness of the thing existing outside soul, just as does sense insofar as it gets an impression of a sensible thing. But when it starts to make a judgment about the thing grasped, then that judgment of understanding is something that is its own and not found outside in the thing. And when what is outside in the thing conforms to it, its judgment is called *true*. Now understanding makes a judgment about the thing grasped at the point when it says something *is* or *is not* so, which is understanding combining or separating. For this reason, the philosopher says in *Metaphysics VI* that combining and separating are in understanding, and not in things. It is for this reason that truth is found in the prior way in understanding's combining and separating.

However *true* is said secondarily and in a posterior way with respect to the understanding formulating definitions, [namely] when a definition is called true or false by reason of a true or false combination — as when it is said to be the definition of something it is not the definition of — for example, if the definition of circle were assigned to a triangle; or else, when the parts of a definition cannot be combined with one another — as if the definition of something were said to be non-sensing animal, since the combination that is entailed, namely that some animal is non-sensing, is false. Thus, a definition is called true or false only as directed to a combination, just as a thing is called true as directed to understanding.

From what has been said it is clear that *true* is said in a prior way of understanding's combining and separating; *secondly*, of definitions of things insofar as a true or false combination is entailed in them; *thirdly*, of things insofar as they conform to human understanding; *fourthly*, of a human being who has chosen to make his statements true or false, or who gives a true or false impression of himself or of others in what he says or does. And truth is predicated of what is spoken in the same way as of the understanding it signifies.

*Aquinas Inspired by the Holy Spirit*

# LANGUAGE IX

### AQUINAS
*Summa theologica* IaIIae Question 9 Article 1 [40]
*Quaestiones de veritate* Question 14 Articles 1-2 [41]

---

### *Summa* IaIIae 9.1 Corpus
### *Whether will is moved by intellect.*

*I reply:* What must be said is that something needs to be moved by something else insofar as it is in potency to a multiplicity, for it is necessary that what is in potency be brought to an act through something which is in act, and this is what it is to move something.

Now any power of soul is found in potency in two ways: one, to acting or not acting; the other, to doing this or doing that. For example, the soul's power of seeing sometimes sees in an act of seeing, and sometimes does not see; and sometimes it is seeing white, and sometimes it is seeing black. It therefore needs a mover in both ways, namely with respect to the exercise or use of an act, and also with respect to determining the act. —Of these two, the first is on the part of the subject, which sometimes is acting and sometimes not acting; but the second is on the part of the object, according to which object the act is specified in kind.

The moving of a subject itself comes from something acting. Since whatever acts acts because of an end, as shown above, the source of this moving comes from the end. Hence is it that an art to which the end pertains moves by command an art to which pertains what leads to the end, as *governing commands shipbuilding*, as said in Physics II.

---

[40] Tr. J. Tomarchio, from the Leonine text in *Summa theologiae* (Marietti, 1953).

[41] Tr. J. Tomarchio, from the Leonine in *Quaestiones disputatae de veritate* (Marietti, 1953).

Good universally, which has the character of an end, is the object of willing. And for its part, will moves other powers of soul to their acts, for we use other powers when we will to. For the ends and enactments of all other powers are included under the object of will as so many particular goods. For it is always the case that an art or power to which a universal end pertains moves to action an art or power to which pertains a particular end included under that universal one, as the leader of an army who intends the common good of the order of the whole army moves by his command one of the tribunes who intends the order of his one battalion.

However, the object of the act moves it by determining the act in the way a formal principle does, by which form an action is specified among natural things, as is heating by heat. Now the primary formal principle is *being* and *truth* universally, which is the object of understanding. Accordingly, it is in that way of acting that understanding moves will, as presenting its object to it.[42]

**In reply to the third objection** it must be said that will moves understanding as far as the exercise of an act goes—for what is true, as the fulfillment of understanding, is itself contained as a particular good under good universally. However, as far as the determination of the act goes, which is on the part of its object, understanding moves will, for what is good is itself apprehended according to a certain specific character included under the character of true universally. Thus, it is clear that there is not something at once moving and moved in the same way.

## De veritate 14.1 Corpus
### To inquire what believing is.

*I reply:* ... According to the philosopher in *De anima*, the activity of our understanding is twofold. By means of one, it formulates the simple kinds that things are, such as *what a man is* or *what an animal is*. There is not found in this activity what is in itself

---

[42] "Understanding rules will, not by inclining it to that toward which it tends, but in showing it what it ought to tend toward." *Quaestiones disputatae de veritate*, qu. 22, ar. 2, ad 5.

true or false, just as it is not found in the simple parts of speech [*e.g.,* the words *human* and *animal*].

There is another activity of understanding in which it combines and separates by affirming or by denying, and in this one there is now found what is true or false, and so also in compounded speech, which is a sign of it. Now belief is not found in the first activity, but only in the second, since we believe what is true, or disbelieve what is false....

The power of understanding, as it is by itself, is in potency relative to all intelligible forms, as primary matter is relative to all sensible forms. Moreover, as it is in itself, it is not more determined to adhere to combining than to separating, nor vice versa. And everything that is undetermined in relation to two comes to be determined to one of them only by something affecting it.

As all this is so, the power of understanding is affected by just two things: namely, by its proper object, which is an intelligible form, or *that which something is*, as is said in *De anima* 3; and by will, which moves all other powers, as Anselm says. In this way, therefore, our power of understanding is disposed in various ways in relation to two contradictories.

Sometimes it does not lean to one more than to the other, either because of a lack in what is affecting it, for example in those problematic claims where we do not have the reasons why; or else because of an apparent equality between the things that are affecting us in either direction. This is the condition of *one who doubts* [*dubitans*], who fluctuates between two contradictories.

But sometimes understanding leans toward one more than the other, although what makes it lean does not affect understanding enough to determine it totally to one side; thus, though it accepts one side, it nevertheless always doubts whether the opposite is not true. This is the condition of *one who supposes* [*opinians*], who accepts one of two contradictories with misgiving about the other.

But sometimes the power of understanding is determined so that it totally adheres to one side; this is sometimes by virtue of what is understandable, sometimes by virtue of will.

When it is by virtue of what is understandable, it is sometimes so mediately, and sometimes immediately. It is so immediately when right away from what themselves are intelligible the truth of the assertions shows unmistakably. This is the condition of *one who understands* [*intelligens*] principles that are known right away in virtue of the recognized terms, as the Philosopher says, so that it is from that itself which something is that understanding is immediately determined to assertions of this sort. However, it happens mediately when after the definitions of the terms are known, understanding is determined in virtue of these first principles to one of the contradictories. And this is the condition of *one who knows* [*sciens*].[43]

But sometimes understanding cannot be determined to one of two contradictories either immediately through the definitions themselves of the terms, as with [first] principles, nor in virtue of principles, as with conclusions of demonstrations; rather it is determined through will, which chooses assent determinedly to one contradictory, but precisely because of something that is enough to affect will, although not to affect understanding[44]— for example, because it seems good or appropriate to assent on this side. This is the condition of *one who believes* [*credens*], as when someone believes the words of a certain man because he seems to him decent or useful.

It is in this way also that we are moved to believe the words of God, in that there is promised to us, if we would believe, the reward of eternal life; and this reward moves our will to will our assent to the things that are said, even if our understanding is not affected by something understood. Thus does Augustine say, *Some things a man can do not wanting to, but he can believe only by wanting to.*

---

[43] An example Aquinas gives elsewhere of an immediate inference is that from understanding what a whole is and what a part is, one knows immediately that a whole is greater than its part. An example of a reasoned inference would be a step of a Euclidean proof that connects this axiom with another premise in order to draw a conclusion.

[44] In a reply to an objection later in this question, Aquinas distinguishes more clearly between the *assent* of understanding and the *consent* of will.

Therefore, it is clear from what has been said that assent is not found in the activity of understanding by which it formulates the simple kinds that things are, since in it there is not what is true or false; for we are not said to assent to something unless we adhere to it as true. Likewise, one who doubts also does not give assent, since he does not adhere to one side rather than to the other. Neither likewise does one who supposes, since his acceptance is not committed to one side.

… One who understands gives assent because he adheres to one side with the greatest certainty, but he does not hold to any thinking, since he is determined to the one without any linking. However, one who knows holds to both thinking and assent, but with thinking causing assent, and assent ending thinking. For it is from linking of principles to conclusions that he assents to the conclusions, from tracing them to their principles, and there the movement of the one thinking is stilled and is contented. For in knowledge the movement of reason begins from an understanding of principles and by way of analysis ends in the same, so that one does not hold to assent and thinking equally, but rather thinking leads to assent, and assent contents thinking.

But in belief, assent and thinking are in a sense on equal footing. For assent is not caused from thinking, but from will, as has been said. But because the intellect does not in this way end at one thing as if led to its proper end—which is the seeing of something knowable—for this reason its movement is not yet contented, and it still holds to thinking and inquiry concerning what it believes, even though it assents to them most firmly. This is so to the extent that it is not from itself that it has satisfied itself or ended at one thing, but rather from something outside.

For this reason, the understanding of one who believes is said to be *captive*, since it is held at limits that are other than its own, as in 2 Corinthians 10:5: *bringing all understanding into captivity*, etc. For this reason, even in one who *believes* there can arise movement contrary to what he so firmly holds, although not in one who understands or one who knows.

## *De veritate* 14.2 Corpus
### *What faith is.*

The Apostle says in Hebrews XI.1 that it is *the substance of the things to be hoped for and proof of the things not appearing.*

*I reply:* ... Now the disposition of one who believes is such that, as stated above, understanding is determined to something through will, and will does nothing except as moved by its object, which is the desirable good and its end. So, for its end a twofold source is needed: the first one is a good moving will, and second, what understanding assents to with will causing it to assent.

Twofold, moreover, is that ultimate good of the human being which primarily moves will as its ultimate end. One of these is proportionate to human nature, for its natural powers suffice for obtaining it, and this is the happiness of which philosophers have spoken—be it the contemplative, which consists in the act of wisdom, or the active, which consists primarily in the act of prudence and following on it the acts of the other moral virtues. The other is the good of the human being exceeding proportion with human nature because natural powers do not suffice to obtain it—or even to know or desire it. Rather, by divine generosity alone is it promised to the human being—*Eye has not seen, ear has not heard, what God has ready for those who love him* (I Cor. II.9)—and this is eternal life. It is from this good that will is inclined toward assenting to the things held by faith: *Everyone who sees the Son and believes in him has eternal life* (John VI.40).

However, nothing can be directed to any end unless there first exist in it that proportion to the end from which may arise in it desire of the end. And this is so insofar as some inception of it comes about, for nothing desires a good except insofar as it possesses some likeness of that good. For this reason is there in human nature a certain inception of the good which is proportionate to the nature, for there naturally first exists in it original principles of demonstration known through themselves that are certain seeds of contemplative wisdom, and original principles of natural right and wrong, which are the seeds of moral virtues.

Hence also for the human to be directed to the good of eternal life, there needs to be a certain inception of it in the one to whom it is promised. Now eternal life consists in knowing God fully, as made clear in John XVII.3—*This is eternal life, that they might know thee the only true God*—and for this there must come to be in us some inception of this supernatural knowing. This comes about through faith, which from infused light holds those things which exceed natural knowing. ... Insofar as faith is a certain inception in us of the eternal life that we hope for from divine promise, it is called the substance [i.e., foundation] of the things to be hoped for. In this point faith is related to a good that *moves* will as determining understanding.

Moreover, *will moved by the good*, it is said, and it puts before natural understanding something that is not apparent to it as worthy for it to assent to. Now an intelligible that is seen by understanding determines understanding, and from this it is said to *prove* it to the mind. Likewise, since something not apparent to understanding also determines it, it *proves* it to the mind by the very fact that it has been accepted from the will as something to assent to. Hence in other writing it is called *conviction*, for it convinces understanding in the way said. On this point of its being called *the proof of things that do not appear*, faith is related to *what* understanding assents to.

Therefore, we have the matter or object of faith given in the phrase *things that do not appear;* and the act given in the *proof;* and the direction to the end given in the *substance of the things to be hoped for.* ... In being said to be of *things that do not appear*, faith is distinguished from *knowledge* and *understanding*. In being called *proof,* it is distinguished from *opinion* and *doubt,* in which the mind is not convinced, i.e. not determined to some one side; it is likewise distinguished from all dispositions that are not cognitive. In being called *the substance of the things to be hoped for,* it is distinguished from *having faith* in the usual sense of the word, by which we are said to believe strongly in our opinions or in the testimony of some person; it is distinguished likewise from *prudence* and other cognitive dispositions that are not directed to things to be hoped for, or if so directed, it is not through them that there comes about in us that very inception of those *things to be hoped for*....

# ORGANON

*Dialectica*, by Hans Sebald Beham

# A Logic Sequence

An Overview of the *Organon*:
Aquinas, *In Posteriorem analyticam*

I. ON DEFINITIONS
*Topics* I.1–9, 141–52

II. ON REASONS
*Posterior Analytics* II.1–10, 153-162

III. ON PREDICATES
*Categories* 1–5, 163–74

IV. ON PROPOSITIONS
*De interpretatione* 1–6 & 11, 175–82

V. OPPOSITION & CONVERSION OF PROPOSITIONS
*De interpretatione* 7–8 & *Prior Analytics* I.1–3, 183–90

VI. ON SYLLOGISM IN GENERAL
*Prior Analytics* I.23–25, 191–98

VII. ON THE FIRST FIGURE OF SYLLOGISM
*Prior Analytics* I.4, 201–06

VIII. ON THE SECOND FIGURE OF SYLLOGISM
*Prior Analytics* I.5, 207–12

IX. ON THE THIRD & FOURTH FIGURES OF SYLLOGISM
*Prior Analytics* I.5–7, 213-18

X. ON DEMONSTRATION
*Posterior Analytics* I.1-4, 219–28

XI. ON PREMISES OF DEMONSTRATION
*Posterior Analytics* I.6–10 & II.19, 229–40

XII. ON THE FIRST PRINCIPLE
*Metaphysics* IV.3–4, 241-52

*On Sophistical Refutations*, Parts 1 & 7, 253–271

# AN OVERVIEW OF THE *ORGANON*

## Thomas Aquinas
**Preface of *Commentary on the Posterior Analytics* [45]**

As the Philosopher says in Metaphysics I, *The human race lives by art and reasonings* (980b26). In this statement the Philosopher seems to touch upon that property whereby man differs from the other animals. For the other animals are prompted to their acts by a natural impulse, but man is directed in his actions by a judgment of reason. And this is the reason why there are various arts devoted to the ready and orderly performance of human acts.

For an art seems to be nothing more than a definite and fixed procedure established by reason whereby human acts reach their due end through apt means. Now reason is not only able to direct the acts of the lower powers but is also director of its own act: for what is peculiar to the intellective part of man is its ability to reflect upon itself. For the intellect knows itself. In like manner reason is able to reason about its own act.

Therefore, just as the art of building or carpentering, through which man is enabled to perform manual acts in an easy and orderly manner, arose from the fact that reason reasoned about manual acts, so in like manner an art is needed to direct the act of reasoning, so that by it a man when performing the act of reasoning might proceed in a manner orderly and easy and without error. And this art is Logic, i.e., the science of reason. And it concerns reason not only because it is according to reason, for that is common to all arts, but also because it is concerned with the very act of reasoning as with its proper matter.

Now the part of Logic which is devoted to the first process is called the judicative part, because it leads to judgments possessed of the certitude of science. And because a certain and sure judgment touching effects cannot be obtained except by analyzing them into their first principles, this part is called *analytical*.

Furthermore, the certitude obtained by such an analysis of a judgment is derived either from the mere form of the syllogism—and to

---

[45] Tr. Fabian R. Larcher, The Thomistic Institute, emended.

this is ordained the book of the PRIOR ANALYTICS which treats of *the syllogism as such*—or from the matter along with the form, because the propositions employed are *per se* and necessary—and to this is ordained the book of the POSTERIOR ANALYTICS which is concerned with the *demonstrative syllogism*.

To the second process of reason another part of Logic called *investigative* is devoted. For investigation is not always accompanied by certitude. Hence in order to have certitude a judgment must be formed bearing on that which has been investigated. But just as in the works of nature which succeed in the majority of cases certain levels are achieved—because the stronger the power of nature the more rarely does it fail to achieve its effect—so too in that process of reason which is not accompanied by complete certitude certain levels are found accordingly as one approaches more or less to complete certitude.

For although science is not obtained by this process of reason, nevertheless belief or opinion is sometimes achieved (on account of the provability of the propositions one starts with), because reason leans completely to one side of a contradiction but with fear concerning the other side. The TOPICS or dialectics is devoted to this. For the *dialectical* syllogism which Aristotle treats in the book of TOPICS proceeds from premises which are provable.

At times, however, belief or opinion is not altogether achieved, but suspicion is, because reason does not lean to one side of a contradiction unreservedly, although it is inclined more to one side than to the other. To this the RHETORIC is devoted.

At other times a mere fancy inclines one to one side of a contradiction because of some representation, much as a man turns in disgust from certain food if it is described to him in terms of something disgusting. And to this is ordained the POETICS. For the poet's task is to lead us to something virtuous by some excellent description.

And all these pertain to the philosophy of the reason, for it belongs to reason to pass from one thing to another.

The third process of reasoning is served by that part of Logic that is called sophistry, which Aristotle treats in the book ON SOPHISTICAL REFUTATIONS.

## On Definition

*What is a human being?*

a rational animal
a political animal
a social animal
a talking animal
a laughing animal
an artistic animal
a semiotic animal
a religious animal

a divine animal
a mortal god
the image of God
a child of God
a sick god

a featherless biped
an upright biped
a great ape

*homo sapiens*   [wise man]
*homo erectus*   [upright man]
*homo habilis*   [handy man]
*homo ergaster*   [working man]

# LOGIC I

## ON DEFINITION

### ARISTOTLE
*Topics* Book I Parts 1-9 [46]

---

### Part 1

Our treatise proposes to find a line of inquiry whereby we shall be able to reason from opinions that are generally accepted about every problem propounded to us, and also shall ourselves when standing up to an argument avoid saying anything that will obstruct us. First, then, we must say what reasoning is, and what its varieties are, in order to grasp dialectical reasoning: for this is the object of our search in the treatise before us.

Now reasoning is an argument in which, certain things being laid down, something other than these necessarily comes about through them. (a) It is a *demonstration* when the premises from which the reasoning starts are true and primary, or are such that our knowledge of them has originally come through premises which are primary and true; (b) reasoning, on the other hand, is *dialectical* if it reasons from opinions that are generally accepted. Things are *true* and *primary* which are believed on the strength not of anything else but of themselves: for in regard to the first principles of science it is improper to ask any further for the why and wherefore of them; each of the first principles should command belief in and by itself. On the other hand, those opinions are generally accepted, which are accepted by everyone or by the majority or by the philosophers—i.e. by all, or by the majority, or by the most notable and illustrious of them.

---

[46] Tr. W.A. Pickard-Cambridge, The Internet Classics Archive, emended.

Again (c), reasoning is *contentious* if it starts from opinions that seem to be generally accepted, but are not really such, or again if it merely seems to reason from opinions that are or seem to be generally accepted. For not every opinion that seems to be generally accepted actually is generally accepted. For in none of the opinions which we call generally accepted is the illusion entirely on the surface, as happens in the case of the principles of contentious arguments; for the nature of the fallacy in these is obvious immediately, and as a rule even to persons with little power of comprehension. So then, of the contentious reasonings mentioned, the former really deserves to be called 'reasoning' as well, but the other should be called 'contentious reasoning', but not 'reasoning', since it appears to reason, but does not really do so.

Further (d), besides all the reasonings we have mentioned there are the misreasonings that start from the premises peculiar to the special sciences, as happens [for example] in the case of geometry and her sister sciences. For this form of reasoning appears to differ from the reasonings mentioned above—the man who draws a false figure reasons from things that are neither true and primary, nor yet generally accepted. For he does not fall within the definition; he does not assume opinions that are received either by everyone or by the majority or by philosophers—that is to say, by all, or by most, or by the most illustrious of them—but he conducts his reasoning upon assumptions which, though appropriate to the science in question, are not true, for he effects his mis-reasoning either by describing the semicircles wrongly or by drawing certain lines in a way in which they could not be drawn.

The foregoing must stand for an outline survey of the species of reasoning. In general, in regard both to all that we have already discussed and to those which we shall discuss later, we may remark that that amount of distinction between them may serve, because it is not our purpose to give the exact definition of any of them; we merely want to describe them in outline; we consider it quite enough from the point of view of the line of inquiry before us to be able to recognize each of them in some sort of way.

## Part 2

Next in order after the foregoing, we must say for how many and for what purposes the treatise is useful. They are three: intellectual training, casual encounters, and the philosophical sciences. That it is useful as a training is obvious on the face of it. The possession of a plan of inquiry will enable us more easily to argue about the subject proposed.

For purposes of casual encounters, it is useful because when we have counted up the opinions held by most people, we shall meet them on the ground not of other people's convictions but of their own, while we shift the ground of any argument that they appear to us to state unsoundly.

For the study of the philosophical sciences it is useful, because the ability to raise searching difficulties on both sides of a subject will make us detect more easily the truth and error about the several points that arise. It has a further use in relation to the ultimate bases of the principles used in the several sciences. For it is impossible to discuss them at all from the principles proper to the particular science in hand, seeing that the principles are prior to everything else: it is through the opinions generally held on the particular points that these have to be discussed, and this task belongs properly, or most appropriately, to dialectic: for dialectic is a process of criticism wherein lies the path to the principles of all inquiries.

## Part 3

We shall be in perfect possession of the way to proceed when we are in a position like that which we occupy in regard to rhetoric and medicine and faculties of that kind: this means the doing of that which we choose with the materials that are available. For it is not every method that the rhetorician will employ to persuade, or the doctor to heal; still, if he omits none of the available means, we shall say that his grasp of the science is adequate.

## Part 4

First, then, we must see of what parts our inquiry consists. Now if we were to grasp with reference to how many and what kind of things arguments take place, and with what materials they start, and how we are to become well supplied with these, we should have sufficiently won our goal. Now the materials with which arguments start are equal in number and identical with the subjects on which reasonings take place. For arguments start with *propositions*, while the subjects on which reasonings take place are called *problems* [or *topics*].

Now every *proposition* and every *problem* indicates either a *genus* or a *property* or an *accident*—for the *differentia*,[47] applying as it does to a class (or genus), should be ranked together with the genus. Since, however, of what is proper to anything, part signifies its essence while part does not, let us divide what is proper to it into both the aforesaid parts, and call that part which indicates the essence a *definition*, while of the remainder let us adopt the terminology which is generally current about these things and speak of it as a *property*.

What we have said, then, makes it clear that according to our present division, the elements turn out to be four, all told, namely either *property* or *definition* or *genus* or *accident*.

Do not let anyone suppose us to mean that each of these enunciated by itself constitutes a proposition or problem, but only that it is from these that both problems and propositions are formed. The difference between a problem and a proposition is a difference in the turn of the phrase. For if it be put in this way, "*An animal that walks on two feet* is the definition of man, is it not?' or "*Animal* is the genus of man, is it not?" the result is a proposition: but if thus, "Is *an animal that*

---

[47] This is a Latin term for the *specific difference* of the genus, with which it constitutes the definition. In Part 5 below Aristotle will define *definition* as a *phrase* signifying an essence: e.g., *rational animal* as a definition of what a human being is, i.e., its nature or essence.

*walks on two feet* a definition of man or not?' [or 'Is *animal* his genus or not?'] the result is a problem. Similarly too in other cases. Naturally, then, problems and propositions are equal in number: for out of every proposition you will make a problem if you change the turn of the phrase.

**Part 5**

We must now say what is *definition, property, genus,* and *accident*.

***A definition is a phrase signifying a thing's essence.*** It is rendered in the form either of a phrase taking the place of a term, or of a phrase taking the place of another phrase; for it is sometimes possible to define the meaning of a phrase as well. People whose rendering consists of a term only, try it as they may, clearly do not render the definition of the thing in question, because a definition is always a phrase of a certain kind.

One may, however, use the word *definitory* also of such a remark as *Becoming is beautiful*, and likewise also of the question, *Are sensation and knowledge the same or different?* For argument about definitions is mostly concerned with questions of sameness and difference. In a word we may call *definitory* everything that falls under the same branch of inquiry as definitions; and that all the above-mentioned examples are of this character is clear on the face of them. For if we are able to argue that two things are the same or are different, we shall be well supplied by the same turn of argument with lines of attack upon their definitions as well: for when we have shown that they are not the same, we shall have demolished the definition.

Observe, please, that the converse of this last statement does not hold, for to show that they are the same is not enough to establish a definition. To show, however, that they are not the same is enough of itself to overthrow it.

*A property is a predicate which does not indicate the essence of a thing,[48] yet belongs to that thing alone, and is predicated convertibly of it.*

Thus, it is a property of man to be capable of learning language: for if A be a man, then he is capable of learning language, and if he be capable of learning language, he is a man.

For no one calls anything a property which may possibly belong to something else, e.g., sleep in the case of man, even though at a certain time it may happen to belong to him alone. That is to say, if any such thing were actually to be called a property, it will be called not a property absolutely, but a temporary or a relative property.

For *being on the right-hand side* is a temporary property, while *two-footed* is in point of fact ascribed as a property in certain relations; e.g., it is a property of man relatively to a horse and a dog. That nothing which may belong to anything else than A is a convertible predicate of A is clear: for it does not necessarily follow that if something is asleep it is a man.

*A genus is what is predicated in the category of essence of a number of things exhibiting differences in kind.*

We should treat as predicates in the category of essence all such things as it would be appropriate to mention in reply to the question, *What is the thing before you?* as, for example, in the case of man, if asked that question, it is appropriate to say, *He is an animal.*

The question, *Is one thing in the same genus as another or in a different one?* is also a question of kind; for that sort of question also falls under the same branch of inquiry as the genus: for having argued that *animal* is the genus of man, and likewise also of ox, we shall have argued that they are in the same genus; whereas if we show that it is

---

[48] Implicit here is a contrast with the *differentia* mentioned in Part 4 as "ranked together with" the genus in the definition. Whereas the specific difference does signify the essence properly, properties do not so distinguish it, although they are convertible with it: e.g., the properties *social* or *political* versus the specific difference *rational* in the case of the human being.

the genus of the one but not of the other, we shall have argued that these things are not in the same genus.

*An accident is something which, though it is none of the foregoing—i.e., neither a definition nor a property nor a genus—yet belongs to the thing; or else something which may possibly either belong or not belong to any one, self-same thing.*

For example, *sitting* may belong or not belong to some self-same thing. Likewise, also whiteness, for there is nothing to prevent the same thing being at one time white, and at another not white.

Of the definitions of accident, the second is the better: for if he adopts the first, any one is bound, if he is to understand it, to know already what *definition* and *genus* and *property* are, whereas the second is sufficient of itself to tell us the essential meaning of the term in question.

To accident are to be attached also all comparisons of things, when expressed in language that is drawn in any way from what happens to be true of them; for example, the question, *Is the honorable or the expedient preferable?* and *Is the life of virtue or the life of self-indulgence the pleasanter?*—and any other problem which may happen to be phrased in terms like these. For in all such cases the question is this: to which of the two does the predicate in question happen to belong more closely?

It is clear on that there is nothing to prevent an accident from becoming a temporary or relative property. Thus, the sitting posture is an accident, but will be a temporary property, whenever a man is the only person sitting, while if he be not the only one sitting, it is still a property relatively to those who are not sitting. So then, there is nothing to prevent an accident from becoming both a relative and a temporary property; but a property absolutely it will never be....

## Part 6

We must not fail to observe that all remarks made in criticism of *property* and *genus* and *accident* will be applicable to definitions as well. For when we have shown that the attribute in question fails to belong only to the term defined, as we do also in the case of a property, or that the genus rendered in the definition is not the true genus, or that any of the things mentioned in the phrase used does not belong, as would be remarked also in the case of an accident, we shall have demolished the definition; so that, to use the phrase previously employed, all the points we have enumerated might in a certain sense be called *definitory*.

But we must not on this account expect to find a single line of inquiry which will apply universally to them all: for this is not an easy thing to find, and, even were one found, it would be very obscure indeed, and of little service for the treatise before us. Rather, a special plan of inquiry must be laid down for each of the classes we have distinguished, and then, starting from the rules that are appropriate in each case, it will probably be easier to make our way right through the task before us. So then, as was said before, we must outline a division of our subject, and other questions we must relegate each to the particular branch to which it most naturally belongs, speaking of them as *definitory* and *generic* questions.[49] The questions I mean have practically been already assigned to their several branches.

## Part 7

First of all, we must define the number of senses borne by the term *sameness*. *Sameness* would be generally regarded as falling roughly into three divisions. We generally apply the term numerically or specifically or generically—*numerically* in cases where there is more than one name but only one thing, e.g., *doublet* and *cloak*; *specifically*, where there is more than one thing, but they present no differences in respect of their species, as one man and another, or one horse and

---

[49] Does "definitory" here mean *specific* in contradistinction to *generic*, i.e., specific differences vs the genera specified by them, e.g., saying *a tomato is a fruit* vs. saying *it is an indehiscent fruit (berry) of the nightshade family*? Consider, more generally, how biology distinguishes genera, species, and varieties, or how *figure* or *line* are defined in geometry.

another: for things like this that fall under the same species are said to be *specifically* the same. Similarly, too, those things are called *generically* the same which fall under the same genus, such as a horse and a man.

It might appear that the sense in which water from the same spring is called *the same water* is somehow different and unlike the senses mentioned above: but really such a case as this ought to be ranked in the same class with the things that in one way or another are called *the same* in view of unity of species. For all such things seem to be of one family and to resemble one another. For the reason that all water is said to be specifically the same as all other water is because of a certain likeness it bears to it, and the only difference in the case of water drawn from the same spring is this, that the likeness is more emphatic—which is why we do not distinguish it from the things that in one way or another are called *the same* in view of unity of species.

It is generally supposed that the term *the same* is most used in a sense agreed on by everyone when applied to what is numerically one. But even so, it is apt to be rendered in more than one sense. Its most literal and primary use is found whenever the sameness is rendered in reference to an alternative name or definition—as when a cloak is said to be the same as a doublet, or an animal that walks on two feet is said to be the same as a man. A second sense is when it is rendered in reference to a property—as when what can acquire knowledge is called the same as a man, and what naturally travels upward the same as fire. A third use is found when it is rendered in reference to some term drawn from accident—as when the creature who is sitting, or who is musical, is called the same as Socrates. For all these uses mean to signify numerical unity.

That what I have just said is true may be best seen where one form of appellation is substituted for another. For often when we give the order to call one of the people who are sitting down, indicating him by name, we change our description, whenever the person to whom we give the order happens not to understand us; he will, we think, understand better from some accidental feature; so we bid him call to us *the man who is sitting* or *who is conversing over there*-clearly supposing ourselves to be indicating the same object by its name and by its accident.

## Part 8

Of *sameness* then, as has been said, three senses are to be distinguished. Now one way to confirm that the elements mentioned above are those out of which and by means of which and to which arguments proceed is by induction: for if anyone was to survey propositions and problems one by one, it would be seen that each was formed either from the definition of something or from its property or from its genus or from its accident.

Another way to confirm it is through reasoning. For every predicate of a subject must of necessity be either convertible with its subject or not: and if it is convertible, it would be its definition or property, for if it signifies the essence, it is the definition; if not, it is a property: for this was what a property is, viz. what is predicated convertibly, but does not signify the essence. If, on the other hand, it is not predicated convertibly of the thing, it either is or is not one of the terms contained in the definition of the subject: and if it be one of those terms, then it will be the genus or the differentia, inasmuch as the definition consists of genus and differentiae; whereas, if it be not one of those terms, clearly it would be an accident, for accident was said to be what belongs as an attribute to a subject without being either its definition or its genus or a property.

## Part 9

Next, then, we must distinguish between the classes of predicates in which the four orders in question are found. These are ten in number: Essence, Quantity, Quality, Relation, Place, Time, Position, State, Activity, Passivity.

For the accident and genus and property and definition of anything[50] will always be in one of these categories: for all the propositions found through these signify either something's essence or its quality or quantity or some one of the other types of predicate.

It is clear, too, on the face of it that the man who signifies something's essence signifies sometimes a substance, sometimes a

---

[50] Come to be called the five *predicables*: genus, species, difference, property, and accident.

quality, sometimes some one of the other types of predicate. For when man is set before him and he says that what is set there is *a man* or *an animal*, he states its essence and signifies a substance; but when a white color is set before him and he says that what is set there is *white* or is *a color*, he states its essence and signifies a quality. Likewise, also, if a magnitude of a cubit be set before him and he says that what is set there is a magnitude of a cubit, he will be describing its essence and signifying a quantity.[51]

Likewise, also, in the other cases: for each of these kinds of predicate, if either it be asserted of itself, or its genus be asserted of it, signifies an essence: if, on the other hand, one kind of predicate is asserted of another kind, it does not signify an essence, but a quantity or a quality or one of the other kinds of predicate.

Such, then, and so many, are the subjects on which arguments take place, and the materials with which they start. How we are to acquire them, and by what means we are to become well supplied with them, falls next to be told.

---

[51] On this account, *a human being* names a kind of thing; *a substance* names a kind of being; and *an essence* names a kind of intelligible. The Greek term here translated *essence* is the interrogative phrase τί ἐστι, or *what it is*. In a parallel listing of ten categories in *The Categories*, in contrast, the first is οὐσία, here translated *substance*, elsewhere translated *essence*.

# Fact & Cause

In *De anima* II.2 Aristotle writes, "The definition not only needs to make clear what something is, as most definitions do, but also needs to include and show the reason. But as things stand, definitions are stated more like conclusions. For example: *What is squaring? —The equality of an equilateral rectangle to an oblong rectangle*. This sort of definition is but a statement as of a conclusion, whereas one who says *Squaring is finding the mean proportional* [*between the sides of a rectangle*] states the cause."

This distinction between factual and causal definitions may be extended to demonstrations of fact and of cause: ὅτι vs. διότι (in Latin, demonstrations *quia* and *propter quid*). In *Elements of Geometry*, Euclid demonstrates in Bk. II Prop. 14 the method of finding a square equal in area to a given rectangle. However, only after introducing his account of proportion in Bk. V does he go on in Bk. VI Prop. 13 to demonstrate the reason why his method of squaring works: because the side of the square found is a mean proportional between the sides of the rectangle. Mean proportionality [*if* a:c::c:b, *then* ab=c²] renders intelligible the equality of square and rectangle—i.e., the geometrical middle supplies the logical middle: the reason for their equality.

Aristotle expounds the differences between definitions ὅτι and διότι, factual and causal, descriptive and ratiocinative, in *Posterior Analytics* II.2, as follows.

# LOGIC II

## ON REASONS

### ARISTOTLE
*Posterior Analytics* Book II Ch. 2 [52]

---

**Part 1**

The kinds of inquiry are as many as the kinds of thing we know. There are four: (1) a fact (2) a reason (3) whether a kind of thing exists; (4) what it is.

So, when our question is about a thing together with its attribute and we ask whether the thing is qualified in that way, or not—e.g., *whether or not the sun suffers eclipse*—then we are asking about a fact. An indication of this is that our inquiry ceases with the discovery that the sun does suffer an eclipse. And when we know from the start that the sun does suffer eclipse, we do not inquire whether it does so or not. On the other hand, when we know a fact, we ask for the reason for it; e.g., when we know that the sun is being eclipsed and that an earthquake is in progress, it is the reason for an eclipse or earthquake we inquire into.

Those are the two questions we ask when a complex of subject and attribute is concerned, but for some objects of inquiry we have a different question to ask, such as *whether or not there is such a thing as a centaur or a god*. I mean whether or not it exists at all, as opposed to whether attributively it *is or is not white*, for example. On the other hand, once we grasp the existing of such a thing, we inquire about its nature, asking for instance, *What, then, is a god?* or *What is a human being?*

---

[52] Retranslated by J. Tomarchio from text of Tr. G.R.G. More, The Internet Classics Archive, extensively emended in light of Loeb text of *Posterior Analytics* edited and translated by H. Tredennick, in Aristotle Vol. II, The Loeb Classical Library (Harvard University Press, 1960).

## Part 2

These, then, are the four kinds of question we ask, and our knowledge consists in answers to these questions. Now, when we ask whether something is a fact or whether something exists, we are really asking whether the fact or thing has a "middle". Once we have ascertained either that something is a fact or that a kind of thing exists—i.e. ascertained either some qualified being of the thing, or the unqualified being of the thing—and we then go on to ask the reason for that fact or for the nature of that kind of thing which exists, then we are asking what the "middle" is.

In distinguishing between a fact about a thing and its existing—i.e., between some partial being of the thing and the unqualified being of the thing—I mean, for example, that if we ask *Does the moon suffer eclipse?* or *Does the moon wax?*, the question concerns a part of the thing's being, for what we are asking in such questions is whether a thing is *like this* or *like that*, i.e., has or has not this or that attribute. However, if we ask whether there is a moon or whether night exists, the question concerns the unqualified being of the thing. We conclude that in all our inquiries we are asking either whether there is a middle or what the middle is. For the middle here is just the cause, and it is the cause that we seek in all our inquiries.[53]

---

[53] As there are different kinds of cause, so too different causal definitions. In *De anima* II.2, Aristotle writes: "A physicist would define a passion of soul differently from a dialectician; the latter would define anger as *appetite for returning pain for pain*, or something like this, while the former would define it as *a boiling of the blood or warm substance around the heart*. The one assigns the material conditions, the other the form or reason, for he states the reason for the fact, though for its actual existence there must be embodiment of it in such matter as described by the other. Again, the reason for a house is assigned in a formula like *shelter against destruction by wind, rain, and heat*, but the physicist would describe it as *stones, bricks, and timbers*.

But there is a third description possible that would say it is *such a form in such material with such a purpose or end*. Which, then, among these three is to be regarded as the genuine physicist? The one who confines himself to the material, or the one who confines himself to the reason? Is it not rather the one who combines both in a single formula?"

Thus, *Does the moon undergo eclipse?* means *Is there or is there not a cause producing eclipse of the moon?* Once we learn that there is, our next question is, *What then is this cause?* For both the cause by which such a thing simply *is* (not is *like this or that*, i.e., has this or that attribute, but simply *is*, without qualification), and also the cause by which it is *like this or that* (as having some attribute, essential or acquired, and not simply *is*, without qualification) are both alike the "middle".

By *what simply is, without qualification,* I mean a subject, e.g., *moon* or *earth* or *sun* or *triangle*. By what the subject is in a partial sense, I mean an attribute, for example, *eclipse, equality* or *inequality, interposition* or *non-interposition*. In all these examples it is clear that *what it is* and *because of what* is the same: the question, *What is eclipse?*, and its answer, *The privation of the moon's light by the interposition of the earth*, are the same thing as the question, *What is the reason for an eclipse?* or *Why does the moon undergo eclipse?*, and the reply, *Because of the failure of light through the earth's shutting it out*. For another example, we may substitute for the question, *What is a harmonic concord?*, and the reply, *A commensurate numerical ratio of a high and a low note,* the question, *What ratio makes a high and a low note concordant?*, and the reply, *Their relation according to a commensurate numerical ratio*. The question, *Are the high and the low note concordant?*, is equivalent to *Is their ratio commensurate?* When we find that it is commensurate, we ask, *What then is their ratio?*

Cases in which the middle is perceptible show that what is sought by inquiry is always the middle. We ask because we have not yet perceived whether or not there is a middle to explain, e.g., an eclipse. But if we were on the moon, we would not ask about either the fact or the reason for it: fact and reason would be obvious at once. For, the act of perceiving it would enable us to know the universal reason for it too, because the present fact of an eclipse being evident to it, perception would at the same time give us the present fact of the earth's screening the sun's light, and from this would arise the universal reason for it. Thus, as we maintain, to know what something is, is to know the reason it is. This is equally true of things insofar as things are said to be *of such a kind* without qualification—as opposed to being possessed of some attribute—and insofar as they are said to be possessed of some attribute, as *equal to right angles, or greater or less*.

## Part 3

It is clear, then, that all questions are a search for a middle. Let us now state how it is shown what a thing is, and in what way it comes from demonstration; and what definition is, and what things are definable. Is it possible to know, one might ask, the same thing in the same respect both by definition and by demonstration? Or is that impossible because there can be no demonstration of the definable? ... The starting points of demonstrations are definitions, and it has been shown that there cannot be demonstration of these, for either these starting points will be demonstrable and so have starting points that are demonstrable, *ad infinitum*[54], or rather the starting points[55] will have to be indemonstrable definitions.

But perhaps there is both definition and demonstration of something, even if not of all? But this is impossible, because a definition is definition of what something is, its essence, and all demonstrations about things clearly posit and take as granted what the thing is—mathematical demonstrations, for example, assume what *unity* is, and what *the odd* is, and all the other sciences do likewise.

Moreover, all demonstration proves that a predicate is or is not predicated of a subject, but in a definition one thing is not predicated of another. We do not, for example, predicate *animal* of *biped* nor *biped* of *animal,* nor do we predicate *figure* of plane, for *plane* is not an attribute of *figure*, nor *figure* of *plane*. Again, to show what a thing is and to demonstrate a fact about it is not the same thing. A definition shows what it is[56] but a demonstration shows that something is or is not predicated of it. However, different things require different demonstrations—unless one demonstration is related to another as part to whole. I add this qualification because if all triangles have been proven to possess angles equal to two right angles, then this has been proven of an isosceles as well; for an isosceles is a part of which all

---

[54] This argument is a *reductio*: the premise is contradicted, for then there are no starting points.

[55] Starting points here translates Greek arche, which also means principles, sources, origins.

[56] The definition is the verbal formulation of some kind of thing's species and genus—e.g., *rational animal*. The thing's essence—*what it is* in itself or of itself—is what a definition aims to show, exhibit, identify, as an object of inquiry and demonstration.

triangles are the whole.[57] But a fact about it and what something is are not so related to one another, since the one is not a part of the other.

It becomes apparent then that not everything definable is demonstrable, nor all the demonstrable definable. It is evident then that it is not possible to have both a definition and a demonstration of the selfsame thing, and that definition and demonstration are neither identical nor is either contained in the other: if they were, their objects would either be identical or else related as whole and part....

## Parts 5-6

[5.] ... Moreover, to state a definition reached by division is not to state a logical inference. When conclusions are drawn without their middle premise, the alleged necessity by which the inference follows is open to the question of the reason for it.[58] Likewise, definitions reached by division invite the same question. Thus, to the question, *What is a human being?*, the divider replies, *Animal, mortal, footed, biped, wingless*. When for each predicate he is asked, *Why?*, he will say, for example, and thinks he proves *that all animal is either mortal or immortal*. But such an explanation taken as a whole is not a definition. So, even if division did demonstrate it, the definition at any rate does not turn out to be a logical inference....

[6.] Is it perhaps possible that we could in fact demonstrate what a thing is essentially by hypothesis, premising that the essential existence proper to it is constituted by the properties included in what it is, and that such and such properties alone are included in what it is, and that the whole of them is proper to the thing, since in this consists the existence of the thing? Or is it not rather obvious that,

---

[57] Note how Aristotle relates a genus to a species as a whole to its part. What sort of whole is a genus? If its species are parts of a sort, what would its specific differences be in this analogy? Elsewhere Aristotle draws an analogy between genus and species as a sort of matter to its forms. However, is not the implicit disanalogy that all these logical things thus related are all formal in character—forms determined by and determining forms through formal determinations?

[58] For example, *If intellect is wholly immaterial, then it cannot be in a place or in time*. The unstated middle is that only a bodily thing can be in a place at a time.

## Part 7

How then shall one who is defining something show its essence or what it is? One cannot show it as a new fact necessarily following from the assumption of admitted facts—the method of demonstration. Nor may one by induction establish a universal on the evidence of particulars which offer no exception, because induction proves not what a thing is but rather the fact that it has or has not some attribute. Since presumably one cannot prove what it is by sense perception or pointing with the finger, then what other way remains?

To put it another way: how shall we demonstrate essence? Anyone who knows what a human being is, or any other kind of thing, must know also that there is such a thing. For no one knows the essence of what does not exist; one can know the meaning of the phrase or name *unicorn*, but not what the essence of a *unicorn* is. If definition can prove what a thing is, can it also prove that it exists? But how will it prove them both by the same reasoning, since definition shows one single thing and demonstration another, and what a human being is and the fact that human beings exist are not the same thing?

We hold it is by demonstration that anything must be proved to exist (unless, indeed, existing were its essence, but since being is not a genus, it is not the essence of anything). Hence the fact that a kind of thing exists is a matter for demonstration. This is the actual procedure of the sciences, for the geometer assumes the meaning of the word *triangle*, but a fact about it he demonstrates. What is it, then, that we shall demonstrate in defining what it is? —What a triangle is? In that case, a man will know by definition what a thing is without knowing whether it exists. But that is impossible.[59]

Moreover, it is clear, if we consider the methods of defining actually in use, that definition does not prove that the thing defined exists: since even if there does actually exist something that is

---

since proof must be through the middle, the definition of what it is, is assumed in this minor premise too? ...

[59] Does Aristotle mean that definitions are but starting points for acquiring knowledge of the essence, attained by demonstration of its properties as well, beginning with its existence?

equidistant from a center, yet why should the thing named in the definition exist? Or for what reason must anything be a circle? One might equally well call it the definition of *mountain copper*. For definitions do not bear evidence that the thing defined can exist or that it is what they claim to define it to be: one can always ask why.... It is clear from these considerations that neither definition and syllogism nor their objects are the same, and that definition neither demonstrates nor proves anything, nor is scientific knowledge of what something is to be obtained either by a definition or by a demonstration.

## Part 8

... When we have the fact we seek the reason for it, and although sometimes the fact and the reason become clear to us simultaneously, yet we cannot discover the reason for it a moment sooner than the fact. In just the same way, clearly, we cannot discover a thing's essential existence without discovering that such a thing exists, for it is impossible to know what it is while we are ignorant whether it is.[60]

Sometimes we have the fact that a thing exists by an attribute, sometimes by some property of the thing. For example, we know of thunder that is a noise in the clouds; of an eclipse that it is a privation of light; or of a human being, that it is a species of animal; or of a soul, that it is self-moving. As often as it is only by an attribute we have it that a thing exists, we are in no state whatever to discover what it is; for we have no sure knowledge even of its existence, and to search for what a thing is when we are unsure that it exists is to search for nothing. But whenever we have some property of the thing, it is easier. Accordingly, the way in which we know that it exists is the way in which we stand to knowing what it is.

Let us take the following as our first example of some property of what it is. Let A be eclipse, C the moon, B the earth's screening. Now to ask whether the moon is eclipsed or not is to ask whether or not B

---

[60] *Essential existence:* τὸ τί ἦν εἶναι. Aristotelian idiolect of notoriously obscure syntax, which I take to be an articular infinitive, τὸ εἶναι, enclosing an indirect question, τί ἦν—in a proleptic imperfect both progressive and persistent—to signify that substantial being of the thing which abides, perdures, makes it the kind of thing it is: *its being what it has kept going to be*.

has occurred. But that is nothing else than asking whether there is a reason for it. And whenever the reasons exist, we assert A also exists.

Again, reasoning may seek which of two contradictories is true: *Are the angles of a triangle equal or not equal to two right angles?* When we have found the answer, if the premises are immediate, we know fact and reason together; if they are not immediate, then we know the fact without the reason, as in the following example: let C be *the moon*, A *an eclipse*, B the fact that *the moon though full fails to produce shadows, with no visible body intervening between us and it*. Then if B—*failure to produce shadows despite absence of any intervening body*—is attributable to C [*the moon*], and A [*eclipse*] is attributable to B, it is clear that the moon is eclipsed, but the reason why is not yet clear, and we know the fact that there exists an eclipse, but we do not know what an eclipse is.

But when it is clear that A is a predicate of C, to ask the reason for this is to ask what B is: *Is it a screening, a rotation or an extinction of the moon?* But in these examples B is the definition of the other term, the major term A, for the eclipse consists in the earth's screening. Thus, *What is thunder?* —*The quenching of fire in cloud*, is equivalent to, *Why does it thunder?* —*Because fire is quenched in the cloud.* Let C be *cloud*, A *thunder*, B *quenching of fire*. Then B is a predicate of C, *cloud*, because fire is quenched in it; and A, *noise*, is a predicate of B; and B is assuredly the definition of the major term A. But if there be a middle definition of B, it will be one of the remaining explanations of A.

We have stated, then, how what a thing is, is grasped and comes to be known, and we see that, while there is no syllogism of what it is (i.e., no demonstrative syllogism), yet it is through syllogism and demonstration that what it is comes to be made clear. So, we conclude that neither can it be known without demonstration what anything is that has a cause distinct from itself, nor can it be demonstrated. And this is what we contended in our preliminary discussion of difficulties.

## Part 9

Now while some things have a cause distinct from themselves, others have not. Hence it is clear that for some things what they are is immediately known and a starting point [of demonstration]. Of these, not only that there is such but what they are must be shown in some other way [than demonstration]—and this is the actual procedure of the arithmetician, who assumes both what the unit is and that it exists. However, as we have said, it is possible through demonstration to exhibit the essence of things that have a middle, i.e., a cause of their essence—although we do not thereby demonstrate it.

## Part 10

Since a definition is an explanation of what something is, it is clear that one kind of definition will be an explanation of the meaning of the name or of some other designation of it. A definition in this sense explains, e.g., what *triangular* means. When we hold that there is such a thing, we ask the reason that there is. But it is difficult to recognize things we do not know to exist, the cause of this difficulty being, as we said, that we only know by an attribute whether such exists or not. Moreover, an explanation may be a unity in either of two ways, by conjunction, like the *Iliad*, or because it exhibits a single predicate as inherent in a single subject not as an attribute.

That is one way of defining definition. Another kind of definition is an explanation that makes clear the reason for what it is. Thus, the former signifies without showing what it is, but the latter is clearly quasi-demonstration, differing from demonstration in the arrangement of its terms. For there is a difference between explaining why it thunders and what thunder is. The former will be *Because fire is quenched in the clouds*, while the explanation of what thunder is will be *The noise of fire being quenched in the clouds*. The same explanation thus takes a different form: in one form it is demonstration through a middle, in the other definition of a middle. Again, thunder can be defined as *noise in the clouds*, which is the conclusion of a demonstration about what it is. On the other hand, the definition of immediate terms is an indemonstrable positing of what they are....

# LOGIC III
# COGITANDA

| | | |
|---|---|---|
| Socrates is *a man*. | A man is *a rational animal*. | A man is *a substance*. |
| Socrates is *five-feet tall*. | A foot is *a length*. | A foot is *a quantity*. |
| Socrates is *snub-nosed*. | Snub is *a shape*. | Snub is *a quality* |
| Socrates is *wiser* than most. | Wiser is *the comparative of wise*. | Wiser is *a relation* |
| Socrates is *in the agora*. | An agora is *a market*. | An agora is *a place*. |
| Socrates is a *5th century* Athenian. | The 5th century is *a historical period*. | The 5th century is a period *of time*. |
| Socrates is *sitting*. | To sit is *to rest on buttocks*. | To sit is *a position*. |
| Socrates is not *shod*. | To be shod is *to wear shoes*. | To be shod is *a condition*. |
| Socrates is *conversing*. | To converse is *to speak with others*. | To converse is *to act*. |
| Socrates *is condemned*. | To be condemned is *to be found guilty in court*. | To be arrested is *to be affected*. |

# LOGIC III
## On Predicates

**Aristotle**
*Categories* Parts 1-4 [61]

---

### Part 1

Things are said to be named equivocally when, though they have a common name, the definition corresponding with the name differs for each. Thus, a real man and a figure in a picture can both lay claim to the name *animal*; yet these are equivocally so named, for, though they have a common name, the definition corresponding with the name differs for each. For should anyone define in what sense each is an animal, his definition in the one case will be appropriate to that case only.

On the other hand, things are said to be named univocally which have both the name and the definition answering to the name in common. A man and an ox are both *animal*, and these are univocally so named, inasmuch as not only the name, but also the definition, is the same in both cases: for if a man should state in what sense each is an animal, the statement in the one case would be identical with that in the other.

Things are said to be named derivatively, which derive their name from some other name, but differ from it by inflection. Thus, the grammarian derives his name from the word grammar, and the courageous from the word courage.

---

[61] Tr. E.M. Edhill, The Project Gutenberg, emended.

## Part 2

Forms of speech are either simple or complex. Examples of the latter are such expressions as *the man runs, the man wins;* of the former *man, ox, runs, wins.*

Of things themselves some are predicable of a subject [in itself] and are never present in a subject [incidentally].[62] Thus *man* is predicable of the individual man and is never only present in its subject [incidentally].

**By being *present in a subject* I do not mean present as parts are present in a whole, but being incapable of existence apart from the said subject.**

Some things, again, are present in a subject [incidentally], but are never predicable of a subject [in itself]. For instance, a certain point of grammatical knowledge is present in a mind incidentally but is not predicable of any [in itself]; or again, a certain whiteness may be present in a body incidentally (for color requires a material basis), yet it is never predicable of any [in itself].

Other things, again, are *both* predicable *of* a subject and present incidentally *in* a subject. For example, while knowledge is present in a human mind incidentally, it is also predicable of *grammar* [in itself].

There is, lastly, a class of things which are neither present incidentally in a subject nor predicable of a subject in itself, such as the individual man or the individual horse. ***To speak more generally, that which is individual and has the character of a unit is never predicable of a subject.*** Yet in some cases there is nothing to prevent its being present in a subject. Thus, a particular point of grammatical knowledge is present in a subject [i.e., a particular man's mind].

---

[62] In Greek, Aristotle simply says *present in* to signify accidental attributes.

NOTE

Aristotle's distinctions can be represented in a Punnett square:

|  | Predicable of a Subject | Not Predicable of a Subject |
|---|---|---|
| Present Incidentally in a Subject (Essential properties of subjects.) | Socrates is *a man*. Grammar is *knowledge.* White is **a color.** | ***Socrates*** is the man talking. The man talking is ***Socrates.*** |
| Present Incidentally in a Subject (Attributes in subjects incidentally) | Socrates is *wise* Socrates knows grammar. Socrates is **white.** | The **whiteness** of that white is very white indeed! [But *not* whiteness is white.] |

Substantive predicates say what the thing is in itself and so predicate properties of their subject *per se*. In contrast, attributive predicates attribute to their subject attributes which it can acquire or lose *per accidens*, which attributes therefore exist in it incidentally.

## Part 3

When something is predicated of something else, all that which is predicable of the predicate will be predicable also of the subject. Thus, *man* is predicated of the individual man; and *animal* is predicated of *man*; it will, therefore, be predicable of the individual man also: for the individual man is both *man* and *animal*.

If genera are different and co-ordinate, their species differences are themselves different in kind. Take as an instance the genus *animal* and the genus *knowledge*. *Footed, two-footed, winged, aquatic* are specific differences of *animal*; the species of knowledge are not distinguished by these same differences. One species of knowledge does not differ from another in being two-footed.

But where one genus is subordinate to another, there is nothing to prevent their having the same specific differences: for the greater class is predicated of the lesser, so that all the differences of the predicate will be differences also of the subject.

## Part 4

Expressions which are in no way composite signify either *Substance, Quantity, Quality, Relation, Place, Tim, Position, State, Action,* or *Passion*. To sketch my meaning roughly:

Examples of SUBSTANCE are *man* or *horse*;
of QUANTITY, such terms as *two cubits long* or *three cubits long*;
of QUALITY, such attributes as *white, grammatical.*

*Double, half, greater,* fall under the category of RELATION;
*in the market place, in the Lyceum,* under that of PLACE;
*yesterday, last year,* under that of TIME;
*Lying, sitting,* are terms indicating POSITION;
*shod, armed,* STATE.

*To lance, to cauterize,* ACTION;
*to be lanced, to be cauterized,* PASSION.

None of these terms, in and by itself, involves an affirmation; it is by the combination of such terms that positive or negative statements arise. For every assertion must, as admitted, be either true or false, whereas expressions that are not in any way composite, like *man, white, runs, wins,* cannot be either true or false.

## Part 5

*Substance*, in the truest and primary and most definite sense of the word, is that which is neither predicable of a subject [in itself] nor present in a subject [incidentally]—e.g., the individual man or horse. But in a secondary sense are called substances those species within which primary substances are included, as well as those genera which include the species. For instance, the individual man is included in the species *man*, and the genus to which the species belongs is *animal*; these, therefore—that is to say, the species *man* and the genus *animal*— are termed *secondary substances*.

It is plain from what has been said that both the name and the definition of the predicate must be predicable of the subject. For instance, *man* is predicted of the individual man. Now in this case the name of the species *man* is applied to the individual, for we use the term *man* in describing the individual; and the definition of *man* will also be predicated of the individual man, for the individual man is both man and animal. Thus, both the name and the definition of the species are predicable of the individual.

With regard, on the other hand, to those things which are present incidentally in a subject, it is generally the case that neither their name nor their definition is predicable of that in which they are present. However, although the definition is never predicable, there is nothing in certain cases to prevent the name being used. For instance, *white* being present in a body is predicated of that in which it is present, for a body is called white: the definition, however, of the color *white* is never predicable of the body [in itself].

Everything except primary substances is either predicable of a primary substance or present in a primary substance. This becomes evident by reference to particular instances. *Animal* is predicated of the species *man*, therefore of the individual man, for if there were no individual man of whom it could be predicated, it could not be predicated of the species *man* at all. Again, color is present in body, therefore in individual bodies, for if there were no individual body in which it was present, it could not be present in body at all.

Thus, everything except primary substances is either predicated of primary substances, or is present in them, and if these last did not exist, it would be impossible for anything else to exist.

Of secondary substances, the species is more truly substance than the genus, being more nearly related to primary substance. For if anyone should render an account of what a primary substance is, he would render a more instructive account and one more proper to the subject by stating the species than by stating the genus. Thus, he would give a more instructive account of an individual man by stating that he was man than by stating that he was animal, for the former description is peculiar to the individual in a greater degree, while the latter is too general. Again, the man who gives an account of the nature of an individual tree will give a more instructive account by mentioning the species *tree* than by mentioning the genus *plant*.

Moreover, primary substances are most properly called substances in virtue of the fact that they are the entities which underlie everything else, and that everything else is either predicated of them [essentially] or present in them [incidentally]. Now the same relation which subsists between primary substance and everything else subsists also between the species and the genus: for the species is to the genus as subject is to predicate, since the genus is predicated of the species, whereas the species cannot be predicated of the genus. Thus, we have a second ground for asserting that the species is more truly substance than the genus.

Of species themselves, except in the case of such as are genera, no one is more truly substance than another. We should not give a more appropriate account of the individual man by stating the species to which he belonged, than we should of an individual horse by adopting the same method of definition. In the same way, of primary substances, no one is more truly substance than another; an individual man is not more truly substance than an individual ox.

It is, then, with good reason that of all that remains, when we exclude primary substances, we concede to species and genera alone the name secondary substance, for these alone of all the predicates convey a knowledge of primary substance. For it is by stating the species or the genus that we appropriately define any individual man; and we shall make our definition more exact by stating the former than by stating the latter. All other things that we state, such as that he is white, that he runs, and so on, are irrelevant to the definition. Thus, it is just that these alone, apart from primary substances, should be called substances.

Further, primary substances are most properly so called because they underlie and are the subjects of everything else. Now the same relation that subsists between primary substance and everything else subsists also between the species and the genus to which the primary substance belongs, on the one hand, as well as to every attribute which is not included within these, on the other. For these are the subjects of all such. If we call an individual man *skilled in grammar*, the predicate is applicable also to the species and to the genus to which he belongs. This law holds good in all cases.

It is a common characteristic of all substance that it is never present in a subject. For primary substance is neither present in a subject nor predicated of a subject; while, with regard to secondary substances, it is clear from the following arguments (apart from others) that they are not present in a subject. For *man* is predicated of the individual man but is not present in any subject [incidentally]: for manhood is not present in the individual man [incidentally]. In the same way, *animal* is also predicated of the individual man, but is not [incidentally] present in him.

Again, when a thing is present in a subject, though the name may quite well be applied to that in which it is present, the definition cannot be applied. Yet of secondary substances, not only the name, but also the definition, applies to the subject: we should use both the definition of the species and that of the genus with reference to the individual man. Thus, substance cannot be present in a subject.

Yet this is not peculiar to substance, for it is also the case that specific differences cannot be present in subjects. The characteristics *terrestrial* and *two-footed* are predicated of the species *man*, but not present in it. For they are not in man. Moreover, the definition of the differences may be predicated of what the specific difference itself is predicated of. For instance, if the characteristic *terrestrial* is predicated of the species *man*, the definition also of that characteristic may be used to form the predicate of the species *man*: for *man* is terrestrial.

The fact that the parts of substances appear to be present in the whole as in a subject should not make us apprehensive lest we should have to admit that such parts are not substances, for in explaining the phrase *being present in a subject*, we stated that we meant *otherwise than as parts in a whole*.

It is the mark of substances and of differences that, in all propositions of which they form the predicate, they are predicated univocally. For all such propositions have for their subject either the individual or the species. It is true that, inasmuch as primary substance is not predicable of anything, it can never form the predicate of any proposition. But of secondary substances, the species is predicated of the individual, the genus both of the species and of the individual. Similarly, the differences are predicated of the species and of the individuals.

Moreover, the definition of the species and that of the genus are applicable to the primary substance, and that of the genus to the species. For all that is predicated of the predicate will be predicated also of the subject. Similarly, the definition of the differences will be applicable to the species and to the individuals. But it was stated above that the word *univocal* was applied to those things which had both name and definition in common. It is, therefore, established that in every proposition, of which either substance or a difference forms the predicate, these are predicated univocally.

All substance appears to signify that which is individual. In the case of primary substance this is indisputably true, for the thing is a unit. In the case of secondary substances, when we speak, for instance, of *man* or *animal*, our form of speech gives the impression that we are here also indicating that which is individual, but the impression is not strictly true; for a secondary substance is not an individual, but a kind with a certain qualification; for it is not one and single as a primary substance is; the words *man, animal*, are predicable of more than one subject.

Yet species and genus do not merely indicate quality, like the term *white*; for *white* indicates quality and nothing further, **but species and genus determine the quality with reference to a substance: they signify substance qualitatively differentiated**. The determinate qualification covers a larger field in the case of the genus that in that of the species: he who uses the word *animal* is using a word of wider extension than he who uses the word *man*.

Another mark of substance is that it has no contrary. What could be the contrary of any primary substance, such as the individual man or animal? It has none. Nor can the species or the genus have a contrary. Yet this characteristic is not peculiar to substance, but is true of many other things, such as quantity. There is nothing that forms the contrary of *two cubits long* or of *three cubits long*, or of *ten*, or of any such term. A man may contend that *much* is the contrary of *little*, or *great* of *small*, but of definite quantitative terms no contrary exists.

Substance, again, does not appear to admit of variation of degree. I do not mean by this that one substance cannot be more or less truly substance than another, for it has already been stated that this is the case; but that no single substance admits of varying degrees within itself.

For instance, one particular substance, *a human*, cannot be more or less human either than himself at some other time or than some other human. One human cannot be more human than another, as that which is white may be more or less white than some other white object, or as that which is beautiful may be more or less beautiful than some other beautiful object. The same quality, moreover, is said to subsist in a thing in varying degrees at different times. A body, being white, is said to be whiter at one time than it was before, or, being warm, is said to be warmer or less warm than at some other time. But substance is not said to be more or less that which it is: a man is not more truly a man at one time than he was before, nor is anything, if it is substance, more or less what it is. Substance, then, does not admit of variation of degree.

The most distinctive mark of substance appears to be that, while remaining numerically one and the same, it is capable of admitting contrary qualities. From among things other than substance, we should find ourselves unable to bring forward any which possessed this mark. Thus, one and the same color cannot be white and black. Nor can the same one action be good and bad: this law holds good with everything that is not substance.

But one and the selfsame substance, while retaining its identity, is yet capable of admitting contrary qualities. The same individual person is at one time white, at another black, at one time warm, at another cold, at one time good, at another bad. This capacity is found nowhere else, though it might be maintained that a statement or opinion was an exception to the rule. The same statement, it is agreed, can be both true and false. For if the statement *He is sitting* is true, yet, when the person in question has risen, the same statement will be false. The same applies to opinions. For if anyone thinks truly that a person is sitting, yet, when that person has risen, this same opinion, if still held, will be false.

Yet although this exception may be allowed, there is, nevertheless, a difference in the manner in which the thing takes place. It is by themselves changing that substances admit contrary qualities. It is thus that that which was hot becomes cold, for it has entered into a different state. Similarly, that which was white becomes black, and that which was bad good, by a process of change; and in the same way in all other cases, it is by changing that substances are capable of admitting contrary qualities. However, statements and opinions themselves remain unaltered in all respects: it is by the alteration in the facts of the case that the contrary quality comes to be theirs. The statement *He is sitting* remains unaltered, but it is at one time true, at another false, according to circumstances....

[I]t is by reason of the modification which takes place within the substance itself that a substance is said to be capable of admitting contrary qualities; for a substance admits within itself either disease or health, whiteness or blackness. It is in this sense that it is said to be capable of admitting contrary qualities.

To sum up, it is a distinctive mark of substance, that, while remaining numerically one and the same, it is capable of admitting contrary qualities, the modification taking place through a change in the substance itself. Let these remarks suffice on the subject of substance.

## Propositions Sundry

### Existential
*Affirms existence of a subject:*

Souls exist.

### *Categorical*
### (a.k.a. Assertoric)
*A predicate is affirmed or denied of a subject simply:*

Souls are immaterial.

### Disjunctive
*Some mutual exclusion of disjuncts is affirmed/denied of subjects or predicates:*

Souls are *either* mortal *or* immortal.

### Conjunctive
*Affirms/denies that two conjuncts can belong to same subject at same time:*

The human soul cannot be *both* mortal *and* immortal.

### Modal
*A proposition qualified for certainty:*

*It is possible that* human soul is not immortal. (*a.k.a. Problematic*)
*It is necessary that* immaterial soul be incorruptible. (*a.k.a. Apodictic*)

### Conditional
*Some conditional relation is affirmed/denied of two propositions:*
*If the antecedent proposition is affirmed/denied,*
*then the consequent is affirmed/denied too:*

*If* something is living, *then* it has a soul.
*If* it is an immaterial soul, *then* it is an immortal soul.

# LOGIC IV

## On Propositions

### Aristotle
*De interpretatione* Parts 1–6 & 11 [63]

#### Part 1

First, we must define the terms 'noun' and 'verb', then the terms 'denial' and 'affirmation', then 'proposition' and 'sentence.'

Spoken words are the symbols of mental experience and written words are the symbols of spoken words. Just as all men have not the same writing, so all men have not the same speech sounds, but the mental experiences, which these directly symbolize, are the same for all, as also are those things of which our experiences are the images. But this matter has been discussed in my treatise about the soul, for it belongs to an investigation distinct from that which lies before us.

As there are in the mind thoughts which do not involve truth or falsity, and also those which must be either true or false, so it is in speech. For truth and falsity imply combination and separation. Nouns and verbs, provided nothing is added, are like thoughts without combination or separation; *man* and *white*, as isolated terms, are not yet either true or false. For proof, consider the word *goat-stag*. It has significance, but there is no truth or falsity about it, unless *is* or *is not* is added, either in the present or in some other tense.

#### Part 2

By a noun we mean a sound significant by convention, which has no reference to time, and of which no part is significant apart from the rest. In the noun *Fairsteed*, the part *steed* has no significance in and

---

[63] Tr. E.M. Edgehill, The Internet Classics Archive, emended.

by itself, as in the phrase *fair steed*. Yet there is a difference between simple and composite nouns; for in the former the part is in no way significant, in the latter it contributes to the meaning of the whole, although it has not an independent meaning. Thus, in the word *pirate-boat* the word *boat* has no meaning except as part of the whole word.

The limitation "by convention" was introduced because nothing is by nature a noun or name—it is only so when it becomes a symbol; inarticulate sounds, such as those which brutes produce, are significant, yet none of these constitutes a noun.

The expression *not-man* is not a noun. There is indeed no recognized term by which we may denote such an expression, for it is not a sentence or a denial. Let it then be called an indefinite noun. The expression *boy's*, *boys'*, and so on, constitute not nouns, but cases of a noun. The definition of these cases of a noun is in other respects the same as that of the noun proper, but, when coupled with *is, was, or will be*, they do not, as they are, form a proposition either true or false, and this the noun proper always does, under these conditions. Take the words *Philo's is* or *Philo's is not*; these words do not, as they stand, form either a true or a false proposition.

## Part 3

A verb is that which, in addition to its proper meaning, carries with it the notion of time. No part of it has any independent meaning, and it is a sign of something said of something else.

I will explain what I mean by saying that it carries with it the notion of time. *Health* is a noun, but *flourishes* is a verb; for besides its proper meaning it indicates the present existence of the state in question. Moreover, a verb is always a sign of something said of something else, i.e., of something either predicable of or present in some other thing.

Such inflections as *is not flourishing*, *is not ailing*, I do not describe as verbs; for though they carry the additional note of time, and always form a predicate, there is no specified name for this variety; but let them be called indefinite verbs, since they apply equally well to that which exists and to that which does not. Similarly, *he was flourishing, he will be flourishing*, are not verbs, but tenses of a verb; the difference lies in the fact that the verb indicates present time, while the tenses of the verb indicate those times which lie outside the present.

Verbs in and by themselves are substantives [i.e., infinitives] and have significance, for he who uses such expressions arrests the hearer's mind, and fixes his attention; but they do not, as they stand, express any judgment, either positive or negative. For neither are the infinitive forms *be* and *not be* or the participle *being* significant of any fact, unless something is added; for they do not themselves indicate anything, but imply a copulation, of which we cannot form a conception apart from the things coupled.

## Part 4

A sentence is a significant portion of speech, some parts of which have an independent meaning, that is to say, as an utterance, though not as the expression of any positive judgment. Let me explain. The words *human being* has a meaning, but do not constitute a proposition, either positive or negative. It is only when other words are added that the whole will form an affirmation or denial. But if we separate one syllable of the word *human* from the other, it has no meaning; similarly, in the word *mouse*, the part *-ouse* has no meaning in itself but is merely a sound. In composite words, indeed, the parts contribute to the meaning of the whole; yet, as has been pointed out, they have not an independent meaning.

Every sentence has meaning, not by a natural organ, as we have said, by convention. Yet every sentence is not a proposition; only such are propositions as have in them either truth or falsity. Thus, a command or wish is a sentence, but is neither true nor false. Let us then dismiss all other types of sentence but the proposition, for it concerns our present inquiry, whereas the investigation of the others belongs rather to the study of rhetoric or of poetry.

## Part 5

The first class of simple propositions is the simple affirmation, the next, the simple denial; all others are only one by conjunction.

Every proposition must contain a verb or the tense of a verb. The phrase which defines the species *man*, if no verb in present, past, or future time be added, is not a proposition. It may be asked how the expression *a footed animal with two feet* can be called single; for it is not the circumstance that the words follow in unbroken succession that effects the unity. This inquiry, however, finds its place in an investigation foreign to that before us. We call those propositions single which indicate a single fact, or the conjunction of the parts of which results in unity: those propositions, on the other hand, are separate and many in number, which indicate many facts, or whose parts have no conjunction.

Let us, moreover, consent to call a noun or a verb an expression only, and not a proposition, since it is not possible for a man to speak in this way when he is expressing something, in such a way as to make a statement, whether his utterance is an answer to a question or an act of his own initiation.

To return: of propositions one kind is simple, i.e., that which asserts or denies something of something, the other composite, i.e. that which is compounded of simple propositions. A simple proposition is a statement, with meaning, as to the presence of something in a subject or its absence, in the present, past, or future, according to the divisions of time.

## Part 6

An affirmation is a positive assertion of something about something, a denial a negative assertion. Now it is possible both to affirm and to deny the presence of something which is present or of something which is not, and since these same affirmations and denials are possible with reference to those times which lie outside the present, it would be possible to contradict any affirmation or denial.

Thus, it is plain that every affirmation has an opposite denial, and similarly every denial an opposite affirmation.

We will call such a pair of propositions a pair of contradictories. Those positive propositions are said to be contradictory which have the same subject and predicate. The identity of subject and of predicate must not be equivocal. Indeed, there are definitive qualifications besides this, which we make to meet the casuistries of sophists.

## Part 11

There is no oneness to an affirmation or denial which, either positively or negatively, predicates one thing of many subjects, or many things of the same subject, unless that which is indicated by the many is really some one thing. Do not apply this word *one* to those things which, though they have a single recognized name, yet do not combine into one. Thus, man may be an animal, and biped, and domesticated, but these three predicates unite into one. On the other hand, the predicates *white, man,* and *walking* do not thus unite. Neither, therefore, if these three forms the subject of an affirmation, nor if they form its predicate, is there any oneness about that affirmation. In both cases the unity is linguistic, but not real.

If therefore the dialectical question is a request for an answer, i.e., either for the admission of a premise or for the admission of one of two contradictories—and the premise is itself always one of two contradictories—the answer to such a question as contains the above predicates cannot be a single proposition. For as I have explained in the *Topics*, a question is not a single one, even though the answer asked for is true.

At the same time, it is plain that a question of the form, *What is it?*, is not a dialectical question, for a dialectical questioner must by the form of his question give his opponent the chance of announcing one of two alternatives, whichever he wishes. He must therefore put the question into a more definite form, and inquire, e.g., whether man has such and such a characteristic or not.

Some combinations of predicates are such that the separate predicates unite to form a single predicate. Let us consider under what conditions this is and is not possible. We may either state in two separate propositions that man is an animal, and that man is a biped, or we may combine the two, and state that man is an animal with two feet. Similarly, we may use *man* and *white* as separate predicates or unite them into one. Yet if a man is a shoemaker and is also good, we cannot construct a composite proposition and say that he is a good shoemaker. For if, whenever two separate predicates truly belong to a subject, it follows that the predicate resulting from their combination also truly belongs to the subject, many absurd results ensue.

For instance, a man is man and white. Therefore, if predicates may always be combined, he is a white man. Again, if the predicate *white* belongs to him, then the combination of that predicate with the former composite predicate will be permissible. Thus, it will be right to say that he is a white man so on indefinitely. Or, again, we may combine the predicates *musical, white,* and *walking,* and these may be combined many times. Similarly, we may say that Socrates is Socrates and a man, and that therefore he is the man Socrates, or that Socrates is a man and a biped, and that therefore he is a two-footed man. Thus, it is manifest that if man states unconditionally that predicates can always be combined, many absurd consequences ensue.

We will now explain what ought to be laid down. Those predicates, and terms forming the subject of predication, which are incidental[64] either to the same subject or to one another, do not unite into one. Take the proposition, *The man is pale and musical*. Being pale and being musical do not combine into one, for they belong only coincidentally to the same subject. Nor yet, if it were true to say that that one who is pale is musical, would the terms *musical* and *white* combine into one, for it is only coincidentally that the one that is musical is white; the combination of the two will, therefore, not unite

---

[64] A traditional translation is *accidental*, which transliterates the Latin term *accidens*, participle of *accidere*, meaning *befall, happen to,* to name what *comes* to be in something, in contrast to what is predicable of it in itself—the former by an acquisition, the latter from its own nature. The categories were Aristotle's attempt to enumerate such attributes as are acquired by and attributed to a substance.

into one. Thus, again, whereas, if a man is both good and a shoemaker, we cannot combine the two propositions and say simply that he is a good shoemaker, we are, at the same time, able to combine the predicates *animal* and *biped* and say that a man is a bipedal animal, for these predicates are not accidental [to one another].

Those predicates, again, cannot unite into one, of which the one is implicit in the other: thus, we cannot combine the predicate *white* again and again with that which already contains the notion *white*, nor is it right to call a man an animal-man or a two-footed man; for the notions *animal* and *biped* are implicit in the word *man*. On the other hand, it is possible to predicate a term simply of any one instance, and to say that some one particular man is a man or that some one pale man is a pale man.

Yet this is not always possible: indeed, when in the adjunct there is some opposite which involves a contradiction, the predication of the simple term is impossible. Thus, it is not right to call a dead man a man. When, however, this is not the case, it is not impossible.

Yet the facts of the case might rather be stated thus: when some such opposite elements are present, resolution is never possible, but when they are not present, resolution is nevertheless not always possible. Take the proposition, *Homer is so-and-so*—say *a poet*—does it follow that Homer is, or does it not? The verb *is*, is here used of Homer only incidentally, the proposition being that Homer is a poet, not that he is, in the independent sense of the word.[65]

Thus, in the case of those predications which have within them no contradiction when the nouns are expanded into definitions, and wherein the predicates belong to the subject in their own proper sense and not in any indirect way, the individual may be the subject of the simple propositions as well as of the composite. But in the case of that which is not, it is not true to say that because it is the object of opinion, it is, for the opinion held about it is that it is not, not that it is.

---

[65] The independent sense in English being *exists*. Greek has one form of the verb which can be either copulative and existential—like the difference in English between *God is good* and *There is a God*.

# EXTENSION

Roses are red. Roses are not red.
*All* roses are red. * *No* roses are red.
*Some* roses are red. * *Some* roses are not red.

*Square of Opposition*

| A<br>*All men are good.* | E<br>*No men are good.* |
|---|---|
| I<br>*Some men are good.* | O<br>*Some men are not good.* |

*Horizontally:* Can **A** and **E** both be true? Can **A** and **E** both be false?
*Vertically:* Can **A** and **I** both be true? both false? one true and one false?
*Diagonally:* Can **A** and **O** both be true? both false? one true and one false?

*Horizontally:* Can **E** and **A** both be false? Can **I** and **O** both be false?
*Vertically:* Can **E** and **O** both be false? Can **E** be false and **O** true?
*Diagonally:* Can **E** and **I** both be false? Can one be true and one false?

*Horizontally:* **A** & **E** are called *contraries*, and **I** & **O** are call *subcontraries*.
*Vertically:* **I** is called *subaltern* of A, and **E** *subaltern* of **O**.
*Diagonally:* **A** & **O** are *contradictories*; and **E** & **I** are *contradictories*.
*Why are these pairs classed together thus?*

|  | LOGICAL ENTAILMENTS ||  INCONCLUSIVE |
|---|---|---|---|
|  | NECESSARILY TRUE | NECESSARILY FALSE | Only Possibly True or False |
| *If A is true, then ...* |  |  |  |
| *If A is false, then ...* |  |  |  |
| *If E is true, then ...* |  |  |  |
| *If E is false, then ...* |  |  |  |
| *If I is true, then ...* |  |  |  |
| *If I is false, then ...* |  |  |  |
| *If O is true, then ...* |  |  |  |
| *If O is false, then ...* |  |  |  |

# LOGIC V

## Opposition & Conversion of Propositions

### ARISTOTLE

*De interpretatione* Parts 7-8 [66]
*Prior Analytics* Book I Parts 1-3 [67]

---

*De interpretatione* 7

Some things are meant universally, others individually. By *a universal* I mean that which is meant to be predicated of many, by *an individual* that which is not. Thus, *a human* is universal, *Callias* is individual. Propositions are necessarily sometimes about a universal and sometimes about an individual.

If then a proposition is made universally about a universal — the one, that something *does* belong to it, and another, that it *does not* — then the propositions will be contrary. By making a universal proposition about a universal I mean such as *Every human is white* or *No human is white*. When, however, the affirmative and negative propositions are about a universal but not themselves universal, they will not be contraries, even though the intentions be sometimes contrary. By making a proposition that is not universal about a universal I mean such as *A human is white* or *A human is not white*. Although *a human* is universal, the proposition is not made universally. For *every* does not signify a universal but rather universally. (And if the predicate be predicated universally as well, then the universal proposition is not true: e.g., *Every man is every animal*.)

---

[66] Tr. J. Tomarchio, from the Greek text of the Loeb Classical Library, *The Categories of Interpretation* (Harvard University Press, 1938)
[67] Tr. A.J. Jenkinson, The Internet Classics Archive.

I say an affirmation is in *contradictory* opposition to a denial when, of the same subject, the affirmation is universal and the negation not, e.g., *Every human is white* and *Not every human is white;* or, *No man is white* and *Some men are white.*

But they are opposed as *contraries* when the affirmation and negation are both universal, e.g., *Every human is white* and *No human is white;* or *Every human is just* and *No human is just.* Therefore these contraries cannot be true at the same time, but the contradictories to them can sometimes be true of the same subject at the same time, i.e., *Not every human is white* and *Some humans are white.*

But when opposite *contradictory* propositions about universals are put universally, it is necessary that one be true and one be false, as well as when they are about individuals, e.g., *Socrates is white* and *Socrates is not white.*

However, when opposite propositions about universals are not put universally, it is not always the case that the one is true and the other false. For it is true at the same time to say *A human being is white* and *A human being is not white,* and *A human being is noble* and *A human being is not noble*—for if he is base, he is also not noble; and also if yet becoming so, he is not. This might at first seem paradoxical, *A human is not white* and *No human is white* appearing to mean the same thing, but they do not mean the same thing, nor necessarily at the same time.

So, it is clear that there is of one affirmation one denial, for the denial must deny that very thing that the affirmation affirms, and about the very same thing, either individuals or universals, and either universally or not universally. I mean, for an example, *Socrates is white* and *Socrates is not white.* But if anything else is denied, or of anything else, it will not be the denial of this but another negation. The denial of *Every human is white* is *Not every human is white;* and of *Some human is white,* it is *No human is white;* but the denial of *A human is white* is *A human is not white.*

So, now it has explained that to one affirmation there is opposed one *contradictory* denial, and which these are; also that other ones are *contrary*, and which they are; moreover, that not every opposite is either true or false, why this is, and when it is either true or false.

## De interpretatione 8

An affirmation or denial is a single one that signifies some one thing about some one thing, whether of a universal universally or not, e.g., *Every man is white* and *Not every man is white*; or *Man is white* and *Man is not white*; or *No man is white* and *Some men are white*—provided that *white* has one meaning. If, however, one word has two meanings that do not unite into one, the affirmation is not a single one.

For example if a man were to establish the signifier *ranger* as signifying both a horse and a human, the proposition *The ranger is white* would not be a single affirmation, nor its opposite a single denial. For it is equivalent to the proposition *A horse and human are white*, which in turn is equivalent to the two propositions, *A horse is white* and *A man is white*. If, then, these two propositions have more than a single significance, and do not form a single proposition, it is clear that the original proposition either has more than one significance or else has none, for there is not any human that is a horse.[68] This, then, is another instance of those propositions of which both the positive and the negative forms may be true or false simultaneously.

---

[68] I have emended Aristotle's strange example: I substitute *ranger* for his *garment: If someone were to establish the name garment for both horse and man ...* I substituted *ranger* as used for either a horse or a man in English. I was tempted to substitute a more clearly equivocal example: the word *bark* signifying both a tree covering and a sound in the affirmation *The bark is rough*. Recall Aristotle's earlier discussion of how some predicates can unite into one and some not: *Those predicates and terms forming the subject of predication that are incidental either to the same subject or to one another, do not unite into one.... Thus, whereas if a man is both good and a shoemaker we cannot combine the two propositions and say simply that he is a good shoemaker, but we are, at the same time, able to combine the predicates animal and biped and say that a man is a bipedal animal, for these predicates are not accidental [to one another].*

## Prior Analytics I.1 [69]

We must first state the subject of our inquiry and the capacity to which it belongs: its subject is demonstration and the capacity that carries it out demonstrative science. We must next define a *premise*, a *term*, and a *syllogism*, and the nature of a *perfect* and of an *imperfect* syllogism; and after that, the inclusion or non-inclusion of one term in another as in a whole, and what we mean by predicating one term of all, or none, of another.

A *premise* then is a sentence affirming or denying one thing of another. This is either universal or particular or indefinite. By *universal* I mean the statement that something belongs to all or none of something else; by *particular*, that it belongs to some or not to some or not to all; by *indefinite*, that it does or does not belong, without any mark to show whether it is universal or particular [i.e., *All*, *None*, *Some*], e.g., *Contraries are subjects of the same science* or *Pleasure is not good*.

The *demonstrative* premise differs from the *dialectical*, because the demonstrative premise is the assertion of one of two contradictory statements (the demonstrator does not ask for his premise [to be granted], but lays it down [as true]), whereas the dialectical premise depends on the adversary's choice between two contradictories. But this will make no difference to the production of a syllogism in either case, for both the demonstrator and the dialectician argue syllogistically after stating that something does or does not belong to something else.

Therefore, a *syllogistic* premise without qualification will be an affirmation or denial of something concerning something else in the way we have described; it will be *demonstrative*, if it is true and obtained through the first principles of its science; while a *dialectical* premise is the giving of a choice between two contradictories, when a man is proceeding by questioning. However, when he is syllogizing, it is the assertion of that which is evident and generally admitted, as

---

[69] Tr. A.J. Jenkinson, The Internet Classics Archive, emended.

has been said in the *Topics*. The nature then of a premise, and the difference between syllogistic, demonstrative, and dialectical premises, may be taken as sufficiently defined by us in relation to our present need, but will be stated more accurately in the sequel.

I call that a *term* into which the premise is resolved, i.e., both the predicate and what it is predicated of [*i.e., subject*], *is* being added and *is not* removed, or vice versa.

A *syllogism* is discourse in which, certain things being stated, something other than what is stated follows *of necessity* from their being so. I mean by the last phrase that they produce the consequence; and by this, that no further term is required from without in order to make the consequence necessary.

I call that a *perfect* syllogism which needs nothing other than what has been stated to make plain what necessarily follows; a syllogism is *imperfect*, if it needs either one or more [other] propositions, which are indeed the necessary consequences of the terms set down but have not been expressly stated as premises.

That one term should be *included* in another as in a whole is the same as for the other to be *predicated* of all of the first. And we say that one term is predicated of all of another, whenever no instance of the subject can be found of which the other [predicated] term cannot be asserted. *To be predicated of none* must be understood in the same way.

## Prior Analytics I.2

Every premise states that something either *is*, or *must be*, or *may be*, the attribute of something else. Of premises of these three kinds, some are *affirmative*, others *negative*, in respect of each of the three modes of attribution. Again, some affirmative and negative premises are *universal*, others *particular*, others *indefinite*.

It is necessary then that in universal attribution the terms of the negative premise should be *convertible*, e.g., *If no pleasure is good, then no good will be pleasure*. The terms of the affirmative must be convertible, not however, universally, but in part, e.g., *If every pleasure, is good, some good must be pleasure*. The particular affirmative must convert in part since, if some pleasure is good, then some good will be pleasure. However, the particular negative need not convert since, *If some animal is not man*, it does not follow that *Some man is not animal*.

First then take a universal negative with the terms A and B. If no B is A, neither can any A be B. For if some A (say C) were B, it would not be true that no B is A; for C is a B. —But if every B is A then some A is B. For if no A were B, then no B could be A. But we assumed that every B is A.

Similarly, too, if the premise is particular. For if some B is A, then some of the As must be B. For if none were, then no B would be A. —But if some B is not A, there is no necessity that some of the as should not be B; e.g., let B stand for animal and A for man. Not every animal is a man; but every man is an animal.

### Prior Analytics I.3

The same manner of conversion will hold good also in respect of *necessary* premises. The universal negative converts universally; each of the affirmatives converts into a particular. If it is necessary that no B is A, then it is necessary also that no A is B. For if it is possible that some A is B, it would be possible also that some B is A. If all or some B is A of necessity, it is necessary also that some A is B: for if there were no necessity, neither would some of the Bs be A necessarily. But the particular negative does not convert, for the same reason which we have already stated.

In respect of *possible* premises, since possibility is used in several senses (for we say that what is necessary, and what is not necessary, and what is potential, is possible), affirmative statements will all convert in a manner similar to those described. For if it is possible that all or some B is A, it will be possible that some A is B. For if that were not possible, then no B could possibly be A. This has been already proved. But in negative statements the case is different.

*A Note*

The four ways of "quantifying" the "extension" of a proposition
can be represented with circles that show whether and how
the proposition places the subject within the predicate:

*Something is affirmed or denied of something else
in whole or in part.*

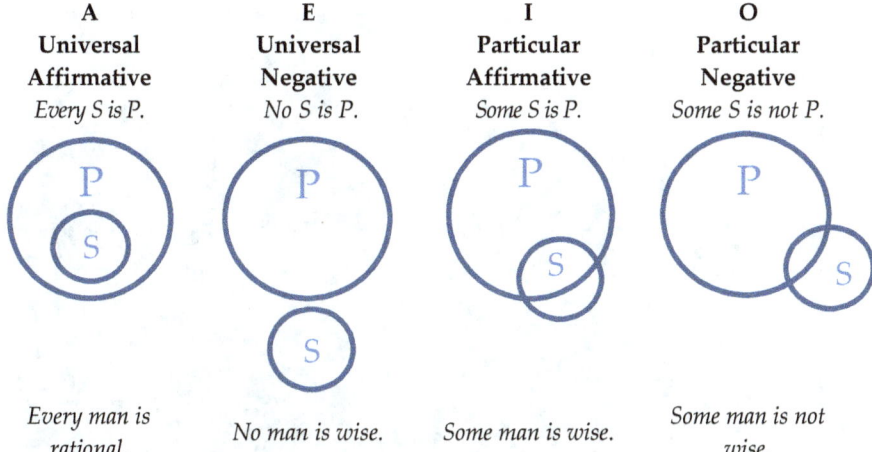

| A | E | I | O |
|---|---|---|---|
| Universal Affirmative | Universal Negative | Particular Affirmative | Particular Negative |
| Every S is P. | No S is P. | Some S is P. | Some S is not P. |
| Every man is rational. | No man is wise. | Some man is wise. | Some man is not wise. |

**Nota bene**
A predicate always extends more widely than its subject,
as a whole including/exluding a part;
e.g., in the proposition All animals are mortals, *mortal* contains *animal*,
whereas in the converse claim, All mortals are animals, *animal* contains *mortal*.

*Allegory of the Seven Liberal Arts,* by Cornelis Schut

# LOGIC VI

## On Syllogism

### ARISTOTLE
*Prior Analytics* Book I Parts 23-25 [70]

---

**Part 23**

... It is necessary that every demonstration and every syllogism should prove either that something belongs or that it does not belong, and this either universally or in part, and either ostensively or hypothetically. One hypothetical proof is the *reductio ad impossibile*. Let us speak first of ostensive syllogisms, for after these have been pointed out, the truth of our contention will be clear with regard to those which are proved *per impossibile*, and in general hypothetically.

If then one wants to prove syllogistically A of B, either as an attribute of it or as not an attribute of it, one must assert something of something else. If now A should be asserted of B, the proposition originally in question will have been assumed. But if A should be asserted of C, but C should not be asserted of anything, nor anything of it, nor anything else of A, no syllogism will be possible. For nothing necessarily follows from the assertion of some one thing concerning some other single thing. Thus, we must take another premise as well.

If then A be asserted of something else, or something of A, or something different of C, nothing prevents a syllogism being formed, but it will not be in relation to B through the premises taken. Nor when C belongs to something else, and that to something else etc., butt no connection being made with B, will a syllogism be possible concerning A in its relation to B. For in general we stated that no syllogism can establish the attribution of one thing to another some middle term is taken, which is somehow related to each by way of predication.

---

[70] Tr. A.J. Jenkinson, The Internet Classics Archive, emended.

For the syllogism in general is made out of premises, and a syllogism [*or conclusion*] referring to *this* out of premises with the same reference, and a syllogism [*or conclusion*] relating *this* to *that* proceeds through premises which relate *this* to *that*. But it is impossible to take a premise in reference to B, if we neither affirm nor deny anything of it; or again to take a premise relating A to B, if we take nothing common, but affirm or deny peculiar attributes of each. So, we must take something midway between the two, which will connect the predications, if we are to have a syllogism relating *this* to *that*.

If then we must take something common in relation to both, and this is possible in three ways—(1) either by predicating A of C, and C of B; (2) or C of both; (3) or both of C—and these are the figures of which we have spoken, then it is clear that every syllogism must be made in one or other of these figures.[71] The argument is the same if several middle terms should be necessary to establish the relation to B; for the figure will be the same whether there is one middle term or many.

It is clear then that the ostensive syllogisms are effected by means of the aforesaid figures; these considerations will show that every *reductio* is also effected in the same way. For all who effect an argument *per impossibile* infer syllogistically what is false, and prove the original conclusion hypothetically when something impossible results from the assumption of its contradictory; e.g., that the diagonal

---

[71] Aristotle names the middle term in each of the 3 figures 'C'. However, let us rename it '**M**'. Naming the subject of the conclusion '**S**', and the predicate of the conclusion '**P**', we can represent the 3 Figures (or "*shapes*") of reasoning as follows:

| Figure I: | Figure II: | Figure III: |
|---|---|---|
| *If* M is P | *If* P is M, | *If* M is P, |
| & S is M, | & S is M, | & M is S, |
| then … | then … | then … |

A conclusion *S is P* will follow in Figure I, e.g., if the two premises are universal affirmations:

*If* All animals (M) are mortal (P),
& All men (S) are animals (M),
*then* All men (S) are mortal (P).

But no conclusion will follow if both premises are universal negatives, for example.

of the square is incommensurate with the side, because odd numbers are equal to evens if it is supposed to be commensurate. One infers syllogistically that odd numbers come out equal to evens, and one proves hypothetically the incommensurability of the diagonal, since a falsehood results through contradicting this. For this we found to be reasoning *per impossibile*, that is, proving something impossible by means of a hypothesis conceded at the beginning.[72]

Consequently, since the falsehood is established in a *reductio ad impossibile* by an ostensive syllogism, and the original conclusion is proved hypothetically, and we have already stated that ostensive syllogisms are affected by means of these figures, it is evident that syllogisms *per impossibile* also will be made through these figures. Likewise, all other hypothetical syllogisms: for in every case the syllogism leads up to the proposition that is substituted for the original thesis; but the original thesis is reached by means of a concession or some other hypothesis. But if this is true, every demonstration and every syllogism must be formed by means of the three figures mentioned above. But when this has been shown it is clear that every syllogism is perfected by means of the first figure and is reducible to the universal syllogisms in this figure.

---

[72] In a pure hypothetical syllogism, both the premises and the conclusion are conditionals, and the antecedent of the one premise must match the consequent of the other. In mixed hypotheticals, one of the premises is a conditional while the other affirms or denies its antecedent or consequent. There are four possible forms, two valid and two invalid.

| *Valid Syllogism* | | *Fallacious Paralogism* | |
|---|---|---|---|
| **Modus ponens** | **Modus tollens** | **Denying the Antecedent** | **Affirming the Consequent** |
| If A, then B. | If A, then B. | If A, then B. | If A, then B. |
| A, | Not-B, | Not-A, | B, |
| Therefore B. | Therefore not-A. | Therefore not-B. | Therefore A. |
| | | Non sequitur! | Non sequitur! |

A **reductio** is a **modus tollens** premised on a necessary disjunction: either A or Not-A, e.g., it must premise that an angle is either equal or unequal to another, not greater or less.

## Part 24

Further, in every syllogism one of the premises must be affirmative, and universality must be present: unless one of the premises is universal, either a syllogism will not be possible, or it will not refer to the subject proposed, or the original position will be begged.

Suppose we have to prove that pleasure in music is good. If one should claim as a premise that pleasure is good without adding *all,* no syllogism will be possible; if one should claim that some pleasure is good, then if it is different from pleasure in music, it is not relevant to the subject proposed; if it is this very pleasure, one is assuming that which was proposed at the outset to be proved.

This is more obvious in geometrical proofs, e.g., that the angles at the base of an isosceles triangle are equal. Suppose the lines A and B have been drawn to the center. If then one should assume that the angle AC is equal to the angle BD, without claiming generally that angles of semicircles are equal; and again if one should assume that the angle C is equal to the angle D, without the additional assumption that every angle of a segment is equal to every other angle of the same segment; and further if one should assume that when equal angles are taken from the whole angles, which are themselves equal, the remainders E and F are equal, he will beg the thing to be proved [i.e., take for granted the very thing to be proved], unless he also states that when equals are taken from equals the remainders are equal.

It is clear then that in every syllogism there must be a universal premise, and that a universal statement is proved only when all the premises are universal, while a particular statement is proved both from two universal premises and from one only: consequently, if the conclusion is universal, the premises also must be universal, but if the premises are universal it is possible that the conclusion may not be universal. And it is clear also that in every syllogism either both or one of the premises must be like the conclusion. I mean not only in being affirmative or negative, but also in being necessary, pure, problematic. We must consider also the other forms of predication.

It is clear also when a syllogism in general can be made and when it cannot; and when a valid, when a perfect syllogism can be formed; and that if a syllogism is formed the terms must be arranged in one of the ways that have been mentioned.

## Part 25

It is clear too that every demonstration will proceed through three terms and no more, unless the same conclusion is established by different pairs of propositions; e.g., the conclusion E may be established through the propositions A and B, and through the propositions C and D, or through the propositions A and B, or A and C, or B and C. For nothing prevents there being several middles for the same terms. But in that case, there is not one but several syllogisms—or again, when each of the propositions A and B is obtained by syllogistic inference, e.g., by means of D and E, and again B by means of F and G; or one may be obtained by syllogistic, the other by inductive inference. But thus, also the syllogisms are many; for the conclusions are many, e.g., A and B and C. But if this can be called one syllogism, not many, the same conclusion may be reached by more than three terms in this way, but it cannot be reached as C is established by means of A and B.

Suppose that the proposition E is inferred from the premises A, B, C, and D. It is necessary then that of these one should be related to another as whole to part: for it has already been proved that if a syllogism is formed, some of its terms must be related in this way. Suppose then that A stands in this relation to B. Some conclusion then follows from them. It must either be E or one or other of C and D, or something other than these.

(1) If it is E, the syllogism will have A and B for its sole premises. But if C and D are so related that one is whole and the other part, then some conclusion will follow from them also; and it must be either E, or one or other of the propositions A and B, or something other than these.

And if it is (i) E, or (ii) A or B, either (i) the syllogisms will be more than one, or (ii) the same thing happens to be inferred by means of several terms only in the sense which we saw to be possible. But if (iii) the conclusion is other than E or A or B, then the syllogisms will be many, and unconnected with one another.

But if C is not so related to D as to make a syllogism, the propositions will have been assumed to no purpose, unless for the sake of induction or of obscuring the argument or something of the sort.

(2) But if from the propositions A and B there follows not E but some other conclusion, and if from C and D either A or B follows or something else, then there are several syllogisms, and they do not establish the conclusion proposed: for we assumed that the syllogism proved E. And if no conclusion follows from C and D, it turns out that these propositions have been assumed to no purpose, and the syllogism does not prove the original proposition.

So, it is clear that every demonstration and every syllogism will proceed through three terms only.

This being evident, it is clear that a syllogistic conclusion follows from two premises and not from more than two. For the three terms make two premises, unless a new premise is assumed, as was said at the beginning, to perfect the syllogisms. It is clear therefore that in whatever syllogistic argument the premises through which the main conclusion follows (for some of the preceding conclusions must be premises) are not even in number, this argument either has not been drawn syllogistically or it has assumed more than was necessary to establish its thesis.

If then syllogisms are taken with respect to their main premises, every syllogism will consist of an even number of premises and an odd number of terms (for the terms exceed the premises by one), and the conclusions will be half the number of the premises. But whenever a conclusion is reached by means of PR syllogisms or by means of several continuous middle terms—e.g., the proposition AB by means of the middle terms C and D—then the number of the terms will similarly exceed that of the premises by one (for the extra term must either be added outside or inserted; but in either case it follows that the relations of predication are one fewer than the terms related), and the premises will be equal in number to the relations of predication.

The premises however will not always be even, the terms odd; but they will alternate—when the premises are even, the terms must be odd; when the terms are even, the premises must be odd. For along with one term one premise is added, if a term is added from any quarter. Consequently, since the premises were (as we saw) even, and the terms odd, we must make them alternately even and odd at each addition.

But the conclusions will not follow the same arrangement, either in respect to the terms or to the premises. For if one term is added, conclusions will be added less by one than the pre-existing terms: for the conclusion is drawn not in relation to the single term last added, but in relation to all the rest, e.g., if to ABC the term D is added, two conclusions are thereby added, one in relation to A, the other in relation to B. Similarly, with any further additions. And similarly, too if the term is inserted in the middle: for in relation to one term only, a syllogism will not be constructed. Consequently, the conclusions will be much more numerous than the terms or the premises.

*Dialectica with magpie, serpent, & toads,
to signify the collecting, convoluting, and controverting of arguments.*

From *Seven Liberal Arts*, by Johann Sadeler.

# LOGIC VII–IX

## A Symbology for the Four Figures of Syllogism

### Types of Categorical Proposition Quantified in Extension
[Something is affirmed/denied of something else in whole or in part.]

| **A** | **E** | **I** | **O** |
|---|---|---|---|
| Universal Affirmative | Universal Negative | Particular Affirmative | Particular Negative |
| All S are P / Every S is P. | No S are P / No S is P. | Some S is/are P. | Some S is/are not P. |

*A predicate always extends more widely than its subject, as a whole including/exluding a part:*
*in* All animals are mortals, *mortal contains animal; in* All mortals are animals, *animal contains mortal.*

### Figures of Syllogism

S = **Subject of the Conclusion** (= the Minor Term [i.e., "smaller term"])
P = **Predicate of the Conclusion** (= the Major Term [i.e., "larger term"])
M = **Middle Term** Common to both of the Premises (i.e., Major & Minor)

| *1st Figure* | *2nd Figure* | *3rd Figure* | *4th Figure* |
|---|---|---|---|
| M is P | P is M | M is P | P is M |
| S is M | S is M | M is S | M is S |
| S is P | S is P | S is P | S is P |
| [ P > M > S ] | [ M > P ≥ S ] | [ P ≥ S > M ] | [ S > M > P ] |

*From which pairs of propositions will* S is P *follow? Which will give valid syllogism?*

### Matter of Syllogisms
[Pairings of Major & Minor Premises]

|  | *A - minor* | *E - minor* | *I - minor* | *O - minor* |
|---|---|---|---|---|
| *A - Major* | A + A = | A + E = | A + I = | A + O = |
| *E - Major* | E + A = | E + E = | E + I = | E + O = |
| *I - Major* | I + A = | I + E = | I + I = | I + O = |
| *O - Major* | O + A = | O + E = | O + I = | O + O = |

### The Valid Moods of Syllogism
*Vowels (a, e, i, o) = Types of Quantified Proposition*

| | |
|---|---|
| *1st Figure* | B<u>a</u>rbara, C<u>e</u>larent, D<u>a</u>rii, F<u>e</u>rio |
| | (& Indirectly: Baralipton, Celantes, Dabitis, Fapesmo, Frisesomorum) |
| *2nd Figure* | Ce<u>s</u>are, Ca<u>m</u>e<u>s</u>tres, Fe<u>s</u>tino, Baro<u>c</u>o |
| *3rd Figure* | Dara<u>p</u>ti, Fela<u>p</u>ton, Di<u>s</u>a<u>m</u>is, Dati<u>s</u>i, Bo<u>c</u>ardo, Feri<u>s</u>on |
| *4th Figure* | Bra<u>m</u>anti<u>p</u>, Ca<u>m</u>ene<u>s</u>, Di<u>m</u>ari<u>s</u>, Fe<u>s</u>a<u>p</u>o, Fre<u>s</u>i<u>s</u>on |

**Consonants <u>s</u>, <u>p</u>, <u>m</u>, & <u>c</u>** = Operations on preceding vowel to reduce to a 1st Figure direct mood (**B, C, D, F**):
<u>s</u> = convert subject & predicate of premise * <u>p</u> = limit premise to its subaltern * <u>m</u> = transpose premises
<u>c</u> = substitute for premise contradictory of conclusion, to derive a contradiction in a *reductio*.
(But a final consonant in the name simply refers to the conclusion of the new syllogism in Figure I.)

# On the First Figure of Syllogism

| Figure I | Valid Moods[73] |
|---|---|
| M is P<br>S is M<br>∴ S is P | **Barbara:** If all M is P, & all S is M, then all S is P. |
| | **Celarent:** If no M is P, & all S is M, then no S is P. |
| | **Darii:** If all M is P, & some S is M, then some S is P. |
| | **Ferio:** If no M is P, & some S is M, then some S is not P. |

---

### Practicum

*In* Prior Analytics *I.4, Aristotle will introduce the First Figure of syllogism and he will identify 4 valid moods of it and 12 invalid ones.*

**Prepare a tripartite presentation of the validity or invalidity of each mood by employing symbols ( M = *Middle Term*, P = *Major Term*, S = *Minor Term*), as well as a Venn-circle diagram and an applied example.**

*For example, the valid mood* Darii *can be exhibited as follows:*

| All M is P<br>Some S is M<br>∴ Some S is P | 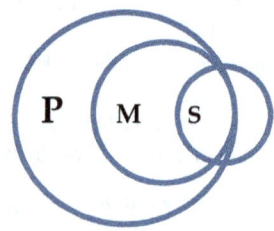 | All smokers are foolish.<br>Some Johnnies are smokers.<br>∴ Some Johnnies are foolish. |

*For another example, that AO does not admit of syllogism can be exhibited as follows:*

| All M is P<br>Some S is not M | 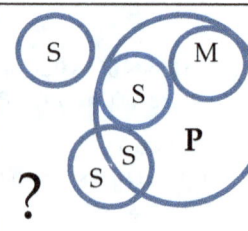 | All smokers are foolish.<br>Some Johnnies are not smokers.<br><br>*So what?* |

---

[73] The vowels of each valid mood name represent one of the four kinds of extensional proposition, as diagrammed on p. 195.

# LOGIC VII

## On the First Figure of Syllogism

### Aristotle
*Prior Analytics* Book I Part 4 [74]

---

### FIRST FIGURE
[ M is P & S is M ]

After these distinctions we now state by what means, when, and how every syllogism is produced; subsequently we must speak of demonstration. Syllogism should be discussed before demonstration because syllogism is the general: the demonstration is a sort of syllogism, but not every syllogism is a demonstration.

Whenever three terms are so related to one another that the last is contained in the middle as in a whole, and the middle is either contained in or excluded from the first as in or from a whole, then the extremes must be related by a perfect syllogism. I call that term *middle* which is itself contained in another and contains another in itself; in position also, this comes in the middle. By *extremes* I mean both that term which is itself contained in another and that in which another is contained.

If A is predicated of all B, and B of all C, A must be predicated of all C [BARBARA] : we have already explained what we mean by *predicated of all*. Similarly, also, if A is predicated of no B, and B of all C, it is necessary that no C will be A [CELARENT].

---

[74] Tr. A.J. Jenkinson, The Internet Classics Archive, emended.

But if the first term belongs to all the middle, but the middle to none of the last term [AE], there will be no syllogism in respect of the extremes; for nothing necessary follows from the terms being so related; for it is possible that the first should belong either to all or to none of the last, so that neither a particular nor a universal conclusion is necessary. But if there is no necessary consequence, there cannot be a syllogism by means of these premises.

As an example of a universal affirmative relation between the extremes we may take the terms *animal, man, horse*; of a universal negative relation, the terms *animal, man, stone*. Nor again can syllogism be formed when neither the first term belongs to any of the middle, nor the middle to any of the last [EE]. As an example of a positive relation between the extremes take the terms *science, line, medicine*: of a negative relation *science, line, unit*.

If then the terms are universally related [AA, EA, AE, EE], it is clear in this figure [MP, SM] when a syllogism will be possible [AAA, EAE], and when not [AE, EE]; and that, if a syllogism is possible, the terms must be related as described, and if they are so related, there will be a syllogism.

But if one term is related universally, the other in part only, to its subject, there must be a perfect syllogism whenever universality is posited with reference to the major term either affirmatively or negatively, and particularity with reference to the minor term affirmatively [AE, EI]. But whenever the universality is posited in relation to the minor term, or the terms are related in any other way, a syllogism is impossible. I call that term the major in which the middle is contained, and that term the minor which comes under the middle.[75]

Let all B be A and some C be B. Then if *predicated of all* means what was said above, it is necessary that some C is A [DARII]. And if no B is A but some C is B, it is necessary that some C is not A [FERIO]. The meaning of *predicated of none* has also been defined. So, there will

---

[75] The premises are likewise named: the premise containing the major term, or predicate of the conclusion, is called the **major premise**; and the premise containing the minor term, or subject of the conclusion, is called the **minor premise**.

be a perfect syllogism. This holds good also if the premise BC should be indefinite, provided that it is affirmative: for we shall have the same syllogism whether the premise is indefinite or particular.

But if the universality is posited with respect to the minor term either affirmatively or negatively, a syllogism will not be possible, whether the major premise is positive or negative, indefinite or particular: e.g., if some B is or is not A, and all C is B [OA]. As an example of a positive relation between the extremes take the terms *good, state, wisdom*: of a negative relation, *good, state, ignorance*.

Again, if no C is B, but some B is or is not A or not every B is A [EI, EO], there cannot be a syllogism. Take the terms *white, horse, swan*: *white, horse, raven*. The same terms may be taken also if the premise BA is indefinite.

Nor when the major premise is universal, whether affirmative or negative, and the minor premise is negative and particular, can there be a syllogism, whether the minor premise be indefinite or particular: e.g., if all B is A and some C is not B, or if not all C is B [AO]. For the major term may be predicable both of all and of none of the minor, to some of which the middle term cannot be attributed. Suppose the terms are *animal, man, white*: next take some of the *white things* of which *man* is not predicated—*swan* and *snow*: *animal* is predicated of all of the one, but of none of the other. Consequently, there cannot be a syllogism.

Again, let no B be A, but let some C not be B [EO]. Take the terms *inanimate, man, white*: then take some *white things* of which *man* is not predicated—*swan* and *snow*: the term *inanimate* is predicated of all of the one, of none of the other.

Further since it is indefinite to say some C is not B [E], and it is true that some C is not B whether no C is B [O], or not all C is B [E], and since if terms are assumed such that no C is B [E], no syllogism follows [OE] (this has already been stated), it is clear that this arrangement of terms will not afford a syllogism: otherwise one would have been possible with a universal negative minor premise.

A similar proof may also be given if the universal premise is negative. Nor can there in any way be a syllogism if both the relations of subject and predicate are particular, either positively or negatively [II or OO], or the one negative and the other affirmative [IO or OI], or one indefinite and the other definite, or both indefinite. Terms common to all the above are animal, white, horse: animal, white, stone.

It is clear then from what has been said that if there is a syllogism in this figure with a particular conclusion, the terms must be related as we have stated: if they are related otherwise, no syllogism is possible anyhow. It is evident also that all the syllogisms in this figure are perfect (for they are all completed by means of the premises originally taken) and that all conclusions are proved by this figure, viz. universal and particular, affirmative and negative. Such a figure I call the first.

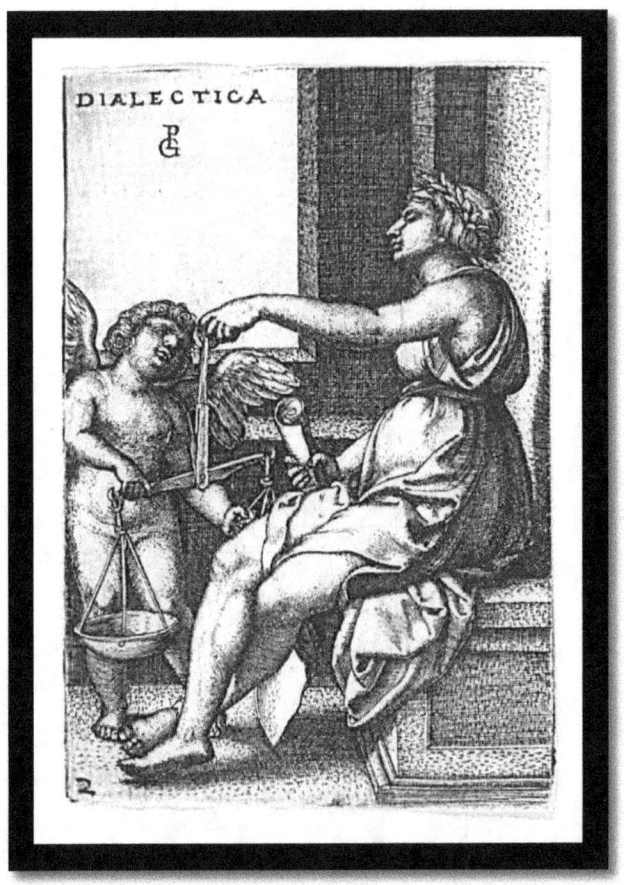

*Dialectica,* from *The Liberal Arts,* by Georg Pencz

# SYLLOGISM
## THE SECOND FIGURE

| FIGURE II | VALID MOODS | |
|---|---|---|
| **P is M**<br>**S is M**<br>∴ **S is P** | **CESARE:** | *If no P is M*<br>*& all S is M,*<br>*then no S is P.* |
| | **CAMESTRES:** | *If all P is M*<br>*& no S is M,*<br>*then no S is P.* |
| | **FESTINO:** | *If no P is M*<br>*& some S is M,*<br>*then some S is not P.* |
| | **BAROCO:** | *If all P is M*<br>*& some S is not M,*<br>*then some S is not P.* |

PRACTICUM

**Prepare a tripartite presentation of the validity or invalidity of each mood with symbols ( M =** *Middle Term,* **P =** *Major Term,* **S =** *Minor Term***),** *as well as with a Venn-circle diagram and an example.*

# LOGIC VIII

## ON THE SECOND FIGURE OF SYLLOGISM

**ARISTOTLE**
*Prior Analytics* Book I Part 5 [76]

---

### SECOND FIGURE
[ P is M & S is M ]

Whenever the same thing belongs to all of one subject and to none of another, or to all of each subject or to none of either, I call such a figure the second. By *middle term* in it I mean that which is predicated of both subjects; by *extremes*, the terms of which this is said; by *major extreme* that which lies near the middle, and by *minor*, further from the middle. The middle term stands outside the extremes and is first in position. A syllogism cannot be perfect in this figure in any mode, but it may be valid whether the terms are related universally or not.

If then the terms are related universally a syllogism will be possible, whenever the middle belongs to all of one subject and to none of another (it does not matter which has the negative relation), but in no other way. Let M be predicated of no N [*major term*], but of all O [*minor term*]. Since, then, the negative relation is convertible, N will belong to no M: but M was assumed to belong to all O: consequently, N will belong to no O [CESARE]. This has already been proved. — Again, if M belongs to all N, but to no O, then N will belong to no O [CAMESTRES]. For if M belongs to no O, O belongs to no M: but M (as was said) belongs to all N: O then will belong to no N: for the first figure has again been formed. But since the negative relation is convertible, N will belong to no O. Thus, it will be the same syllogism that proves both conclusions. It is possible to prove these results also by *reductio ad impossibile*.

---

[76] Tr. A.J. Jenkinson, The Internet Classics Archive, emended.

It is clear then that a syllogism is formed when the terms are so related, but not a perfect syllogism; for necessity is not perfectly established merely from the original premises; others also are needed.

But if M is predicated of every N and O, there cannot be a syllogism [AA]. Terms to illustrate a positive relation between the extremes are substance, animal, man; a negative relation, *substance, animal, number*—substance being the middle term. Nor is a syllogism possible when M is predicated neither of any N nor of any O [EE]. Terms to illustrate a positive relation are *line, animal, man*: a negative relation, *line, animal, stone*.

It is clear then that if a syllogism is formed when the terms are universally related, the terms must be related as we stated at the outset: for if they are otherwise related no necessary consequence follows.

If the middle term is related universally to one of the extremes, a particular negative syllogism must result whenever the middle term is related universally to the major whether positively or negatively, and particularly to the minor and in a manner opposite to that of the universal statement: by an opposite manner I mean, if the universal statement is negative, the particular is affirmative: if the universal is affirmative, the particular is negative.

For if M belongs to no N, but to some O, it is necessary that N does not belong to some O [FESTINO]. For since the negative statement is convertible, N will belong to no M: but M was admitted belonging to some O: therefore, N will not belong to some O: for the result is reached by means of the first figure. —

Again, if M belongs to all N, but not to some O, it is necessary that N does not belong to some O [BAROCO]: for if N belongs to all O, and M is predicated also of all N, M must belong to all O: but we assumed that M does not belong to some O. And if M belongs to all N but not to all O, we shall conclude that N does not belong to all O: the proof is the same as the above. —But if M is predicated of all O [*minor term*], but not of all N [*major term*], there will be no syllogism [OA]. Take the terms *animal, substance, raven; animal, white, raven*.

Nor will there be a conclusion when M is predicated of no O [minor term], but of some N [IE]. Terms to illustrate a positive relation between the extremes are *animal, substance, unit*: a negative relation, *animal, substance, science*.

If then the universal statement is opposed to the particular, we have stated when a syllogism will be possible and when not: but if the premises are similar in form, I mean both negative or both affirmative, a syllogism will not be possible in any mode.

First let them be negative, and let the major premise be universal, e.g., let M belong to no N, and not to some O [EO]. It is possible then for N to belong either to all O or to no O. Terms to illustrate the negative relation *are black, snow, animal*. But it is not possible to find terms of which the extremes are related positively and universally, if M belongs to some O, and does not belong to some O. For if N belonged to all O, but M to no N, then M would belong to no O: but we assumed that it belongs to some O. In this way then it is not admissible to take terms: our point must be proved from the indefinite nature of the particular statement. For since it is true that M does not belong to some O, even if it belongs to no O, and since if it belongs to no O a syllogism is (as we have seen) not possible, clearly it will not be possible now either.

Again, let the premises be affirmative, and let the major premise be universal, as before, e.g., let M belong to all N and to some O [AI]. It is possible then for N to belong to all O or to no O. Terms to illustrate the negative relation are *white, swan, stone*. But it is not possible to take terms to illustrate the universal affirmative relation, for the reason already stated: the point must be proved from the indefinite nature of the particular statement.

But if the minor premise is universal, and M belongs to no O, and not to some N [OE], it is possible for N to belong either to all O or to no O. Terms for the positive relation are *white, animal, raven:* for the negative relation, *white, stone, raven*. If the premises are affirmative [IA], terms for the negative relation are *white, animal, snow;* for the positive relation, *white, animal, swan*. Evidently then, whenever the premises are similar in form, and one is universal, the other particular, a syllogism cannot be formed in any mode. Nor is one possible if the middle term belongs to some of each of the extremes [II], or does not belong to some of either [OO], or belongs to some of the one and not to some of the other [IO & OI], or belongs to neither universally [EE], or is related to them indefinitely. Common terms for all the above are *white, animal, man*: *white, animal, inanimate*.

It is clear then from what has been said that if the terms are related to one another in the way stated, a syllogism results of necessity; and if there is a syllogism, the terms must be so related. But is evident also that all the syllogisms in this figure are imperfect: for all are made perfect by certain supplementary statements, which either are contained in the terms of necessity or are assumed as hypotheses, i.e., when we prove *per impossibile*. And it is evident that an affirmative conclusion is not attained by means of this figure, but all are negative, whether universal or particular.

Detail of The Seven Liberal Arts, by Virgilius Solis

| M = Middle Term, P = Major Term, S = Minor Term | | |
|---|---|---|
| FIGURE II | FIGURE III | FIGURE IV |
| P is M<br>S is M<br>∴ S is P | M is P<br>M is S<br>∴ S is P | P is M<br>M is S<br>∴ S is P |
| VALID MOODS | VALID MOODS | VALID MOODS |
| CE<u>S</u>ARE<br>CA<u>M</u>E<u>S</u>TRE<u>S</u><br>FE<u>S</u>TINO<br>BARO<u>C</u>O | DARA<u>P</u>TI<br>FELA<u>P</u>TON<br>DI<u>S</u>A<u>M</u>I<u>S</u><br>DATI<u>S</u>I<br>BO<u>C</u>ARDO<br>FERI<u>S</u>ON | BRA<u>M</u>ANTI<u>P</u><br>CA<u>M</u>ENE<u>S</u><br>DI<u>M</u>ARI<u>S</u><br>FE<u>S</u>A<u>P</u>O<br>FRE<u>S</u>I<u>S</u>ON |

| REDUCTION TO THE FIRST FIGURE | | |
|---|---|---|
| *Four consonants of the mood-names encode the conversions needed on its preceding vowel:*<br>**S**   *Invert the subject and predicate of the premise (e.g., M is P >> P is M)*<br>**P**   *Limit the premise to its subaltern (i.e., A>>I or E>>O)*<br>**M**  *Transpose the two premises (e.g., S is M & M is P >> M is P & S is M)*<br>**C**   *Do a reductio by substituting the contradictory of the conclusion.*<br>(*Except:* a final consonant refers to the conclusion of the new syllogism in Figure I.) | | |
| DARA<u>P</u>TI<br>(reducible to DARII) | All M is P<br>All M is S >><br>∴ Some S is P | All M is P<br>>> Some S is M<br>∴ Some S is P |
| BARO<u>C</u>O<br>(*reductio ad absurdum*<br>via BARBARA) | All P is M<br>*Some S is not M*<br>∴ *Some S is not P* >> | All P is M<br>>> *All S is P*<br>∴ *All S is M*<br>*But it was premised that<br>Some S is not M* |

PRACTICUM

Display each valid mood using symbols (M, P, & S) and a Venn diagram,
and then reduce it to the First Figure.

# LOGIC IX

## On the Third and Fourth Figures of Syllogism

### ARISTOTLE
*Prior Analytics* Book I Part 6-7 [77]

---

**Part 6**

THIRD FIGURE
[M is P & M is S]

But if one term belongs to all, and another to none, of a third, or if both belong to all, or to none, of it, I call such a figure the third. By *middle term* in it I mean that of which both the predicates are predicated; by *extremes* I mean the predicates [P & S]; by the *major extreme*, that which is further from the middle [P], and by *the minor* that which is nearer to it [S]. The middle term stands outside the extremes and is last in position. A syllogism cannot be perfect in this figure either, but it may be valid whether the terms are related universally or not to the middle term.

If they are universal, whenever both P and R belong to S, it follows that P will necessarily belong to some R. For, since the affirmative statement is convertible, S will belong to some R: consequently, since P belongs to all S, and S to some R, P must belong to some R: for a syllogism in the first figure is produced.

It is possible to demonstrate this also *per impossibile* and by exposition. For if both P and R belong to all S, should one of the Ss, e.g., N, be taken, both P and R will belong to this, and thus P will belong to some R.

---

[77] Tr. A.J. Jenkinson, The Internet Classics Archive, emended.

If R belongs to all S, and P to no S, there will be a syllogism to prove that P will necessarily not belong to some R. This may be demonstrated in the same way as before by converting the premise RS. It might be proved also *per impossibile*, as in the former cases. But if R belongs to no S, P to all S, there will be no syllogism. Terms for the positive relation are animal, horse, man: for the negative relation animal, inanimate, man. Nor can there be a syllogism when both terms are asserted of no S. Terms for the positive relation are animal, horse, inanimate; for the negative relation *man, horse, inanimate—inanimate* being the middle term.

It is clear then in this figure also when a syllogism will be possible and when not, if the terms are related universally. For whenever both the terms are affirmative, there will be a syllogism to prove that one extreme belongs to some of the other; but when they are negative, no syllogism will be possible. But when one is negative, the other affirmative, if the major is negative, the minor affirmative, there will be a syllogism to prove that the one extreme does not belong to some of the other: but if the relation is reversed, no syllogism will be possible. If one term is related universally to the middle, the other in part only, when both are affirmative there must be a syllogism, no matter which of the premises is universal. For if R belongs to all S, P to some S, P must belong to some R. For since the affirmative statement is convertible S will belong to some P: consequently, since R belongs to all S, and S to some P, R must also belong to some P: therefore, P must belong to some R.

Again, if R belongs to some S, and P to all S, P must belong to some R. This may be demonstrated in the same way as the preceding. And it is possible to demonstrate it also *per impossibile* and by exposition, as in the former cases. But if one term is affirmative, the other negative, and if the affirmative is universal, a syllogism will be possible whenever the minor term is affirmative. For if R belongs to all S, but P does not belong to some S, it is necessary that P does not belong to some R. For if P belongs to all R, and R belongs to all S, then P will belong to all S: but we assumed that it did not. Proof is possible also without *reductio ad impossibile*, if one of the Ss be taken to which P does not belong.

But whenever the major is affirmative, no syllogism will be possible, e.g., if P belongs to all S and R does not belong to some S. Terms for the universal affirmative relation are animate, man, animal. For the universal negative relation, it is not possible to get terms, if R belongs to some S, and does not belong to some S. For if P belongs to all S, and R to some S, then P will belong to some R: but we assumed that it belongs to no R. We must put the matter as before. Since the expression *It does not belong to some* is indefinite, it may be used truly of that also which belongs to none. But if R belongs to no S, no syllogism is possible, as has been shown. Clearly then no syllogism will be possible here.

But if the negative term is universal, whenever the major is negative and the minor affirmative there will be a syllogism. For if P belongs to no S, and R belongs to some S, P will not belong to some R: for we shall have the first figure again, if the premise RS is converted.

But when the minor is negative, there will be no syllogism. Terms for the positive relation are *animal, man, wild*: for the negative relation, *animal, science, wild*—the middle in both being the term wild.

Nor is a syllogism possible when both are stated in the negative, but one is universal, the other particular. When the minor is related universally to the middle, take the terms animal, science, wild; animal, man, wild. When the major is related universally to the middle, take as terms for a negative relation, *raven, snow, white*. For a positive relation, terms cannot be found, if R belongs to some S, and does not belong to some S. For if P belongs to all R, and R to some S, then P belongs to some S: but we assumed that it belongs to no S. Our point, then, must be proved from the indefinite nature of the particular statement.

Nor is a syllogism possible anyhow, if each of the extremes belongs to some of the middle or does not belong, or one belongs, and the other does not to some of the middle, or one belongs to some of the middle, the other not to all, or if the premises are indefinite. Common terms for all are animal, man, white: animal, inanimate, white.

It is clear then in this figure also when a syllogism will be possible, and when not; and that if the terms are as stated, a syllogism results of necessity, and if there is a syllogism, the terms must be so related. It is clear also that all the syllogisms in this figure are imperfect (for all are made perfect by certain supplementary assumptions), and that it will not be possible to reach a universal conclusion by means of this figure, whether negative or affirmative.

## Part 7

### FOURTH FIGURE
### [ P is M & M is S ]

It is evident also that in all the figures, whenever a proper syllogism does not result, if both the terms are affirmative or negative nothing necessary follows at all, but if one is affirmative, the other negative, and if the negative is stated universally, a syllogism always results relating the minor to the major term, e.g., if A belongs to all or some B, and B belongs to no C: for if the premises are converted, it is necessary that C does not belong to some A. Similarly, also in the other figures: a syllogism always results by means of conversion.

It is evident also that the substitution of an indefinite for a particular affirmative will affect the same syllogism in all the figures. *It is clear too that all the imperfect syllogisms are made perfect by means of the First Figure. For all are brought to a conclusion either ostensively or per impossibile.* In both ways the first figure is formed:

—if they are made perfect ostensively, because (as we saw) all are brought to a conclusion by means of conversion, and conversion produces the first figure;

—if they are proved *per impossibile*, because on the assumption of the false statement [*i.e., the contradictory of the conclusion*], the syllogism comes about by means of the first figure,

e.g., in the last figure, if A and B belong to all C, it follows that A belongs to some B: for if A belonged to no B, and B belongs to all C, A would belong to no C: but (as we stated) it belongs to all C. Similarly, also with the rest.

It is possible also to reduce all syllogisms to the universal syllogisms in the first figure. Those in the second figure are clearly made perfect by these, though not all in the same way; the universal syllogisms are made perfect by converting the negative premise, each of the particular syllogisms by *reductio ad impossibile*.

In the first figure particular syllogisms are indeed made perfect by themselves, but it is possible also to prove them by means of the second figure, reducing them *ad impossibile*, e.g., if A belongs to all B, and B to some C, it follows that A belongs to some C. For if it belonged to no C, and belongs to all B, then B will belong to no C: this we know by means of the second figure.

Similarly, also demonstration will be possible in the case of the negative. For if A belongs to no B, and B belongs to some C, A will not belong to some C: for if it belonged to all C, and belongs to no B, then B will belong to no C: and this (as we saw) is the middle figure.

Consequently, since all syllogisms in the middle figure can be reduced to universal syllogisms in the first figure, and since particular syllogisms in the first figure can be reduced to syllogisms in the middle figure, it is clear that particular syllogisms can be reduced to universal syllogisms in the first figure.

Syllogisms in the third figure, if the terms are universal, are directly made perfect by means of those syllogisms; but, when one of the premises is particular, by means of the particular syllogisms in the first figure: and these (we have seen) may be reduced to the universal syllogisms in the first figure: consequently, also the particular syllogisms in the third figure may be so reduced. It is clear then that all syllogisms may be reduced to the universal syllogisms in the first figure.

We have stated then how syllogisms which prove that something belongs or does not belong to something else are constituted, both how syllogisms of the same figure are constituted in themselves, and how syllogisms of different figures are related to one another.

# The Four Quadrivial Arts

*As number is the object of Arithmetic and number in motion of Music, so is magnitude of Geometry and magnitude in motion, of Astronomy.*

From *The Seven Liberal Arts*, by Hans Sebald Beham

# LOGIC X
## On Demonstration

**ARISTOTLE**
*Posterior Analytics* Book I, Parts 1-4 [78]

### Part 1

All teaching or learning by way of reasoning comes from previous knowing. This becomes clear if we consider all kinds of learning. For knowledge of mathematical sciences comes about in this way, as does knowledge of each of the other arts. This is also the case for the arguments both of syllogism and induction, since both bring learning about by means of things recognized beforehand—logical argument, by taking for granted what those who are present accept as true; and inductive argument, by showing what is universal through what is evident in the individual. Rhetorical argument persuades in just the same way: either through examples, which is induction; or by way of enthymemes, which are a kind of syllogism.

There are two ways in which previous knowing is needed: sometimes what is true needs to be taken for granted, and sometimes what is being signified needs to be taken for granted, and sometimes both. It must be assumed, for example, that either an affirmation or its denial must be true; and what *triangle* means must be taken for granted; and in the case of *unit*, both what it means and that there is one must be taken for granted.

Now, each of these is not evident to us in the same way.

---

[78] Tr. J. Tomarchio, from the Greek text of The Loeb Classical Library, *Posterior Analytics,* Ed. Hugh Tredennick (Harvard University Press, 1960).

Sometimes the knowing needed is of things recognized beforehand, and sometimes recognition is needed of things being understood in the moment, namely individuals falling under a known universal. For example, by knowing that every triangle has angles equal to two right angles, we are led to recognize that this figure being inscribed in a semicircle is a triangle. For some learning happens only in this way, namely learning about individual things which, not being predicable of any subject, are not known through any middle term.

Before being led to recognize a thing or to grasp a syllogism, there is knowledge in some way, and in another way not. For if it is not yet known absolutely that this figure being inscribed in the semicircle is a triangle, how could it be known absolutely that its angles are equal to two right angles? Clearly, it is not yet known absolutely that the figure being inscribed is a triangle, but because the universal is known, it is known in some way. For, if not, then we face the dilemma in the *Meno*: one can only learn either nothing or what is already known.

There is a solution that some people offer for this dilemma that is not acceptable. A man is asked, *Do you know, or do you not know, that every pair is even?* He says that he does know it. The questioner then produces a particular pair which the man did not know to exist and therefore which he did not know to be even. The solution which some people offer is to assert that they do not know that every pair is even, but only that everything which they know to be a pair is even. However, what they know to be even is what they have demonstrated to be even, *i.e.*, what they took to be the subject of their premise—not merely every triangle or number they know to be even, but rather absolutely *any* number or triangle. For no premise is ever formulated, *Every number that you know to be such*, or *Every rectilinear figure that you know to be such*, but rather all.

I maintain that there is nothing to prevent a man from in one way knowing about what he is learning, and in another way not knowing about it. What would be untoward is, not his already knowing what he was learning in some way, but his already knowing it *in that very way* in which he was learning about it.

## Part 2

We think ourselves to know a thing absolutely, rather than outwardly according to an attribute, whenever we think ourselves to know what the reason is on account of which it is the thing that it is and cannot be otherwise. It is clear that knowing is this sort of thing, as those who only imagine they know think they have this, and those who do know do have this. Accordingly, anything about which there is absolute knowledge is something which cannot be otherwise.

Now, whether there may be another way of knowing will be discussed later, but for now at any rate we shall state that through demonstration we do indeed know. By *demonstration* I mean scientific syllogism. By *scientific* I mean that it is by our possessing the syllogism that we know by means of it.

Now if knowing is like what we have stated, it is necessary that scientific demonstration be from what is true as well as primary and immediate; and from what is known better than the conclusion and what is prior to the conclusion; and from what are the reasons for the conclusion. In this way will the premises be apt for what is being demonstrated. Without these, there may be syllogism, but not demonstration, for they will not cause knowledge.

They must be true, because there's no knowing what is not true (e.g., *that the diameter of the square is commensurable with its side*). They must also be primary and so indemonstrable; for, if not, then what is being demonstrated will not be known for not having demonstration of the premises; since not to know the things the demonstration is from is to have demonstration only incidentally.

They must also be the reasons for it both known better than and prior to what is being demonstrated—reasons, because we know something when we see the reason for it; and if known reasons, then known prior—and known not only in the sense that what is signified by them is known, but known to be true as well.

Now *prior* and *known better* have a twofold sense, for what is prior *by nature* and prior *for us* are not the same, nor what is known better and better known to us. I mean that what is nearer to sense perception is prior for us and better known for us, but what is prior and known better as such is further from sense perception. For what is most universal is furthest away, and the individual nearest, and these are opposites of one another.

From a primary premise means from an apt original principle, as I mean the same thing by *primary* and by *original*. An original principle of a demonstration is a proposition known immediately— immediate because there is none prior to it. The proposition is either of the forms of predication, i.e., either affirming or denying one thing of another. A dialectical proposition premises either side equally, but a demonstrative one premises definitively that one is true. The proposition is the one side or other of a contradiction. A contradiction is an opposition such that there is no middle. One part of a contradiction is the affirmation of one thing of another, and the other part is the denial of the one thing of the other.

An immediate principle of syllogism for which there is no proof and the learner has no need I call a presupposition. When it is necessary for the learner's learning anything, I call it an axiom, since there are such principles, and we are used to giving this name to such. A presupposition that puts forward one side or other of a proposition—i.e., *that this is so* or *that this is not so*—I call a hypothesis, and one that does not, a definition. For a definition is also a presupposition—the arithmetician states that the unit *is* what is indivisible in quantity, but this is not a hypothesis, for to state what a unit is and that there is a unit is not the same thing.

Now since both to be certain and to know a thing is necessarily through having a syllogism of the kind we are calling demonstrative, and since the syllogism is of this sort by virtue of the sort of things it comes from, it is necessary not only to know these first things, whether all or some, but also to know them better. For something always applies all the more to that because of which it applies to something else, e.g., that because of which we love something, we love the more.

Consequently, if it is through the first things that we know and are certain, we also both know and believe those first things more, since it because of them we believe those that follow.

But it is not possible for a man to believe anything more than the things he knows, if it's the case that he neither knows them nor is in a better state than if he did know them. But this is what will come about if he does not know something prior to what he believes through demonstrating. Rather, it is necessary to believe in the original principles, in some if not in all, more than in the conclusions. And if a man is going to have knowledge through demonstration, not only is it necessary that he acknowledge original principles and believe in them more than in what is being proven, it is also necessary that for him nothing of what is in opposition to these original principles could be more certain or better known, as sources of contradictory syllogism. For it is necessary that one who knows absolutely be unshakeable.

## Part 3

Because of the need to know primary principles, to some it seems that knowledge does not exist; to others it seems to exist because of their having demonstrations. Neither is either true or necessary.

Those who propose that knowing does not exist altogether think that we are led on infinitely, never knowing what follows from what precedes without there being among them what is first—speaking rightly, for it is impossible to traverse infinites—and if thinking does come to a stop and if there are primary sources, then they are unknowable, there being no demonstration of them, which they say is the only knowing. And if there is no knowing of primary principles, then there is no knowing absolutely what follows from them, strictly speaking, but only from presupposing, if those are true.

The others agree about knowing's being only through demonstration, but think nothing prevents there being demonstration of all premises, for demonstration is possible from one another in a circle.

However, we say that not all knowledge is demonstrable, but rather that knowledge of what is immediate is indemonstrable. That this is necessary is evident, for if it is indeed necessary to know what precedes and from which demonstration comes, and this comes to a stop at what is immediate, that these be indemonstrable is necessary. And we state that these are so and we say not only that there is knowledge but that there is even a certain primary principle of knowledge by which we recognize limits.

It is clear that demonstration in a circle is impossible, absolutely speaking, if indeed demonstration must be from what precedes and is better known. For it is impossible for the same things at the same time to precede and to follow from each other, unless in a different way—e.g., what is prior *for us* and what is prior absolutely, the different way of being prior that induction makes known to us. If there is such a difference, then either knowing absolutely would not be well defined but be ambivalent, or else that "demonstration" that comes by induction from things better known to us is not demonstration absolutely speaking.

It is clear that demonstrating in a circle is not possibly absolutely speaking, if in fact demonstration is from what is prior and better known. For it is impossible for the same things to be prior and posterior to the same things at the same time, unless it be in different ways, for example for us versus in itself, in the way that induction makes for recognition. But defined in this way, knowing absolutely would not be well defined but ambivalent. For this other kind of knowing that comes from what is better known to us is not knowing absolutely speaking.

Besides what has just been said, it will also happen to those who say that circular demonstration does exist that they are saying nothing more than, *It is if it is*. But in this way it is easy to prove anything. That this happens is made clear by taking any three terms. It makes no difference whether the circle be made by many terms or by a few not fewer than two. For, if of necessity B must be whenever A is, and C be when B is, then if A be, C will be. Now, if when A is it is necessary that B be, and when B is that A be—for this is what was meant by *in a circle*—then let A be put in place of C. In that case, to say that when B is, C is, is to say that when B is, A is—which is to say that when A is, C is. But C is the same as A, so that those who say that the demonstration is circular are saying nothing more than that if A is, A is. But it is easy to show anything this way.

Nor is any such demonstration possible except in the case of things that follow from each other, such as essential properties. Now, it has been shown that nothing ever follows of necessity from stating one thing—I mean by one either stating one definition or one proposition—and that at least two first propositions are needed for anything to follow, if there is in fact to be linking of their terms. Thus, if A follows both from B and from C, and if these two from one another as well as from A, then it is possible in the first figure to prove reciprocally all assumptions made, as shown in my writings on syllogism. However, it has also been shown that in the other figures no syllogism occurs, or none concerning the premised assumptions. There can be no demonstrating in a circle of any things that are not convertible, and since there are very few such things in demonstrations, clearly it is in vain as well as impossible to say that there is demonstration of them from one another and therefore that demonstration of all things is possible.

## Part 4

Since it is impossible for that of which we have knowledge absolutely to be other than it is, what is known through demonstrative knowledge is always what is necessary. Now knowledge is demonstrative only by having a demonstration. Therefore, a demonstration is a syllogism from necessary premises. So, we must consider from premises of what sort demonstration comes.

In the first place, let us define what we mean by predicating a predicate: 1) of the whole; 2) of a thing in itself; and 3) as its universal.

By predicated of the whole I mean what is not predicated of one part but not another, or at one time and not another. For example, if animal is predicated of man as a whole, then if it is true to say that this thing is a man, then it is also true to say that he is an animal, and whenever the former is true, the latter is too; likewise, if in every line there is a point. An indication of this is that when questioning a predication of a whole, we bring as objections either some thing of which it is not predicated or some time when it is not predicated.

Those things belong to something in itself which are part of what it is, for example, a line in a triangle and a point in a line, for their substance is made up of these and these are included in the explanation defining what it is.

Also, of attributes belonging to other things, they are predicated in itself of those other things they include in the statement defining what each is, for example, straight or curved belong to line in itself, and odd or even, prime or compound, square or oblong, to number in itself; so, *line* on one part and *number* on the other are contained in each case in the definition stating what each predicate is.[79]

Accordingly, I say predicated in itself of all such things that in either way do not belong incidentally as attributes, as do *musical* or *white* to *animal*.

Moreover, there is predicated in itself what is not said of something incidentally as its subject—as it is one thing for a walker to be a walker and another for him to be white. Now, its substance and whatever signifies a kind of thing is not predicated of a thing as something other than what the thing itself is. Thus, those things predicated of something not as *in the subject* I call predicated *in itself*, and as *in a subject*, predicated *as an attribute*.[80]

---

[79] Thus, the definition of "straight" is the points of a line lying evenly on it.

[80] Thus, Socrates being a man is predicated of him in himself, as what he is, and his being snub-nosed is predicated of him as an attribute in a subject.

I note that some translators here use the expression an "essential" attribute or predication, but I would distinguish between a "substantive" and "essential" one: a substantive predication predicates of a subject in itself, such as *Socrates is a man*, whereas an essential predication predicates properties of an essence as such, such as *A man is a rational or political animal*. Aristotle's categories enumerate such essential predicates: a man is a substance, white a color, conversing an action.

In yet another way, what belongs to a thing because of it is predicated of it in itself, and what not, is attributed as incidental. For example, if it dawned while he was walking, it did not dawn because he was walking; rather, we say this happened. But when it is because of him, we say it of him in himself, for example, if something strangled dies from the strangling, then because it happened through being strangled, the strangled thing did not just happen to die.

Therefore, what is said in themselves of things that are known absolutely are such as to include or be included in their predicates both of themselves and of necessity. For it is not possible for the attributes not to belong, either absolutely or as opposites—for example, to line, either straight or curved; or to number, either odd or even. For the privation or the contrary within a same genus is an opposite—for example, among numbers, what is not odd is even as a consequence. As a result, if it is necessary either to affirm or to deny attributes, then it is necessary also that they belong to their subjects in themselves.

In this way, then, do I distinguish between what is predicated of something *as whole* and what is predicated of something *in itself*. But I call universal what belongs to something both as a whole and in itself and also of itself *as such*. Therefore, it is clear that what is their universal belongs to things by necessity. For what is said of something *as a whole* is said insofar as it is said of it *as such*—for example, having a point or being straight belong to a line in itself, insofar precisely as it is a line; and it is to a triangle insofar as it is a triangle that three angles equaling two right angles belong.

A universal applies when a predicate belongs primarily to any one of a kind. For example, having angles equal to two right angles is not universal for figure, even though it is possible to prove there is a kind of figure that has angles equaling two right angles—but not just any figure, for a square is a figure, but does not have angles equaling two right angles. Now, any isosceles does have angles equaling two right angles, but it is not the primary figure, because triangle is prior. So, whatever figure can be shown to have angles equal to two right angles, or any such attribute, in any one of its kind, that is the primary figure to which it belongs as universal, and the demonstration that this belongs to it *in itself* is also universal, but the demonstration of it in other figures in a certain respect is not, for it is not for example universal of isosceles, but of more than isosceles.[81]

*Ars Dialectica,* by Giulio Bonasone

---

[81] Accordingly, if one happens to use a figure of an isosceles triangle in a demonstration of the equality of a triangle's three angles to two right angles, it would be in virtue of its being a triangle rather than its being isosceles that it would serve to prove this property necessarily and universally true of all triangles.

I note that "universal" can apply in one sense adverbially to the extension of a proposition or proof—what is universally true of all triangles—and in another sense adjectivally to the defining properties of an essence or kind—a universal property of triangles as such. To call a defining difference of a thing its universal is an uncommonly precise use of the term in English. Modern logicians will speak more technically of such definitively universal properties as "commensurate" with their essence or kind.

# LOGIC XI

## On Premises of Demonstration

**Aristotle**
*Posterior Analytics*
Book I Parts 6-10 & Book II Part 19 [82]

---

**Part I.6**

Demonstrative knowledge must rest on necessary primary principles; for the object of scientific knowledge cannot be other than it is. Now attributes attaching essentially to their subjects attach necessarily to them: for essential attributes are either elements in the essential nature of their subjects or contain their subjects as elements in their own essential nature. (The pairs of opposites which the latter class includes are necessary because one member or the other necessarily inheres.) It follows from this that premises of the demonstrative syllogism must be connections essential in the sense explained: for all attributes must inhere essentially or else be accidental, and accidental attributes are not necessary to their subjects.

We must either state the case thus, or else premise that the conclusion of demonstration is necessary and that a demonstrated conclusion cannot be other than it is, and then infer that the conclusion must be developed from necessary premises. For though you may reason from true premises without demonstrating, yet if your premises are necessary, you will assuredly demonstrate—in such necessity you have at once a distinctive character of demonstration. That demonstration proceeds from necessary premises is also indicated by the fact that the objection we raise against a professed demonstration is that a premise of it is not a necessary truth—whether we think it altogether devoid of necessity, or at any rate so far as our opponent's previous argument goes.

---

[82] Tr. G.R.G. More, The Internet Classics Archive, emended.

This shows how naive it is to suppose one's primary principles rightly chosen if one starts with a proposition which is both popularly accepted and also true, such as the sophists' assumption that to know is the same as to possess knowledge. For popular acceptance or rejection is no criterion of a basic truth, which can only be the primary law of the genus constituting the subject matter of the demonstration; and not all truth is 'appropriate'.

A further proof that the conclusion must be the development of necessary premises is as follows. Where demonstration is possible, one who can give no account which includes the cause has no scientific knowledge. If, then, we suppose a syllogism in which, though A necessarily inheres in C, yet B, the middle term of the demonstration, is not necessarily connected with A and C, then the man who argues thus has no reasoned knowledge of the conclusion, since this conclusion does owe its necessity to the middle term; for though the conclusion is necessary, the mediating link is a contingent fact.

Or again, if a man is without knowledge now, though he still retains the steps of the argument, though there is no change in himself or in the fact and no lapse of memory on his part; then neither had he knowledge previously. But the mediating link, not being necessary, may have perished in the interval; and if so, though there be no change in him nor in the fact, and though he will still retain the steps of the argument, yet he has not knowledge, and therefore had not knowledge before. Even if the link has not actually perished but is liable to perish, this situation is possible and might occur. But such a condition cannot be knowledge.

When the conclusion is necessary, the middle through which it was proved may yet quite easily be non-necessary. You can in fact infer the necessary even from a non-necessary premise, just as you can infer the true from the not true. On the other hand, when the middle is necessary the conclusion must be necessary; just as true premises always give a true conclusion. Thus, if A is necessarily predicated of B and B of C, then A is necessarily predicated of C. But when the conclusion is non-necessary the middle cannot be necessary either. Thus, let A be predicated non-necessarily of C but necessarily of B, and let B be a necessary predicate of C; then A too will be a necessary predicate of C, which by hypothesis it is not.

To sum up, then, demonstrative knowledge must be knowledge of a necessary link, and therefore must clearly be obtained through a necessary middle term; otherwise, its possessor will know neither the cause nor the fact that his conclusion is a necessary connection. Either he will mistake the non-necessary for the necessary and believe the necessity of the conclusion without knowing it, or else he will not even believe it—in which case he will be equally ignorant, whether he actually infers the mere fact through middle terms or the reasoned fact and from immediate premises.

Of accidents that are not essential according to our definition of essential there is no demonstrative knowledge; for since an accident, in the sense in which I here speak of it, may also not inhere, it is impossible to prove its inherence as a necessary conclusion.

A difficulty, however, might be raised as to why in dialectic, if the conclusion is not a necessary connection, such and such determinate premises should be proposed in order to deal with such and such determinate problems. Would not the result be the same if one asked any questions whatever and then merely stated one's conclusion? The solution is that determinate questions have to be put, not because the replies to them affirm facts which necessitate facts affirmed by the conclusion, but because these answers are propositions which if the answerer affirm, he must affirm the conclusion and affirm it with truth if they are true.

Since it is just those attributes within every genus which are essential and possessed by their respective subjects as such that are necessary it is clear that both the conclusions and the premises of demonstrations which produce scientific knowledge are essential. For accidents are not necessary: and, further, since accidents are not necessary one does not necessarily have reasoned knowledge of a conclusion drawn from them (this is so even if the accidental premises are invariable but not essential, as in proofs through signs; for though the conclusion be actually essential, one will not know it as essential nor know its reason); but to have reasoned knowledge of a conclusion is to know it through its cause. We may conclude that the middle must be consequentially connected with the minor, and the major with the middle.

## Part I.7

It follows that we cannot in demonstrating pass from one genus to another. We cannot, for instance, prove geometrical truths by arithmetic. For there are three elements in demonstration: (1) what is proved, the conclusion—an attribute inhering essentially in a genus; (2) the axioms, the ones namely which are premises of demonstration; (3) the subject-genus whose attributes, i.e. essential properties, are revealed by the demonstration. The axioms which are premises of demonstration may be identical in two or more sciences: but in the case of two different genera such as arithmetic and geometry you cannot apply arithmetical demonstration to the properties of magnitudes unless the magnitudes in question are numbers. How in certain cases transference is possible I will explain later.

Arithmetical demonstration and the other sciences likewise possess, each of them, their own genera; so that if the demonstration is to pass from one sphere to another, the genus must be either absolutely or to some extent the same. If this is not so, transference is clearly impossible, because the extreme and the middle terms must be drawn from the same genus: otherwise, as predicated, they will not be essential and will thus be accidents.

That is why it cannot be proved by geometry that opposites fall under one science, nor even that the product of two cubes is a cube. Nor can the theorem of any one science be demonstrated by means of another science, unless these theorems are related as subordinate to superior (e.g., as optical theorems to geometry, or harmonic theorems to arithmetic). Geometry again cannot prove of lines any property which they do not possess qua lines, i.e., in virtue of the fundamental truths of their peculiar genus: it cannot show, for example, that the straight line is the most beautiful of lines or the contrary of the circle; for these qualities do not belong to lines in virtue of their peculiar genus, but according to some property which it shares with other genera.

## Part I.8

It is also clear that if the premises from which the syllogism proceeds are commensurately universal, the conclusion of such i.e., in the unqualified sense—must also be eternal. Therefore, no attribute can be demonstrated nor known by strictly scientific knowledge to inhere in perishable things. The proof can only be accidental, because the attribute's connection with its perishable subject is not commensurately universal but temporary and special. If such a demonstration is made, one premise must be perishable and not commensurately universal (perishable because only if it is perishable will the conclusion be perishable; not commensurately universal, because the predicate will be predicable of some instances of the subject and not of others); so that the conclusion can only be that a fact is true at the moment—not commensurately and universally.

The same is true of definitions, since a definition is either a primary premise or a conclusion of a demonstration, or else only differs from a demonstration in the order of its terms. Demonstration and science of merely frequent occurrences—e.g., of eclipse as happening to the moon-are, as such, clearly eternal: whereas so far as they are not eternal they are not fully commensurate. Other subjects too have properties attaching to them in the same way as eclipse attaches to the moon.

## Part I.9

It is clear that if the conclusion is to show an attribute inhering as such, nothing can be demonstrated except from its appropriate primary principles. Consequently, a proof even from true, indemonstrable, and immediate premises does not constitute knowledge. Such proofs are like Bryson's method of squaring the circle; for they operate by taking as their middle a common character—a character, therefore, which the subject may share with another—and consequently they apply equally to subjects different in kind. They therefore afford knowledge of an attribute only as inhering accidentally, not as belonging to its subject as such: otherwise, they would not have been applicable to another genus.

Our knowledge of any attribute's connection with a subject is accidental unless we know that connection through the middle term in virtue of which it inheres, and as an inference from basic premises essential and appropriate to the subject—unless we know, e.g., the property of possessing angles equal to two right angles as belonging to that subject in which it inheres essentially, and as inferred from basic premises essential and appropriate to that subject: so that if that middle term also belongs essentially to the minor, the middle must belong to the same kind as the major and minor terms.

The only exceptions to this rule are such cases as theorems in harmonics which are demonstrable by arithmetic. Such theorems are proved by the same middle terms as arithmetical properties, but with a qualification—the fact falls under a separate science (for the subject genus is separate), but the reasoned fact concerns the superior science, to which the attributes essentially belong. Thus, even these apparent exceptions show that no attribute is strictly demonstrable except from its 'appropriate' primary principles, which, however, in the case of these sciences have the requisite identity of character.

It is no less evident that the peculiar primary principles of each inhering attribute are indemonstrable; for primary principles from which they might be deduced would be primary principles of all that is, and the science to which they belonged would possess universal sovereignty. This is so because he knows better whose knowledge is deduced from higher causes, for his knowledge is from prior premises when it derives from causes themselves uncaused: hence, if he knows better than others or best of all, his knowledge would be science in a higher or the highest degree. But, as things are, demonstration is not transferable to another genus, with such exceptions as we have mentioned of the application of geometrical demonstrations to theorems in mechanics or optics, or of arithmetical demonstrations to those of harmonics.

It is hard to be sure whether one knows or not; for it is hard to be sure whether one's knowledge is based on the primary principles appropriate to each attribute—the differentia of true knowledge. We think we have scientific knowledge if we have reasoned from true and primary premises. But that is not so: the conclusion must be homogeneous with the basic facts of the science.

## Part I.10

I call the primary principles of every genus those elements in it the existence of which cannot be proved. As regards both these primary truths and the attributes dependent on them the meaning of the name is assumed. The fact of their existence as regards the primary truths must be assumed; but it has to be proved of the remainder, the attributes. Thus, we assume the meaning alike of unity, straight, and triangular; but while as regards unity and magnitude we assume also the fact of their existence, in the case of the remainder proof is required.

Of the primary principles used in the demonstrative sciences some are peculiar to each science, and some are common, but common only in the sense of analogous, being of use only in so far as they fall within the genus constituting the province of the science in question. Peculiar truths are, e.g., the definitions of line and straight; common truths are such as, *Take equals from equals and equals remain*. Only so much of these common truths is required as falls within the genus in question: for a truth of this kind will have the same force even if not used generally but applied by the geometer only to magnitudes, or by the arithmetician only to numbers.

Also peculiar to a science are the subjects the existence as well as the meaning of which it assumes, and the essential attributes of which it investigates, e.g., in arithmetic units, in geometry points and lines. Both the existence and the meaning of the subjects are assumed by these sciences; but of their essential attributes only the meaning is assumed. For example, arithmetic assumes the meaning of odd and even, square and cube, geometry that of incommensurable, or of deflection or verging of lines, whereas the existence of these attributes is demonstrated by means of the axioms and from previous conclusions as premises. Astronomy too proceeds in the same way. For indeed every demonstrative science has three elements: (1) that which it posits, the subject genus whose essential attributes it examines; (2) the so-called axioms, which are primary premises of its demonstration; (3) the attributes, the meaning of which it assumes.

Yet some sciences may very well pass over some of these elements; e.g., we might not expressly posit the existence of the genus if its existence were obvious (for instance, the existence of hot and cold is more evident than that of number); or we might omit to assume expressly the meaning of the attributes if it were well understood—in the way that the meaning of axioms such as *Take equals from equals and equals remain* is well known and so not expressly assumed. Nevertheless, in the nature of the case the essential elements of demonstration are three: the subject, the attributes, and the basic premises.

That which expresses necessary self-grounded fact, and which we must necessarily believe, is distinct both from the hypotheses of a science and from illegitimate postulate—I say must believe, because all syllogism, and therefore *a fortiori* demonstration, is addressed not to the spoken word, but to the discourse within the soul, and though we can always raise objections to the spoken word, to the inward discourse we cannot always object.

That which is capable of proof but assumed by the teacher without proof is, if the pupil believes and accepts it, hypothesis, though only in a limited sense hypothesis—that is, relatively to the pupil; if the pupil has no opinion or a contrary opinion on the matter, the same assumption is an illegitimate postulate. Therein lies the distinction between hypothesis and illegitimate postulate: the latter is the contrary of the pupil's opinion, demonstrable, but assumed and used without demonstration.

The definition—viz. those which are not expressed as statements that anything is or is not—are not hypotheses: but it is in the premises of a science that its hypotheses are contained. Definitions require only to be understood, and this is not hypothesis—unless it be contended that the pupil's hearing is also a hypothesis required by the teacher. Hypotheses, on the contrary, postulate facts on the being of which depends the being of the fact inferred.

Nor are the geometer's hypotheses false, as some have held, urging that one must not employ falsehood and that the geometer is uttering falsehood in stating that the line which he draws is a foot long or straight, when it is actually neither. The truth is that the geometer does not draw any conclusion from the being of the particular line of which he speaks, but from what his diagrams symbolize. A further distinction is that all hypotheses and illegitimate postulates are either universal or particular, whereas a definition is neither.

## Part II.19

As regards syllogism and demonstration, the definition of, and the conditions required to produce each of them, are now clear, and with that also the definition of, and the conditions required to produce, demonstrative knowledge, since it is the same as demonstration. As to the basic premises, how they become known and what is the developed state of knowledge of them is made clear by raising some preliminary problems.

We have already said that scientific knowledge through demonstration is impossible unless a man knows the primary immediate premises. But there are questions which might be raised in respect of the apprehension of these immediate premises: one might not only ask whether it is of the same kind as the apprehension of the conclusions, but also whether there is or is not scientific knowledge of both; or scientific knowledge of the latter, and of the former a different kind of knowledge; and, further, whether the developed states of knowledge are not innate but come to be in us, or are innate but at first unnoticed.

Now it is strange if we possess them from birth; for it means that we possess apprehensions more accurate than demonstration and fail to notice them. If on the other hand we acquire them and do not previously possess them, how could we discover and learn without a basis of pre-existent knowledge? For that is impossible, as we used to find in the case of demonstration. So, it emerges that neither can we possess them from birth, nor can they come to be in us if we are without knowledge of them to the extent of having no such developed state at all. Therefore, we must possess a capacity of some sort, but not such as to rank higher in accuracy than these developed states.

And this at least is an obvious characteristic of all animals, for they possess a congenital discriminative capacity which is called sense-perception. But though sense-perception is innate in all animals, in some the sense-impression comes to persist, in others it does not. So animals in which this persistence does not come to be have either no knowledge at all outside the act of perceiving, or no knowledge of objects of which no impression persists; animals in which it does come into being have perception and can continue to retain the sense-impression in the soul: and when such persistence is frequently repeated, a further distinction at once arises between those which from the persistence of such sense-impressions develop a power of systematizing them and those which do not.

So out of sense-perception comes to be what we call memory, and out of frequently repeated memories of the same thing develops experience; for a number of memories constitute a single experience. From experience again—i.e. from the universal now stabilized in its entirety within the soul, the one beside the many which is a single identity within them all—originate the skill of the craftsman and the knowledge of the man of science, skill in the sphere of coming to be and science in the sphere of being.

We conclude that these states of knowledge are neither innate in a determinate form, nor developed from other higher states of knowledge, but from sense-perception. It is like a rout in battle stopped by first one man making a stand and then another, until the original formation has been restored. The soul is so constituted as to be capable of this process.

Let us now restate the account given already, though with insufficient clearness. When one of a number of logically indiscriminable particulars has made a stand, the earliest universal is present in the soul: for though the act of sense-perception is of the particular, its content is universal—is man, for example, not the man

Callias. A fresh stand is made among these rudimentary universals, and the process does not cease until the indivisible concepts, the true universals, are established: e.g., such and such a species of animal is a step towards the genus animal, which by the same process is a step towards a further generalization.

Thus, it is clear that we must get to know the primary premises by induction; for the method by which even sense-perception implants the universal is inductive. Now of the thinking states by which we grasp truth, some are unfailingly true, others admit of error—opinion, for instance, and calculation, whereas scientific knowing and intuition are always true: further, no other kind of thought except intuition is more accurate than scientific knowledge, whereas primary premises are more knowable than demonstrations, and all scientific knowledge is discursive.

From these considerations it follows that there will be no scientific knowledge of the primary premises, and since except intuition nothing can be truer than scientific knowledge, it will be intuition that discovers the primary premises—a result which also follows from the fact that demonstration cannot be the originative source of demonstration, nor, consequently, scientific knowledge of scientific knowledge. If, therefore, it is the only other kind of true thinking except scientific knowing, intuition will be the originative source of scientific knowledge. And the originative source of science grasps the original basic premise, while science as a whole is similarly related as originative source to the whole body of fact.

*Dialectica*, by Virgilius Solis

# LOGIC XII

## On the First Principle

**Aristotle**
*Metaphysics* Book IV Parts 3-4 [83]

### Part 3

We must state whether it belongs to one or to different sciences to inquire into the truths that are called axioms in mathematics and into substance. Clearly the inquiry into these axioms also belongs to one science, the science namely of the philosopher, since these truths hold good for everything that is, and not for some special genus apart from others. All men use them because they are true of being *qua* being and every genus has being. But men use them only so far as to satisfy their purposes, that is, as far as the genus to which their demonstrations refer extends.

Therefore, since these truths clearly hold good for all things *qua* being—for this is what is common to them—the inquiry into these belongs to him as well who studies being *qua* being. And for this reason, no one who is conducting a special inquiry tries to say anything about their truth or falsity—neither the geometer nor the arithmetician. Some natural philosophers have in fact done so, and their approach was intelligible enough, given that they thought that they alone were inquiring about the whole of nature and about being.

But since there is one kind of thinker who is above even the natural philosopher—since nature is only one particular genus of being—the discussion of these truths also will belong to the one whose inquiry is universal and deals with primary substance. Physics is also a kind of wisdom, but it is not the first kind.

---

[83] Tr. W.D. Ross, The Internet Classics Archive, emended.

And the attempts of some of those who discuss the terms on which truth should be accepted are due to a want of training in Logic; for they should know these things already when they come to a special study, and not be inquiring into them while they are listening to lectures on it.

Evidently then it belongs to the philosopher, i.e., to him who is studying the nature of all substance, to inquire also into the principles of syllogism. But he who knows best about each genus must be able to state the most certain principles of his subject, so that he whose subject is existing things qua existing must be able to state the most certain principles of all things. This is the philosopher, and the most certain principle of all is that regarding which it is impossible to be mistaken; for such a principle must be both the best known (for all men may be mistaken about things which they do not know), and non-hypothetical. For a principle which everyone must have who understands anything that is, is not a hypothesis; and that which everyone must know who knows anything, he must already have when he comes to a special study. Evidently then such a principle is the most certain of all. Which principle this is, let us proceed to say.

It is, that *the same attribute cannot at the same time belong and not belong to the same subject and in the same respect;* we must presuppose, to guard against dialectical objections, any further qualifications which might be added. This, then, is the most certain of all principles, since it answers to the definition given above. For it is impossible for anyone to believe the same thing to be and not to be, as some think Heraclitus says.

For what a man says, he does not necessarily believe; and if *it is impossible that contrary attributes should belong at the same time to the same subject* (the usual qualifications must be presupposed in this premise too), and if an opinion which contradicts another is contrary to it, obviously it is impossible for the same man at the same time to believe the same thing to be and not to be; for if a man were mistaken on this point he would have contrary opinions at the same time. It is for this reason that all who are carrying out a demonstration reduce it to this as an ultimate belief; for this is naturally the starting-point even for all the other axioms.

## Part 4

There are some who, as we said, both themselves assert that it is possible for the same thing to be and not to be, and who say that people can judge this to be the case. And among others many writers about nature use this language. But we have now posited that *it is impossible for anything at the same time to be and not to be*, and by this means have shown that this is the most indisputable of all principles.

Some indeed demand that even this shall be demonstrated, but this they do through want of education, for not to know of what things one should demand demonstration, and of what one should not, argues want of education. For it is impossible that there should be demonstration of absolutely everything (there would be an infinite regress, so that there would still be no demonstration); but if there are things of which one should not demand demonstration, these persons could not say what principle they maintain to be more self-evident than the present one.

We can, however, demonstrate negatively even that this view is impossible, if our opponent will only say something; and if he says nothing, it is absurd to seek to give an account of our views to one who cannot give an account of anything, in so far as he cannot do so. For such a man, as such, is from the start no better than a vegetable. Now negative demonstration I distinguish from demonstration proper, because in a demonstration one might be thought to be begging the question, but if another person is responsible for the assumption we shall have negative proof, not demonstration.

The starting point for all such arguments is not the demand that our opponent shall say that something either is or is not (for this one might perhaps take to be a begging of the question), but that he shall say something which is significant both for himself and for another; for this is necessary, if he really is to say anything. For, if he means nothing, such a man will not be capable of reasoning, either with himself or with another. But if anyone grants this, demonstration will be possible; for we shall already have something definite. The person responsible for the proof, however, is not he who demonstrates but he who listens; for while disowning reason he listens to reason. And again, he who admits this has admitted that something is true apart from demonstration (so that not everything will be 'so and not so').

First then this at least is obviously true, that the word *be* or *not be* has a definite meaning, so that not everything will be *so* and *not so*. Again, if *man* has one meaning, let this be *two-footed animal*; by having one meaning I understand this:—if *man* means 'X', then if A is a man, 'X' will be what being a man means for him. It makes no difference even if one were to say a word has several meanings, if only they are limited in number; for to each definition there might be assigned a different word. For instance, we might say that *man* has not one meaning but several, one of which would have one definition, viz. *two-footed animal*, while there might be also several other definitions if only they were limited in number; for a peculiar name might be assigned to each of the definitions.

If, however, they were not limited but one were to say that the word has an infinite number of meanings, obviously reasoning would be impossible; for not to have one meaning is to have no meaning, and if words have no meaning our reasoning with one another, and indeed with ourselves, has been annihilated; for it is impossible to think of anything if we do not think of one thing; but if this is possible, one name might be assigned to this thing.

Let it be assumed then, as was said at the beginning, that the name has a meaning and has one meaning; it is impossible, then, that *being a man* should mean precisely *not being a man*, if *man* not only signifies something about one subject but also has one significance (for we do not identify having one significance with signifying something about one subject, since on that assumption even *musical* and *white* and *man* would have had one significance, so that all things would have been one; for they would all have had the same significance).

And it will not be possible to be and not to be the same thing, except in virtue of an ambiguity, just as if one whom we call *man*, others were to call *not-man*; but the point in question is not this, whether the same thing can at the same time be and not be a man in name, but whether it can in fact.

Now if *man* and *not-man* mean nothing different, obviously *not being a man* will mean nothing different from *being a man*; so that *being a man* will be *not being a man*; for they will be one. For being one means this—being related as *raiment* and *garment* are, if their definition is one. And if *being a man* and *being a non-man* are to be one, they must mean one thing. But it was shown earlier that they mean different things.

Therefore, if it is true to say of anything that it is a man, it must be a two-footed animal (for this was what *man* meant); and if this is necessary, it is impossible that the same thing should not at that time be a two-footed animal; for this is what being necessary means—that it is impossible for the thing not to be. It is, then, impossible that it should be at the same time true to say the same thing is a man and is not a man.

The same account holds good with regard to *not being a man*, for *being a man* and *being a non-man* mean different things, since even *being white* and *being a man* are different; for the former terms are much more different so that they must a fortiori mean different things. And if anyone says that *white* means one and the same thing as *man*, again we shall say the same as what was said before, that it would follow that all things are one, and not only opposites. But if this is impossible, then what we have maintained will follow, if our opponent will only answer our question.

And if, when one asks the question simply, he adds the contradictories, he is not answering the question. For there is nothing to prevent the same thing from being both a man and white and countless other things: but still, if one asks whether it is or is not true to say that this is a man, our opponent must give an answer which means one thing, and not add, *It is also white and large*. For, besides other reasons, it is impossible to enumerate its accidental attributes, which are infinite in number; let him, then, enumerate either all or none. Similarly, therefore, even if the same thing is a thousand times a man and a not-man, he must not, in answering the question whether this is a man, add that it is also at the same time a not-man, unless he is bound to add also all the other accidents, all that the subject is or is not; and if he does this, he is not observing the rules of argument.

And in general, those who say this do away with substance and essence. For they must say that all attributes are accidents, and that there is no such thing as being essentially a man or an animal. For if there is to be any such thing as being essentially a man this will not be being a non-man or not being a man (yet these are negations of it); for there was one thing which it meant, and this was the substance of something. And denoting the substance of a thing means that the essence of the thing is nothing else. But if its being essentially a man is to be the same as either being essentially a not-man or essentially not being a man, then its essence will be something else.

Therefore, our opponents must say that there cannot be such a definition of anything, but that all attributes are accidental; for this is the distinction between substance and accident—*white* is accidental to man, because though he is white, whiteness is not his essence. But if all statements are accidental, there will be nothing primary about which they are made, if the accidental always implies predication about a subject. The predication, then, must go on *ad infinitum*. But this is impossible; for not even more than two terms can be combined in accidental predication.

For (1) an accident is not an accident of an accident, unless it be because both are accidents of the same subject. I mean, for instance, that the white is musical, and the latter is white, only because both are accidental to man. But (2) Socrates is musical, not in this sense, that both terms are accidental to something else. Since, then, some predicates are accidental in this and some in that sense, (a) those which are accidental in the latter sense, in which white is accidental to Socrates, cannot form an infinite series in the upward direction; e.g., Socrates the white has not yet another accident; for no one can be got out of such a sum. Nor again (b) will *white* have another term accidental to it, e.g., *musical*. For this is no more accidental to that than that is to this; and at the same time we have drawn the distinction, that while some predicates are accidental in this sense, others are so in the sense in which *musical* is accidental to Socrates; and the accident is an accident of an accident not in cases of the latter kind, but only in cases of the other kind, so that not all terms will be accidental. There must, then, even so be something which denotes substance. And if this is so, it has been shown that contradictories cannot be predicated at the same time.

Again, if all contradictory statements are true of the same subject at the same time, evidently all things will be one. For the same thing will be a trireme, a wall, and a man, if of everything it is possible either to affirm or to deny anything (and this premise must be accepted by those who share the views of Protagoras). For if anyone thinks that the man is not a trireme, evidently he is not a trireme; so that he also is a trireme, if, as they say, contradictory statements are both true. And we thus get the doctrine of Anaxagoras, that all things are mixed together; so that nothing really exists.

They seem, then, to be speaking of the indeterminate, and, while fancying themselves to be speaking of being, they are speaking about non-being; for it is that which exists potentially and not in complete reality that is indeterminate. But they must predicate of every subject the affirmation or the denial of every attribute. For it is absurd if of each subject its own negation is to be predicable, while the denial of something else which cannot be predicated of it is not to be predicable of it; for instance, if it is true to say of a man that he is not a man, evidently it is also true to say that he is either a trireme or not a trireme. If, then, the affirmative can be predicated, the negative must be predicable too; and if the affirmative is not predicable, the negative, at least, will be more predicable than the negative of the subject itself. If, then, even the latter negative is predicable, the negative of *trireme* will be also predicable; and, if this is predicable, the affirmative will be so too.

Those, then, who maintain this view are driven to this conclusion, and to the further conclusion that it is not necessary either to assert or to deny. For if it is true that a thing is a man and a not-man, evidently also it will be neither a man nor a not-man. For to the two assertions there answer two negations, and if the former is treated as a single proposition compounded out of two, the latter also is a single proposition opposite to the former.

Again, either the theory is true in all cases, and a thing is both white and not-white, and existent and non-existent, and all other assertions and negations are similarly compatible, or the theory is true of some statements and not of others. And if not of all, the exceptions will be contradictories of which admittedly only one is true; but if of all, again either the denial will be true wherever the assertion is, and the assertion true wherever the denial is, or the denial will be true where the assertion is, but the assertion not always true where the denial is. And (a) in the latter case there will be something which fixedly is not, and this will be an indisputable belief; and if non-being is something indisputable and knowable, the opposite assertion will be more knowable. But (b) if it is equally possible also to assert all that it is possible to deny, one must either be saying what is true when one separates the predicates (and says, for instance, that a thing is white, and again that it is not-white), or not.

And if (i) it is not true to apply the predicates separately, our opponent is not saying what he professes to say, and also nothing at all exists; but how could non-existent things speak or walk, as he does? Also, all things would on this view be one, as has been already said, and man and God and trireme and their contradictories will be the same. For if contradictories can be predicated alike of each subject, one thing will in no wise differ from another; for if it differs, this difference will be something true and peculiar to it. And (ii) if one may with truth apply the predicates separately, the above-mentioned result follows none the less, and, further, it follows that all would then be right and all would be in error, and our opponent himself confesses himself to be in error.

And at the same time our discussion with him is evidently about nothing at all; for he says nothing. For he says neither yes nor no, but yes and no; and again, he denies both of these and says neither yes nor no; for otherwise there would already be something definite.

Again, if when the assertion is true, the denial is false, and when this is true, the affirmation is false, it will not be possible to assert and deny the same thing truly at the same time. But perhaps they might say this was the very question at issue.

Again, is he in error who judges either that the thing is so or that it is not so, and is he right who judges both? If he is right, what can they mean by saying that the nature of existing things is of this kind? And if he is not right, but righter than he who judges in the other way, being will already be of a definite nature, and this will be true, and not at the same time also not true. But if all are alike both wrong and right, one who is in this condition will not be able either to speak or to say anything intelligible; for he says at the same time both yes and no. And if he makes no judgement but thinks and does not think, indifferently, what difference will there be between him and a vegetable?

Thus, then, it is in the highest degree evident that neither any one of those who maintain this view nor anyone else is really in this position. For why does a man walk to Megara and not stay at home, when he thinks he ought to be walking there? Why does he not walk early some morning into a well or over a precipice, if one happens to be in his way? Why do we observe him guarding against this, evidently because he does not think that falling in is alike good and not good? Evidently, then, he judges one thing to be better and another worse. And if this is so, he must also judge one thing to be a man and another to be not-a-man, one thing to be sweet and another to be not-sweet. For he does not aim at and judge all things alike, when, thinking it desirable to drink water or to see a man, he proceeds to aim at these things; yet he ought, if the same thing were alike a man and not-a-man. But, as was said, there is no one who does not obviously avoid some things and not others. Therefore, as it seems, all men make unqualified judgments, if not about all things, still about what is better and worse.

And if this is not knowledge but opinion, they should be all the more anxious about the truth, as a sick man should be more anxious about his health than one who flourishes; for he who has opinions is, in comparison with the man who knows, not in a healthy state as far as the truth is concerned.

Again, however much all things may be *so* and *not so*, still there is a more and a less in the nature of things; for we should not say that two and three are equally even, nor is he who thinks four things are five equally wrong with him who thinks they are a thousand. If then they are not equally wrong, obviously one is less wrong and therefore more right. If, then, that which has more of any quality is nearer the norm, there must be some truth to which the more true is nearer. And even if there is not, still there is already something better founded and more like the truth, and we shall have got rid of the unqualified doctrine which would prevent us from determining anything in our thought.

*The Sciences,* by Stefano della Bella

*Dialectic and Logic,*
by Giovanni Antonio da Brescia.

# SOPHISTICAL FALLACIES

**Aristotle**
*On Sophistical Refutations* Parts I & VII [84]

Followed by *Recollections of the MENO*
J. Tomarchio

### Part I

Let us now discuss sophistic refutations, i.e., what appear to be refutations but are really fallacies instead. We will begin in the natural order with the first.

That some reasonings are genuine, while others seem to be so but are not, is evident. This happens with arguments, as also elsewhere, through a certain likeness between the genuine and the sham. For physically some people are in a vigorous condition, while others merely seem to be so by blowing and rigging themselves out as the tribesmen do their victims for sacrifice; and some people are beautiful thanks to their beauty, while others seem to be so, by dint of embellishing themselves. So, it is, too, with inanimate things; for of these, too, some are really silver and others gold, while others are not and merely seeming to be such to our sense; e.g., things made of litharge and tin seem to be of silver, while those made of yellow metal look golden.

In the same way both reasoning and refutation are sometimes genuine, sometimes not, though inexperience may make them appear so: for inexperienced people obtain only, as it were, a distant view of these things. For reasoning rests on certain statements such that they involve necessarily the assertion of something other than that which has

---

[84] Tr. W.A. Pickard, The Internet Classics Archive, emended.

been stated, through what has been stated: refutation is reasoning involving the contradictory of the given conclusion.

Now some of them do not really achieve this, though they seem to do so for a number of reasons; and of these the most prolific and usual domain is the argument that turns upon names only. It is impossible in a discussion to bring in the actual things discussed: we use their names as symbols instead of them; and therefore, we suppose that what follows in the names, follows in the things as well, just as people who calculate suppose in regard to their counters. But the two cases (names and things) are not alike.

For names are finite and so is the sum-total of formulae, while things are infinite in number. Inevitably, then, the same formulae, and a single name, have a number of meanings. Accordingly, just as, in counting, those who are not clever in manipulating their counters are taken in by the experts, in the same way in arguments too those who are not well acquainted with the force of names reason amiss both in their own discussions and when they listen to others.

For this reason, then, and for others to be mentioned later, there exists both reasoning and refutation that is apparent but not real. Now for some people it is better worthwhile to seem to be wise, than to be wise without seeming to be (for the art of the sophist is the semblance of wisdom without the reality, and the sophist is one who makes money from an apparent but unreal wisdom); for them, then, it is clearly essential also to seem to accomplish the task of a wise man rather than to accomplish it without seeming to do so.

To reduce it to a single point of contrast it is the business of one who knows a thing, himself to avoid fallacies in the subjects which he knows and to be able to show up the man who makes them; and of these accomplishments the one depends on the faculty to render an answer, and the other upon the securing of one. Those, then, who would be sophists are bound to study the class of arguments aforesaid: for it is worth their while: for a faculty of this kind will make a man seem to be wise, and this is the purpose they happen to have in view.

Clearly, then, there exists a class of arguments of this kind, and it is at this kind of ability that those aim whom we call sophists. Let us now go on to discuss how many kinds there are of sophistical arguments, and how many in number are the elements of which this faculty is composed, and how many branches there happen to be of this inquiry, and the other factors that contribute to this art.

## Part 7

Deception comes about in the case of arguments that depend on *ambiguity of words* and of *ambiguity of phrases* because we are unable to divide up the ambiguous term (for some terms it is not easy to divide, e.g., *unity*, *being*, and *sameness*), while in those that depend on *ambiguous combination and division*, it is because we suppose that it makes no difference whether the phrases be combined or divided, as is in fact the case with most phrases.

Likewise, also with those ambiguities that depend on *accentuation:* for the emphatic lowering or raising of the voice upon a phrase is thought not to alter its meaning—with any phrase, or not with many. With those ambiguities that depend on the *form of expression* it is because of likeness of expression. For it is hard to distinguish what kind of things are signified by the same and what by different kinds of expression; for a man who can do this is practically next door to the understanding of the truth.

A special reason why a man is liable to be hurried into assent to fallacy is that we suppose every predicate of everything to be an individual thing, and we understand it as being one with the thing: and we therefore treat it as a substance: for it is to that which is one with a thing or substance, as also to substance itself, that 'individually' and 'being' are deemed to belong in the fullest sense.

For this reason, too, this type of fallacy is to be ranked among those that depend on language; in the first place, because the deception is effected the more readily when we are inquiring into a problem in company with others than when we do so by ourselves (for an inquiry with another person is carried on by means of speech, whereas an inquiry by oneself is carried on quite as much by means of the object itself); secondly a man is liable to be deceived, even when inquiring by himself, when he takes speech as the basis of his inquiry: moreover the deception arises out of the likeness (of two different things), and the likeness arises out of the language.

With those fallacies that depend upon an *accident*, deception comes about because we cannot distinguish the sameness and otherness of terms, i.e., their unity and multiplicity, or what kinds of predicate have all the same accidents as their subject. Likewise, also with those that depend on a *consequent:* for the consequent is a branch of accident. Moreover, in many cases appearances point to this—the claim is made that if A is inseparable from B, so also is B from A.

With those that depend upon *a defective definition of refutation*, and with those that depend upon the difference between *a qualified and an absolute statement*, the deception consists in the smallness of the difference involved; for we treat the limitation to the particular thing or respect or manner or time as adding nothing to the meaning, and so grant the statement universally.

Likewise, also in the case of those fallacies that *beg the original point*, and those of *mistaken cause*, and all that treat *a multiplicity of questions* as one: for in all of them the deception lies in the smallness of the difference: for our failure to be quite exact in our definition of premises and of proof is due to the aforesaid reason.

*Dialectic teaches the human being how to make use of reasoning, for which reason the great Plato rightly calls it the apex of Arts.*

*Dialectic*a with magpie, serpent, and toads, in conversation with a philosopher, Netherlandish engraving after Franz Floris.

## RECOLLECTIONS OF PLATO'S *MENO*
### Revisiting Plato's **Meno** Logically And Rhetorically
### In Light of Aristotle's 12 Sophistical Fallacies

---

### FIVE LINGUISTIC FALLACIES
*Failing to indicate the same thing by the same words.*

1. **ACCENT / EMPHASIS:**
   **Adds to or alters a word's meaning by an emphasis.**

   *At any rate, I know <u>their</u> kind, whether I've had experience or not.* Anytus, Meno 92c.

   Anytus calls Sophists *the ruin and corruption of anyone who comes into contact with them.* However, he admits to having no experience of them at all. Socrates asks, *How can you know what is good or bad in something when you have no experience of it?* Anytus replies, *I know <u>their</u> kind, at any rate, ....* Does Anytus' emphasis add to or alter the meaning of his words? Does it answer Socrates' question?

2. **AMBIGUITY OF FORM:**
   **Plays on ambiguous features of morphology, e.g., case of noun or voice of verb.**

   *"Is there the same virtue for a boy and a slave both to be able to rule over the master, and would the ruler then seem to you to be the slave?* Socrates, *Meno*, 73d1

   Why does Socrates use the dual form of *boy and slave* here—rendered in English by *both: for a boy and a slave both to be able to rule.* In Attic Greek, the dual is used for natural pairs, like eyes, ears, legs, and twins. Why does he make the boy and the slave a natural pair with this use of the dual?

## 3. AMBIGUITY OF WORD / EQUIVOCATION:
Plays on multiple meanings of a word.

*But will you yourself Meno, by god, answer what is virtue?*

Is not Socrates' question grammatically ambivalent, insofar as the interrogative pronoun *what* can refer either materially to subjects or formally to predicates? In other words, does the question ask for what is a virtue or for what a virtue is, *i.e.*, for what kind of things *are virtue* or for what kind of thing *virtue is*?

Meno at first takes the pronoun in the substantive sense and names particular subjects and kinds of virtue, such as men and justice. Socrates at first goes along with Meno's reply: *Rather we may say that whatever is accompanied by justice is virtue …* (79a). He goes on, however, to complain that justice is only a part of virtue, but what he wants rather is a definition of the *whole* of virtue, its *nature*, the *common* characteristic of virtues. But was this obvious in his question from the start? Why didn't he from the start ask Meno unambiguously for *a definition*—as in geometry?

Later, when Meno insists on returning to the original question he had put to Socrates, namely whether virtue can be taught, does Socrates return to another ambivalent form of speech: *If virtue is some sort of knowledge, clearly it could be taught* (87c)? What is the difference between their saying before that *justice is virtue* and saying now *virtue is knowledge* or *a sort of wisdom*? Does the former subject name a "part" of virtue but the latter two predicate nouns a definitional genus? Socrates offers two examples of the sort of definition he seeks: *shape* he defines as *the only thing that always accompanies color* or *the limit of a solid*. Is it clear how Meno's last attempted definition in reply to this fails of this *form* of definition: *Virtue consists in a wish for good things plus the power to accompany them* (78b)?

In any case, the ambivalent reference of the pronoun *what* once clarified become horns of dilemma. On one hand, can one know what are virtues without knowing what virtue is—but, on the other, can one know what virtue is without knowing what is a virtue or who is virtuous? Socrates doesn't seem to challenge Meno's beliefs about that.

## 4. AMBIGUITY OF PHRASE / AMPHIBOLY:
Plays on ambiguous meaning of a phrase.

*Now, then, try to tell me how long each of its sides will be. The present figure has a side of 2 feet. What will be the side of the double-sized one? ... But we haven't yet got the square of 8 feet even from a 3-foot side? Then what length will it be? Try to tell exactly. If you don't want to count it up, just show us on the diagram.* Socrates, Meno 82e & 84a

What precisely does Socrates mean by the interrogative phrase *How long?* In ordinary experience, would not the slave boy expect the question *How long is it?* to be answered in terms of some conventional unit-measure, like feet? Instead, Socrates has divided up the side of a given square into two parts (*feet,* as it were) and asked the slave boy *how long* the side of its double will be. What Socrates means, *stated more precisely*, is how much *longer* will the side of its double be?

However, the boy finds he can't double the area of the given square by doubling its side, so he tries other multiples. *If you don't want to count it up, then just show us*, says Socrates, knowing well that the boy cannot count it up because it is not countable. It is the notorious geometrical scandal of the incommensurability of a side of a square with its diagonal. Socrates is asking the boy a question that he knows geometry demonstrates to be unanswerable. *Why?*

However, Socrates also gives the slave boy a way out in the second form of his question: *Just show us on the diagram.* Geometry can indeed find the determinate side of the double. Socrates re-draws the diagram in such a way as to show the boy that the diagonal of the half-square is the side of the double asked for. But does Socrates' graphic solution to the problem answer his original question **as asked**: *Now then, try to tell me how long each of its sides will be?*

Socrates generates the slave-boy's perplexity by the way he asks his question. The question to ask about his question is how the interrogative adverb *how* modifies the adjective *long?* If *How long?* means *How much longer?*, then geometry can demonstrate that the question is unanswerable. But if *How long?* just means *Show me how long*, then geometrical construction can indeed find and show the line asked for.

Now the rhetorical question to ask in turn about the logical question raised by the ambiguity in Socrates' geometrical question is this: is he misleading the boy when he asks *how long* and *what length* the side of the double will be? If misleading, misleading intentionally? If intentionally, to what end?

5. **AMBIGUITY OF COMPOSITION / DIVISION OF PHRASES: Plays on ambiguous sentence syntax.**

*Since there is the same virtue for all of them, try to say and recall what Gorgias says the thing is, and you along with him.* Socrates, Meno 73b

Presumably what Socrates means to say is that *virtue for all of them is the same thing*, rather than *there is the same virtue for all of them*. (Moreover, surely, he means, *Try to recall and say what Gorgias says it is*, rather than, *Try to say and recall*). Yet Socrates puts *same* in the attributive position: *theirs is the same virtue*. Why not put it in the predicate position: *their virtue is the same*?

Meno's first attempt to say what virtue is had taken the form of a list that contradistinguishes a man's virtue from a woman's, a child's, and an old man's. Socrates, to explain that he seeks the essence and character common to these virtues, askes Meno whether he thinks health or strength differ in a man and in a woman. When Meno agrees that they do not, Socrates asks, *And will virtue insofar as it is virtue differ in any way, be it in a boy or in an old man, or in a woman or in a man?* Meno responds, *To me, Socrates, this case doesn't seem to be at all the same as those others*. Meno resists Socrates' comparison between a same meaning of 'health' as applied to man and woman and the differing meanings Meno wants to assign the 'virtue' of each.

Socrates doesn't seem interested in inquiring into Meno's reservation about his analogy between virtue and health. Might not Meno have responded Socratically, *Socrates, do you for your part think health is the same in a man, in his diet, and in his complexion, for do we not call all these 'healthy'? And is health the very same, moreover, in his body, in his soul, and in his city?* With this question Meno could challenge Socrates' unexamined premise that virtue is a univocal term with one selfsame meaning, rather than an analogical term with a primary and derivative meanings. Had Socrates inquired further into Meno's reservation, we might have learned if Meno perhaps believes that virtue in its complete and proper sense applies only to a man active in a *polis*, and only secondarily and analogically to a woman in her homemaking, a child in his schooling, or an elder in his senescence.

Socrates goes on, rather, to ask Meno whether both a man and a woman, in order to direct either a city or a household well, will need to so do temperately and justly? When Meno agrees they will, Socrates converts his adverbs to substantives: *that means with temperance and justice.* Is it valid for Socrates thus to reify the adverb, thereby converting a manner of acting to a quality? The conversion proves consequential for his next inference: *Then both man and woman need the same things, justice and temperance, if they are to be good.* The reified adverbs become predicates in an apodosis, the protasis of which introduces a term of which we could likewise ask: is *good* here assumed to be univocal rather than analogical? After all, the logical validity of any subsequent reasoning hangs on whether all the terms are predicated univocally of the same things in the same way throughout the syllogisms.

Moreover, even granting that man and woman both require temperance and justice, is not the question at issue whether or not that temperance and justice are one and the same in a man governing a city well and in a woman governing a house well, or whether the one is manly temperance and justice, and the other womanly—specified not only by their subjects, *man* and *woman*, but also by their objects, *city* and *household*? Does virtue lie in the subjects, in a quality of theirs, in their manner of acting, in their relation to the object of their activity? Is that question being begged by Socrates' way of framing his questions for Meno?

Socrates goes on to conclude further, *So all human beings are good in the same way, since it happens that they become good from the same things.* What does *the same things* refer to? Are these *same things* the particular virtues of temperance and justice? And are these the only virtues necessary for human beings to *become good*? Further, are all human beings good in the *same* way by virtue of the *same* temperance and the *same* justice? What does *same* mean here, precisely? If Meno doesn't ask, should not we readers?

Socrates goes on to say that they would not be good in *the same way* if *the same virtue* did not belong to all of them. He then carries over this attributive use of *same* to our theme-quotation: *Since, then, there is the same virtue for all of them, try to say and recall what Gorgias says the thing is, and you along with him.* Does Socrates mean to say that justice is the same virtue as temperance? And not only that justice and temperance are the same as one another, but the same as virtue itself as well—sundry names for one and the same thing?

Presumably not. Presumably Socrates means that virtue is the same in a man and woman, and the same in justice and temperance, with the consequence that the particular virtues of justice and temperance do not differ in *essence* or *character* in a man and in a woman, any more than virtue as a whole does. But is his phrasing ambiguous on purpose? If so, with what purpose?

Now when Socrates goes on to ask Meno what Gorgias thinks, he uses the pronominal form of *the same* in the neuter rather than feminine to refer to virtue—rendered here as *what Gorgias says the thing is*, the *thing* being virtue. Why all these grammatical ambiguities in Socrates' phrasing? Why not predicate *the same* of virtue as subject, rather than predicate *the same virtue* of all virtue's subjects? Why go on to refer to virtue with a neuter pronoun rather than a feminine one when asking Meno what Gorgias says it is? And why, for good measure, enclose between the two clauses the rhetorical flourish of a *hysteron proteron*: *Tell me and recall what Gorgias says*?

*I distinguish the false account from true.
Through me doubtful matters are tested by trained reasoning.*

*Dialectic*a in conversation with a philosopher, Netherlandish engraving.

## SEVEN LOGICAL FALLACIES
*Reasoning from what's incidental —
resulting in paralogism.*

6. **BASED ON ACCIDENT**
   *A dicto simpliciter/ad dictum secundum quid*: **Plays on what is incidental to subject and predicates in the predication.**

   *Ought we not to reckon those men divine who with no conscious thought are repeatedly and outstandingly successful in what they do or say? – Certainly. We are right therefore to give this title to the oracular priests and the prophets that I mentioned, and to poets of every description. Statesmen too, when by their speeches they get great things done yet know nothing of what they are saying, are to be considered as acting no less under divine influence, inspired and possessed by the divinity. – Certainly.* Socrates, Meno 99c

   Meno concedes that men thought virtuous are colloquially called *divine*. Such an epithet of praise seems accidental either to the men who are virtuous or to their virtue—not to mention to Meno's question about virtue's origin or Socrates' question about its essence. Yet Socrates goes on to fallaciously extend this accidental attribute to both the subject and predicate of their dialogue: he ascribes to virtuous men (as well as successful orators, like Meno), not even the word's primary meaning, *having the nature of a god*, but the derivative meaning, *by a god's influence or inspiration*.

   Socrates will go on to conclude both this argument and the dialogue with, *Whoever gets virtue has it by divine dispensation*. The fallacious equivocation and inference Socrates indulges in here is perhaps more ironic than disingenuous, and this may well not escape the rhetor Meno, but the question remains, what is Socrates' rhetorical aim in culminating his dialogue with Meno with an equivocation and consequently fallacious syllogism?

## 7. BASED ON AFFIRMING THE CONSEQUENT:
Infers an antecedent from its consequent

*So, we may say in general that the goodness of non-spiritual assets depends on our spiritual character, and the goodness of that on wisdom. This argument shows that the advantageous element must be wisdom, and virtue, we agree, is advantageous; so that amounts to saying that virtue, either in whole or in part, is wisdom.* Socrates, *Meno* 89a

How so? If wisdom is always advantageous, does that entail that because virtue is likewise advantageous it will be identical with wisdom—whether in whole or only in part? Is that not the fallacy of affirming the consequent: *Where there is wisdom, there is always advantage; therefore, wherever there is advantage, there is also wisdom?*

Looking at the argument in another way, as a syllogism, if both wisdom and virtue are affirmed to be always advantageous, then the advantageous is posited as a whole of which wisdom and virtue are parts. Those parts need not overlap, nor exclude other parts. If wisdom is always advantageous, and virtue is always advantageous, no syllogism follows: it does not follow that they are identical with one another, either in whole or in part, nor that whatever else is advantageous is identical with either of them, either in whole or in part, logically speaking.

In fact, Socrates himself will later overturn the premise that virtue is knowledge on the basis of the experience that right opinion has proven no less advantageous than knowledge or wisdom in virtuous actions. But was his logical argument valid in the first place for identifying virtue with wisdom on the basis of a commonly predicated middle term of advantageousness? If not, why did he make it, only to overturn it?

## 8. IN A CERTAIN RESPECT VS. SIMPLY
*Secundum quid et simpliciter*: **Plays on applications of a term with and without qualification, often fallaciously extending an attribute of an individual or part to its kind or whole.**

*I have just asked you not to break virtue up into fragments, and given you models of the type of answer I wanted, but taking no notice of this, you tell me that virtue consists in the acquisition of good things with justice, and justice, you agree, is a part of virtue.... The point I want to make is that whereas I asked you to give me an account of virtue as a whole, far from telling me what it is itself, you say that every action is virtue which exhibits a part of virtue, as if you had already told me what the whole is ...* Socrates, Meno 79b

Socrates complains that he is asking for virtue simply, but Meno keeps giving him virtue in some respect; he claims that Meno in his latest definition extends what is virtue in one respect, namely justice, to all other virtues and all virtue. However, it is Socrates himself who added the phrase *just and righteous* to Meno's definition of virtue. Meno defined virtue as *a wish for good things plus the power to acquire them*. Socrates asks of this definition, *Do you add "just" and "righteous" to the word "acquisition," or doesn't it make any difference to you?* Meno replies that it certainly does make a difference, from which qualification Socrates infers a substantive "part" of virtue: *We may say that whatever is accompanied by justice is virtue, whatever is without qualities of that sort is vice.* Meno replies, *I agree that your conclusion is inescapable,* whereupon Socrates offers the above complaint of Meno's confusing the whole of virtue with its parts, which are virtue in various respects.

But, who confused what? Why did Socrates introduce a problematic qualification to Meno's definition, only to complain about the very thing he himself added, the very thing that restricted Meno's definition of virtue as *a wish* and *a power* to justice as but one part of virtue by qualifying the qualifying object *of acquiring*. Did Socrates treat the attempted definition justly? What if Meno had said *wish for the good and power to acquire it*? Would that need qualification?

9. **IGNORANCE OF REFUTATION / IRRELEVANT CONCLUSION: Invalidly offers an argument for a conclusion that does not follow from it.**

*If all we have said in this discussion and the questions we have asked have been right, virtue will be acquired neither by nature nor by teaching. Whoever has it gets it by divine dispensation without taking thought, unless he be the kind of statesman who can create another like himself.* Socrates, *Meno* 99e-100a

How would valid arguments for virtue's not being acquired by nature and for its not being acquired by teaching lead to the conclusion that it is acquired by divine dispensation? To be a valid *reductio ad absurdum*, would not Socrates' conclusion have to assume an exhaustive disjunction: virtue must necessarily either come by nature, or by teaching, or by divine dispensation? If so, whence this premise?

It does not seem to be the premise of Meno's question at the start, which leaves an opening for yet unconceived alternatives: *Can you tell me Socrates—is virtue something that can be taught? Or does it come by practice? Or is it neither teaching nor practice that gives it to a man but natural aptitude, or something else?* (70a). Without a premise of an exhaustive disjunction accepted, doesn't Socrates' argument leave us with a rhetorical absurdity, not a plausible conclusion? If so, why end the dialogue on that note?

10. **BEGGING THE QUESTION / CIRCULAR REASONING
Assumes its own conclusion, the very point in dispute.**

*Do you realize that that what you are bringing up is the trick argument that a man cannot try to discover either what he knows or what he does not know? He would not seek what he knows, for since he knows it, there is no need of the inquiry; nor what he does not know, for in that case he does not even know what he is to look for.* Socrates, *Meno* xxx

Does not Socrates' question beg the question of whether Meno's question is fallacious or not? Doesn't Socrates' asking if Meno realizes that it's "a trick" assume it is one? At issue in Meno's question, after all, is Socrates' own credibility as an inquirer who claims that he knows nothing at all about what he is inquiring into. In any case, Meno ingenuously reasserts the question Socrates disingenuously begs, saying, *Well, do you think it is a good argument?*

To explain why he thinks that it is not, Socrates offers, not an argument, but rather a story that some priests and priestesses tell about the immortality of the soul—of which story he later says, *I shouldn't like to take my oath on the whole story* (86b).

## 11. MISTAKEN CAUSE
*Cum hoc, ergo propter hoc*: **Asserts a causal relation where only a correlation has been established.**

*Well now, let's try to tell you what shape is. See if you accept this definition. Let us define it as the only thing which always accompanies color. Does that satisfy you, or do you want it in some other way? I should be content if your definition of virtue were on similar lines.*
Socrates, Meno 75b

Socrates asked Meno for a definition of virtue's *essence*, i.e., *that common character* with respect to which particular virtues don't differ at all. So why does he here say that he will be content if Meno offers a definition of virtue that states what it always accompanies? Indeed, it is not clear whether in Socrates' definition of shape *always* even entails *necessarily*, for shape may well always accompany color in perception, but is not color abstracted from in geometrical considerations of shape itself in itself?

In any case, even if virtue always necessarily accompanies something else, or is always necessarily accompanied by something else, will such a correlation define what virtue is in itself? Any such necessary relation to a different thing will not be the cause of virtue's being virtue, will it? What could be the relation between such a necessary relation and the defining characteristic of virtue such that Meno's stating this relation could stand in for his stating the formal cause of virtues' being virtues, *i.e.*, the defining characteristic that makes all virtues virtue?

## 12. MULTIPLICITY OF QUESTIONS
*Plurium interrogationum*: **Conflating questions confusingly or distractingly.**

*I share the poverty of my fellow countrymen in this respect and confess to my shame that I have no knowledge about virtue at all. And how can I know a property of something when I don't even know what it is? Do you suppose that somebody entirely ignorant who Meno is could say whether he is handsome and rich and wellborn or the reverse? Is that possible, do you think?* Socrates, *Meno* 71a-b.

Is Socrates asking one question in many ways, or many questions at once? If many at once, how are they related?

Having just stated, *Far from knowing whether it can be taught, I have no idea what virtue itself is,* Socrates goes on to state, *I have no knowledge about virtue at all.* Is he saying that his ignorance of what virtue is, is but one part of his total ignorance of virtue? How can he ask about virtue at all if he has no knowledge of virtue at all?

In any case, he goes on to pose a question about the relation between knowing *what* things are to know *what they are like*. By way of example, he relates the question of *what* virtue is to *who* Meno is—rather than to *what* Meno is—and then relates this question of *who* Meno is to such individual and variable attributes of Meno as being rich and handsome, rather than such essential properties as his being rational or living. Is Socrates conflating questions of essential nature with questions of individual identity, and variable attributes with defining characteristics? If so, on purpose? If so, with what purpose?

*Socrates in the Agora,* by Harry Bates

www.ingramcontent.com/pod-product-compliance
Lightning Source LLC
Chambersburg PA
CBHW051802100526
44592CB00016B/2528